# THE NEW FOLGER LIBRARY SHAKESPEARE

Designed to make Shakespeare's great plays available to all readers, the New Folger Library edition of Shakespeare's plays provides accurate texts in modern spelling and punctuation, as well as scene-by-scene action summaries, full explanatory notes, many pictures clarifying Shakespeare's language, and notes recording all significant departures from the early printed versions. Each play is prefaced by a brief introduction, by a guide to reading Shakespeare's language, and by accounts of his life and theater. Each play is followed by an annotated list of further readings and by a "Modern Perspective" written by an expert on that particular play.

Barbara A. Mowat is Director of Research *emerita* at the Folger Shakespeare Library, Consulting Editor of *Shakespeare Quarterly,* and author of *The Dramaturgy of Shakespeare's Romances* and of essays on Shakespeare's plays and their editing.

Paul Werstine is Professor of English at the Graduate School and at King's University College at Western University. He is a general editor of the New Variorum Shakespeare and author of *Early Modern Playhouse Manuscripts and the Editing of Shakespeare* and of many papers and articles on the printing and editing of Shakespeare's plays.

# Folger Shakespeare Library

The Folger Shakespeare Library in Washington, D.C., is a privately funded research library dedicated to Shakespeare and the civilization of early modern Europe. It was founded in 1932 by Henry Clay and Emily Jordan Folger, and incorporated as part of Amherst College in Amherst, Massachusetts, one of the nation's oldest liberal arts colleges, from which Henry Folger had graduated in 1879. In addition to its role as the world's preeminent Shakespeare collection and its emergence as a leading center for Renaissance studies, the Folger Shakespeare Library offers a wide array of cultural and educational programs and services for the general public.

EDITORS

BARBARA A. MOWAT
*Director of Research emerita*
*Folger Shakespeare Library*

PAUL WERSTINE
*Professor of English*
*King's University College at Western University, Canada*

FOLGER SHAKESPEARE LIBRARY

The Tragedy of

# King Lear

By
## WILLIAM SHAKESPEARE

AN UPDATED EDITION

EDITED BY BARBARA A. MOWAT
AND PAUL WERSTINE

SIMON & SCHUSTER PAPERBACKS
NEW YORK LONDON TORONTO SYDNEY NEW DELHI

Simon & Schuster
Avenue of the Americas
New York, NY 10020

Copyright © 1993, 2015 by The Folger Shakespeare Library

This Simon & Schuster trade paperback edition October 2015

SIMON & SCHUSTER and colophon are registered trademarks of Simon & Schuster, Inc.

For information about special discounts for bulk purchases, please contact Simon & Schuster Special Sales at 1-866-506-1949 or business@simonandschuster.com.

The Simon & Schuster Speakers Bureau can bring authors to your live event. For more information or to book an event, contact the Simon & Schuster Speakers Bureau at 1-866-248-3049 or visit our website at www.simonspeakers.com.

Manufactured in the United States of America

10  9  8  7  6  5  4  3  2

ISBN 978-1-5011-1811-1
ISBN 978-1-4516-8239-7 (ebook)

# From the Director of the Folger Shakespeare Library

It is hard to imagine a world without Shakespeare. Since their composition more than four hundred years ago, Shakespeare's plays and poems have traveled the globe, inviting those who see and read his works to make them their own.

Readers of the New Folger Editions are part of this ongoing process of "taking up Shakespeare," finding our own thoughts and feelings in language that strikes us as old or unusual and, for that very reason, new. We still struggle to keep up with a writer who could think a mile a minute, whose words paint pictures that shift like clouds. These expertly edited texts, presented here with accompanying explanatory notes and up-to-date critical essays, are distinctive because of what they do: they allow readers not simply to keep up, but to engage deeply with a writer whose works invite us to think, and think again.

These New Folger Editions of Shakespeare's plays are also special because of where they come from. The Folger Shakespeare Library in Washington, D.C., where the Editions are produced, is the single greatest documentary source of Shakespeare's works. An unparalleled collection of early modern books, manuscripts, and artwork connected to Shakespeare, the Folger's holdings have been consulted extensively in the preparation of these texts. The Editions also reflect the expertise gained through the regular performance of Shakespeare's works in the Folger's Elizabethan Theater.

I want to express my deep thanks to editors Barbara

Mowat and Paul Werstine for creating these indispensable editions of Shakespeare's works, which incorporate the best of textual scholarship with a richness of commentary that is both inspired and engaging. Readers who want to know more about Shakespeare and his plays can follow the paths these distinguished scholars have tread by visiting the Folger itself, where a range of physical and digital resources (available online) exist to supplement the material in these texts. I commend to you these words, and hope that they inspire.

*Michael Witmore*
Director, Folger Shakespeare Library

# Contents

# Editors' Preface

In recent years, ways of dealing with Shakespeare's texts and with the interpretation of his plays have been undergoing significant change. This edition, while retaining many of the features that have always made the Folger Shakespeare so attractive to the general reader, at the same time reflects these current ways of thinking about Shakespeare. For example, modern readers, actors, and teachers have become interested in the differences between, on the one hand, the early forms in which Shakespeare's plays were first published and, on the other hand, the forms in which editors through the centuries have presented them. In response to this interest, we have based our edition on what we consider the best early printed version of a particular play (explaining our rationale in a section called "An Introduction to This Text") and have marked our changes in the text—unobtrusively, we hope, but in such a way that the curious reader can be aware that a change has been made and can consult the "Textual Notes" to discover what appeared in the early printed version.

Current ways of looking at the plays are reflected in our brief introductions, in many of the commentary notes, in the annotated lists of "Further Reading," and especially in each play's "Modern Perspective," an essay written by an outstanding scholar who brings to the reader his or her fresh assessment of the play in the light of today's interests and concerns.

As in the Folger Library General Reader's Shakespeare, which this edition replaces, we include explanatory notes designed to help make Shakespeare's language clearer to a modern reader, and we place the notes on the page facing the text that they explain. We also follow the earlier edition in including illustrations—of objects, of clothing, of mythological figures—from books and manuscripts in the Folger Shakespeare Library collection. We provide fresh accounts of the life of Shakespeare, of the publishing of his plays, and of the theaters in which his plays were performed, as well as an introduction to the text itself. We also include a section called "Reading Shakespeare's Language," in which we try to help readers learn to "break the code" of Elizabethan poetic language.

For each section of each volume, we are indebted to a host of generous experts and fellow scholars. The "Reading Shakespeare's Language" sections, for example, could not have been written had not Arthur King, of Brigham Young University, and Randal Robinson, author of *Unlocking Shakespeare's Language*, led the way in untangling Shakespearean language puzzles and shared their insights and methodologies generously with us. "Shakespeare's Life" profited by the careful reading given it by S. Schoenbaum; "Shakespeare's Theater" was read and strengthened by Andrew Gurr, John Astington, and William Ingram; and "The Publication of Shakespeare's Plays" is indebted to the comments of Peter W. M. Blayney. We, as editors, take sole responsibility for any errors in our editions.

We are grateful to the authors of the "Modern Perspectives"; to Leeds Barroll and David Bevington for their generous encouragement; to the Huntington and Newberry Libraries for fellowship support; to King's University College for the grants it has provided to Paul Werstine; to the Social Sciences and Humanities Research Council of Canada, which provided him with Research Time Stipends; to R. J. Shroyer of Western University for essential computer support; and to the Folger Institute's Center for Shakespeare Studies for its fortuitous sponsorship of a workshop on "Shakespeare's Texts for Students and Teachers" (funded by the National Endowment for the Humanities and led by Richard Knowles of the University of Wisconsin), a workshop from which we learned an enormous amount about what is wanted by college and high-school teachers of Shakespeare today.

In preparing this preface for the publication of *King Lear* in 1993, we wrote: "Our biggest debt is to the Folger Shakespeare Library: to Werner Gundersheimer, Director of the Library, who has made possible our edition; to Jean Miller, the Library's Art Curator, who combed the Library holdings for illustrations, and to Julie Ainsworth, Head of the Photography Department, who carefully photographed them; to Peggy O'Brien, Director of Education, who gave us expert advice about the needs being expressed by Shakespeare teachers and students (and to Martha Christian and other 'master teachers' who used our texts in manuscript in their classrooms); to the staff of the Academic Programs Division, especially Paul Menzer (who drafted 'Further Reading' material), Mary Tonkinson, Lena Cowen Orlin, Molly Haws, and Jessica Hymowitz; and, finally, to the staff of the Library Reading Room, whose patience and support have been invaluable.

"Special thanks are due Richard Knowles, who allowed us to see his commentary on Acts 1 and 2 for his forthcoming New Variorum edition of *King Lear.*"

As we revise the play for publication in 2015, we add to the above our gratitude to Michael Witmore, Director of the Folger Shakespeare Library, who brings to our work a gratifying enthusiasm and vision; to Gail Kern Paster, Director of the Library from 2002 until July 2011, whose interest and support have been unfailing and whose scholarly expertise continues to be an invaluable resource; to Jonathan Evans and

Alysha Bullock, our production editors at Simon & Schuster, whose expertise, attention to detail, and wisdom are essential to this project; to the Folger's Photography Department; to Deborah Curren-Aquino, for continuing superb editorial assistance; to Alice Falk for her expert copyediting; to Michael Poston for unfailing computer support; to Anna Levine; and to Rebecca Niles (whose help is crucial). We are grateful to Leslie Thomson and Roslyn L. Knutson for theater history expertise. Among the editions we consulted, we found René Weis's *Parallel Text Edition* (2010) and R. A. Foakes's Arden edition (1997) especially useful. Finally, we once again express our gratitude to the late Jean Miller for the wonderful images she unearthed, to Stephen Llano for twenty-five years of invaluable assistance as our production editor, and to the ever-supportive staff of the Library Reading Room.

Barbara A. Mowat and Paul Werstine
2015

# Shakespeare's *King Lear*

So great is the suffering depicted in Shakespeare's *King Lear* that one has trouble finding the words to write about it. It is a play that relentlessly challenges its readers and theater audiences with the magnitude, intensity, and sheer duration of the pain that it represents. While other tragedies, including many of Shakespeare's, depict their characters experiencing a measure of joy and satisfaction before the onset of their misery, *King Lear* offers us no such relief. From beginning to end, all of its figures suffer, and all attempt various strategies to escape their suffering—some hardening their hearts, others engaging in orgies of violence, many devoting themselves to alleviating the suffering of others, Lear himself raging against his own pain until his sanity cracks. In this play only death seems to provide escape from "the rack of this tough world."

What, then, keeps bringing us back to *King Lear*? There is, of course, the power of the language. Once one has absorbed this play, one can articulate one's own suffering; one can put language to one's horror in the face of human cruelty and poverty; one has words to express the depths of grief that follow on extreme loss. But the fact that *King Lear* is almost equally powerful when translated (for example, into Japanese), converted to film, and set in lands far different from ancient Britain makes it likely that it is the story told in *Lear* that, in large part, draws us to the play. Within *Lear* are stories of two families, each caught up in a struggle between greed and cruelty, on the one hand, and support and consolation on the other. Each family is centered in an aging father, one an imperious near-tyrant, the other a gullible sensualist, each of whom sees his children through a distorted lens and, turning against the child who truly loves him, unleashes in his other child (or, in Lear's case, children) enormous greed, lust, and ambition.

This double story draws us because it tells us about families—about fathers and daughters, fathers and sons, sisters and their husbands and lovers, brothers natural and unnatural. In this play, ordinary jealousies, demands for love, sibling rivalries, desire for money and power, petty cruelties are all taken to the extreme; we can see ourselves and our small vices magnified to gigantic proportions. Also in this play we can see the end of our lives, with old age portrayed in all its vulnerability, helplessness, pride, and, finally, perhaps, wisdom. Lear had envisioned a world in which old men would continue to be respected even after giving away their money and their power, a world in which everyone would behave as Kent does, continuing to admire and obey because of the authority that inheres in Lear himself. Lear learns that once time and age have weakened one, without money and power one is almost helpless against the ravages of greed and power-hunger—but his final speech to Cordelia suggests that he also learns that, finally, greed and power-hunger do not really matter. Lear moves out of the world of the young and the middle-aged and into an old-age world of letting go. This play's special understanding of old age explains in part why this most devastating of Shakespeare's tragedies is also perhaps his most moving.

For a "Modern Perspective" on *King Lear*, we invite you, after you have read the play, to read the essay by the late Professor Susan Snyder of Swarthmore College, printed at the back of this book.

# Reading Shakespeare's Language: *King Lear*

For many people today, reading Shakespeare's language can be a problem—but it is a problem that can be solved. Those who have studied Latin (or even French or German or Spanish) and those who are used to reading poetry will have little difficulty understanding the language of poetic drama. Others, though, need to develop the skills of untangling unusual sentence structures and of recognizing and understanding poetic compressions, omissions, and wordplay. And even those skilled in reading unusual sentence structures may have occasional trouble with Shakespeare's words. More than four hundred years of "static"—caused by changes in language and in life—intervene between his speaking and our hearing. Most of his immense vocabulary is still in use, but a few of his words are no longer used, and many of his words now have meanings quite different from those they had in the sixteenth and seventeenth centuries. In the theater, most of these difficulties are solved for us by actors who study the language and articulate it for us so that the essential meaning is heard—or, when combined with stage action, is at least *felt*. When we are reading on our own, we must do what each actor does: go over the lines (often with a dictionary close at hand) until the puzzles are solved and the lines yield up their poetry and the characters speak in words and phrases that are, suddenly, rewarding and wonderfully memorable.

## Shakespeare's Words

As you begin to read the opening scenes of a Shakespeare play, you may notice occasional unfamiliar words. Some are unfamiliar simply because we no longer use them. In the opening scenes of *King Lear*, for example, we find such words as *haply* (perchance, perhaps), *sith* (since), and *sirrah* (a term of address that shows the speaker's position of authority). Words of this kind are explained in notes to the text and will become familiar the more of Shakespeare's plays you read.

In *King Lear*, as in all of Shakespeare's writing, more problematic are words that are still in use but that now have different meanings. In the opening line of *King Lear*, the word *affected* is used where we would say "been partial to." Later in the first scene, we find *several* where we would use "separate," *addition* where we would use "title," *owes* where we would use "owns," and *plighted* where we would use "pleated" or "folded." In the play's second scene, *character* means "handwriting," *closet* means "private room," and *practices* means "plots." Again, such words will be explained in the notes to this text, but they, too, will become familiar as you continue to read Shakespeare's language.

Some words are strange not because of the "static" introduced by changes in language over the past centuries but because these are words that Shakespeare is using to build a dramatic world that has its own space, time, history, and background mythology. *King Lear* is a particularly interesting example of this practice, in that, in this play, Shakespeare creates two worlds separated by centuries of time but that seem to exist simultaneously. One of these worlds is that of the Britain inhabited by the legendary King Leir, who, in the histories of Shakespeare's time, came to power "in the year of the world 3105"—i.e., in 845 B.C.E., many years before the founding of Rome. This world is created through references to "the mysteries of Hecate," to "Scythians" and other barbaric peoples who "make their generations messes [i.e., eat their own young]," to "Apollo" and "Jupiter" (both of whom play important parts in the stories of early Britain). This world is recalled throughout the play in references to "Sarum Plain" (the prehistoric name for Salisbury Plain) and "Camelot," in repeated references to "the gods," and in dialogue about astrology (reportedly of wide influence in the early days of Britain), including such terms as "sectary astronomical," "the operations of the orbs," and "under the Dragon's tail."

At the same time, the early scenes of the play create a court and a political world that linguistically reflect Shakespeare's own time. This is a world of "dukes," "princes," "kings"; it is a world of courtly phrases ("My services to your lordship," "I must love you and sue to know you better," "I shall study deserving") and of formal courtly orders ("Attend the lords of Burgundy and France," "To thine and Albany's issue be this perpetual"). The two worlds of the play are linked through words that describe the land of Britain—"shadowy forests," "wide-skirted meads," "champains riched, with plenteous rivers"—words that could describe both ancient and seventeenth-century Britain. It is possible that, in part, *King Lear*'s seeming timelessness is a function of this double world created by the play's diction.

## Shakespeare's Sentences

In an English sentence, meaning is quite dependent on the place given each word. "The dog bit the boy" and

"The boy bit the dog" mean very different things, even though the individual words are the same. Because English places such importance on the positions of words in sentences, on the way words are arranged, unusual arrangements can puzzle a reader. Shakespeare frequently shifts his sentences away from "normal" English arrangements—often in order to create the rhythm he seeks, sometimes to use a line's poetic rhythm to emphasize a particular word, sometimes to give a character his or her own speech patterns or to allow the character to speak in a special way. When we attend a good performance of the play, the actors will have worked out the sentence structures and will articulate the sentences so that the meaning is clear. When reading the play, we need to do as the actor does: that is, when puzzled by a character's speech, check to see if the words are being presented in an unusual sequence.

Often Shakespeare places the verb before the subject (i.e., instead of "He goes" we find "Goes he"). In the opening scene of *King Lear*, when Gloucester says "yet was his mother fair" (instead of "yet his mother was fair"), he is using such a construction. Such inversions rarely cause much confusion. More problematic is Shakespeare's frequent placing of the object before the verb and sometimes before the subject and verb (i.e., instead of "I hit him," we might find "Him I hit"). When Lear says "That we our largest bounty may extend," he is using such an inverted construction (the normal order would be "that we may extend our largest bounty"). Lear uses another such inversion later in the same scene when he says "Ourself . . . shall our abode / Make with you," and again with "Five days we do allot thee for provision." The king of France uses a similar inversion when he says to Cordelia "Thee and thy virtues here I seize upon." *King Lear* is among those plays of Shakespeare that make frequent use of this more complicated kind of inversion. In this play, in fact, Shakespeare sometimes complicates his sentences yet further by combining subject/verb/object inversions with subject/verb inversions—as in Goneril's remark to Regan: "Such unconstant starts are we like to have from him" (where the normal order would be "We are like [i.e., likely] to have such unconstant starts from him").

Inversions are not the only unusual sentence structures in Shakespeare's language. Often in his sentences words that would normally appear together are separated from each other. (This may be done to create a particular rhythm or to stress a particular word.) In Lear's command to his daughters in the opening scene, "Tell me, my daughters— / Since now we will divest us both of rule, / Interest of territory, cares of state— / Which of you shall we say doth love us most," the phrase "tell me . . . which" is interrupted by Lear's explanation of why he is giving this command. Later in the scene he separates subject from verb when he says "Ourself by monthly course, / With reservation of an hundred knights / By you to be sustained, shall our abode / Make with you by due turn," where "ourself [i.e., I] . . . shall our abode / Make" is interrupted by a series of phrases, and the verb and its object, as noted above, are themselves inverted. In order to create for yourself sentences that seem more like the English of everyday speech, you may wish to rearrange the words, putting together the word clusters and placing the remaining words in their more normal order. You will usually find that the sentence will gain in clarity but will lose its rhythm or shift its emphasis.

Locating and, if necessary, rearranging words that "belong together" is especially necessary in passages that separate subjects from verbs and verbs from objects by long delaying or expanding interruptions—

a structure that is used frequently in *King Lear.* For example, when Lear asks Burgundy whether he wants to marry the now dowerless Cordelia, he uses such an interrupted construction:

> *Will you,* with those infirmities she owes,
> Unfriended, new-adopted to our hate,
> Dowered with our curse and strangered with our oath,
> *Take her or leave her?* (1.1.231–35)

The king of France answers Lear's charges against Cordelia with a speech containing a similarly interrupted clause:

> This is most strange,
> That *she* whom even but now was your best object,
> The argument of your praise, balm of your age,
> The best, the dearest, *should* in this trice of time
> *Commit* a thing so monstrous to dismantle
> So many folds of favor. (1.1.245–51)

Cordelia herself responds to France's speech with a plea to Lear built around an interrupted structure:

> *I* yet *beseech your Majesty*—
> If for I want that glib and oily art
> To speak and purpose not, since what I well intend
> I'll do 't before I speak—*that you make known*
> It is no vicious blot, murder, or foulness,
> No unchaste action or dishonored step
> That hath deprived me of your grace and favor. . . .
> (1.1.257–64)

In each of these cases—and similar constructions occur throughout the play—the interruption of the main sentence elements serves to heighten emotional intensity. The separation of the basic sentence

elements—"will you . . . take her or leave her," "she . . .
should . . . commit," "I beseech your Majesty . . . that
you make known"—forces the audience to attend to
the characters' accusations and explanations, and to
feel the power of emotion conveyed in the interrupting
material, while waiting for the basic sentence elements
to come together.

Occasionally, rather than separating basic sentence
elements, Shakespeare simply holds them back, delaying them until much subordinate material has already
been given. Again, emotional intensity is heightened
for an audience as it listens and waits for the sentence's
subject and verb. Lear uses such a delaying structure
when he says to Cordelia, at 1.1.121–28,

> For by the sacred radiance of the sun,
> The mysteries of Hecate and the night,
> By all the operation of the orbs
> From whom we do exist and cease to be,
> Here *I disclaim all my paternal care,*
> *Propinquity, and property of blood,*
> *And as a stranger* to my heart and me
> *Hold thee* from this forever.

Again, in his speech banishing Kent, Lear uses a similar delaying structure:

> That [i.e., because] thou hast sought to make us
>        break our vows—
> Which we durst never yet—and with strained pride
> To come betwixt our sentence and our power,
> Which nor our nature nor our place can bear,
> Our potency made good, *take thy reward.* . . .
>                                          (1.1.192–96)

Shakespeare's sentences are sometimes complicated
not because of unusual structures or interruptions or

delays but because he omits words and parts of words that English sentences normally require. (In conversation, we, too, often omit words. We say "Heard from him yet?" and our hearer supplies the missing "Have you.") Frequent reading of Shakespeare—and of other poets—trains us to supply such missing words. In plays written five or ten years earlier than *King Lear*, omissions seem to be used primarily for rhythmic effects. In *King Lear*, however, Shakespeare uses omissions—of verbs, of nouns, of prepositions, of parts of words— as an integral part of the language world he is creating. Often the omission is uncomplicated, as in Kent's "My life I never held but as a pawn / To wage against thine enemies, nor fear to lose it," where "nor do I fear" becomes "nor fear." A similarly uncomplicated omission is found in Lear's "Therefore beseech you" (1.1.241), a compression of "therefore I beseech you," as well as in France's "Commit a thing so monstrous to dismantle" (1.1.250), where one needs to supply an "as" before "to dismantle."

Many times in *Lear*, however, omissions are coupled with inversions or other dislocations of language. When Cordelia says, at line 317, "But yet, alas, *stood I* within his grace," the word "if" has been omitted and the subject and verb inverted. When Regan replies to her, at line 320, "*Prescribe not us* our duty," omission has again been combined with subject/verb inversion. (The normal structure would be "Do not prescribe our duty to us.") Gloucester's "Why so earnestly seek you to put up that letter?" (1.2.29–30) combines two inversions and an omission. (The normal order would be "Why do you seek to put up . . . ? ") Since these omissions and inversions occur as often in prose as they do in verse, they seem to be used not only for rhythmic effects but also to create a language world of unusually complicated syntax.

## Shakespearean Wordplay

Shakespeare plays with language so often and so variously that books are written on the topic. His wordplay in *King Lear* is particularly interesting in the way it varies Shakespeare's usual use of puns and figurative language. A pun is a play on words that sound the same but that have different meanings. In many of Shakespeare's plays (*Romeo and Juliet* and *Taming of the Shrew* are good examples), puns are used frequently. In *King Lear* they are used less often; when they are used, they carry interesting ambiguities, often conveying what may be sophisticated courtly wit or may be somewhat crass double entendre. For example, in the opening lines of the play, Gloucester responds to Kent's question "Is not this your son, my lord?" with the statement "His breeding, sir, hath been at my charge," a sentence that plays on two meanings of "breeding" and two meanings of "at my charge," so that Gloucester can be heard to say, simultaneously, "I have been accused of begetting him" and "I have had to pay for his education." In response to Kent's "I cannot conceive you" (in which *cannot conceive* means "do not understand"), Gloucester replies "Sir, this young fellow's mother could," pretending to understand *conceive* to mean "conceive a child." When Gloucester asks Kent "Do you smell a fault?" Kent replies "I cannot wish the fault undone, the issue of it being so proper," playing with *issue* as meaning both "result" and "offspring" and with *proper* as meaning both "appropriate, fitting" and "handsome," so that Kent's words say both that the outcome is fitting and the offspring attractive. In a more serious passage near the end of the same scene, Cordelia leaves her sisters with the statement "Time shall unfold what plighted cunning hides," where *plighted* has the primary meaning of "pleated, folded," and *unfold* is a pun on "unpleat" and "reveal"; the statement carries an additional resonance in that *plighted* can also be used in reference to someone who has pledged her word or her honesty, so that Cordelia can be heard to say that her sisters, who have outwardly plighted their truth and love to Lear, have actually pledged instead their cunning.

Not only are puns used rarely and complexly in *King Lear*, but figurative language is also shifted away from Shakespeare's customary use of metaphors (i.e., plays on words in which one object or idea is expressed as if it were something else, something with which it is said to share common features). Occasionally one does find straightforward metaphoric language. For example, as the characters' suffering intensifies near the end of the play, their anguish is expressed through metaphors about instruments of torture. Lear says to Cordelia, for instance, near the end of Act 4, "I am bound / Upon a wheel of fire, that mine own tears / Do scald like molten lead"; a similar metaphor of torture is used at the end of the play when Kent urges Edgar to let Lear die: "O, let him pass! He hates him / That would upon the rack of this tough world / Stretch him out longer."

These straightforward metaphors are, however, relatively rare in *King Lear*. More often the metaphors are either displaced or are placed slightly beneath the surface of the language. Most of the Fool's speeches can be seen as examples of displaced and extended metaphor—as analogies in which the listener must provide the sometimes difficult connections between Lear's situation and the Fool's seemingly random comments. To take only two of many examples: In 1.4, Goneril addresses Lear as if he were her dependent, threatening him with "censure" and "redresses":

I had thought by making this well known unto you
To have found a safe redress, but now grow fearful,
By what yourself too late have spoke and done,
That you protect this course and put it on
By your allowance; which if you should, the fault
Would not 'scape censure, nor the redresses sleep
Which in the tender of a wholesome weal
Might in their working do you that offense,
Which else were shame, that then necessity
Will call discreet proceeding.        (1.4.210–19)

In response to this speech, the Fool comments:

The hedge-sparrow fed the cuckoo so long,
That it's had it head bit off by it young.
So out went the candle, and we were left darkling.
(1.4.221–23)

Metaphorically, according to the Fool, Lear is a hedge-sparrow, Goneril the cuckoo that the sparrow has fed, thinking it his; like the sparrow, Lear is now being attacked by his young. As Goneril continues her attack, the Fool comments: "May not an ass know when the cart draws the horse?" Metaphorically, Lear and Goneril are a horse and cart whose functions have gotten reversed.

Often the play's language contains metaphors that do not lie clearly on the surface of the play but, when discovered, make the characters' speeches much more vivid. When Edmund says, in the play's second scene, "This is the excellent foppery of the world, that when we are sick in fortune (often the surfeits of our own behavior) we make guilty of our disasters the sun, the moon, and stars," just under the surface of his language is a metaphor in which bad luck is imaged as a sickness caused by our own "surfeits"—i.e., overindulgences. (These lines also contain an amusing play on the word *disasters*, a word of astrological origin meaning, literally, "from the stars.") In the opening scene, Lear's "'tis our fast intent / To shake all cares and business from our age, / Conferring them on younger strengths, while we / Unburdened crawl toward death" (1.1.40–43) carries within it a metaphor in which man is pictured as a pack-animal that, in its old age, shakes off its heavy load. Later in the same scene, within Lear's "I do invest you jointly with my power, / Preeminence, and all the large effects / That troop with majesty" (1.1.146–48), the word *troop* metaphorically makes "power" and "preeminence" and other "large effects" into companions that march along with "majesty."

In this final example we see not only a metaphor (in which the attributes of kingship are likened to the king's traveling companions) but also personification, a kind of figurative language used with unusual frequency and power in *King Lear*. In personification, abstract qualities or natural objects are given human characteristics (so that "power" is allowed to "troop"). Kent uses personification when he says to Lear:

> Think'st thou that duty shall have dread to speak
> When power to flattery bows? To plainness honor's
>   bound
> When majesty falls to folly.          (1.1.164–67)

In these lines, *duty, power, flattery, honor,* and *majesty* are given the ability to speak, to feel dread, to fall, to bow, to receive bows, to remain loyal.

Some of the most powerful scenes in *King Lear* depend heavily on personification. Lear responds to Goneril's initial attack on him with his personification of "ingratitude":

Ingratitude, thou marble-hearted fiend,
More hideous when thou show'st thee in a child
Than the sea monster!    (1.4.270–72)

His powerful speeches in 4.6 on "how this world goes"
depend heavily on the personification of such abstrac-
tions as *vices, sin,* and *justice,* to which he attributes
the ability to wear clothing and to be dressed in gold-
plated armor:

Through tattered clothes small vices do appear.
Robes and furred gowns hide all. Plate sin with gold,
And the strong lance of justice hurtless breaks.
Arm it in rags, a pygmy's straw does pierce it.
                                    (4.6.180–84)

Most importantly, his speeches in the storm scenes of
Act 3 are built around personifications in which wind,
rain, lightning, and thunder are given cheeks that can
crack, emotions that can rage; the elements, in these
speeches, experience "horrible pleasures" and become
"servile ministers" who have joined with Goneril and
Regan to destroy him.

## Implied Stage Action

Finally, in reading Shakespeare's plays we should
always remember that what we are reading is a performance script. The dialogue is written to be spoken
by actors who, at the same time, are moving, gestur-
ing, picking up objects, weeping, shaking their fists.
Some stage action is described in what are called
"stage directions"; some is suggested within the dialogue itself. We must learn to be alert to such signals
as we stage the play in our imaginations. When, in the

second scene of *King Lear*, Gloucester says to Edmund "Why so earnestly seek you to put up that letter?" it is clear that Edmund puts away the piece of paper he has been holding; Gloucester's following question, "What needed then that terrible dispatch of it into your pocket?" lets us know that Edmund's putting away of the letter was done obtrusively and that he put it in his pocket, not on a shelf or in a book. When in 2.4 Goneril enters and Lear says "O, Regan, will you take her by the hand?" the stage action is obvious. It is less obvious in 2.1 exactly how we are to imagine Edmund's actions when he says "Some blood drawn on me would beget opinion / Of my more fierce endeavor. I have seen drunkards / Do more than this in sport." Since a few lines later he says to his father "Look, sir, I bleed," he has clearly wounded himself in some fashion, but the director and the actor (and the reader, in imagination) must decide on his precise action. Which weapon he uses and how and where he wounds himself will be answered variously from production to production. Learning to read the language of stage action repays one many times over when one reaches a crucial scene like that of the blinding of Gloucester (3.7) or the play's final scene with its sequence of duels, exits, entrances, and deaths, in both of which scenes implied stage action vitally affects our response to the play.

It is immensely rewarding to work carefully with Shakespeare's language so that the words, the sentences, the wordplay, and the implied stage action all become clear—as readers for the past four centuries have discovered. It may be more pleasurable to attend a good performance of a play—though not everyone has thought so. But the joy of being able to stage one of Shakespeare's plays in one's imagination, to return to passages that continue to yield further meanings (or further questions) the more one reads them—these are pleasures that, for many, rival (or at least augment) those of the performed text, and certainly make it worth considerable effort to "break the code" of Elizabethan poetic drama and let free the remarkable language that makes up a Shakespeare text.

# Shakespeare's Life

Surviving documents that give us glimpses into the life of William Shakespeare show us a playwright, poet, and actor who grew up in the market town of Stratford-upon-Avon, spent his professional life in London, and returned to Stratford a wealthy landowner. He was born in April 1564, died in April 1616, and is buried inside the chancel of Holy Trinity Church in Stratford.

We wish we could know more about the life of the world's greatest dramatist. His plays and poems are testaments to his wide reading—especially to his knowledge of Virgil, Ovid, Plutarch, Holinshed's *Chronicles*, and the Bible—and to his mastery of the English language, but we can only speculate about his education. We know that the King's New School in Stratford-upon-Avon was considered excellent. The school was one of the English "grammar schools" established to educate young men, primarily in Latin grammar and literature. As in other schools of the time, students began their studies at the age of four or five in the attached "petty school," and there learned to read and write in English, studying primarily the catechism from the Book of Common Prayer. After two years in the petty school, students entered the lower form (grade) of the grammar school, where they began the serious study

Title page of a 1573 Latin and Greek catechism for children.
From Alexander Nowell, *Catechismus paruus pueris
primum Latine* . . . (1573).

of Latin grammar and Latin texts that would occupy most of the remainder of their school days. (Several Latin texts that Shakespeare used repeatedly in writing his plays and poems were texts that schoolboys memorized and recited.) Latin comedies were introduced early in the lower form; in the upper form, which the boys entered at age ten or eleven, students wrote their own Latin orations and declamations, studied Latin historians and rhetoricians, and began the study of Greek using the Greek New Testament.

Since the records of the Stratford "grammar school" do not survive, we cannot prove that William Shakespeare attended the school; however, every indication (his father's position as an alderman and bailiff of Stratford, the playwright's own knowledge of the Latin classics, scenes in the plays that recall grammar-school experiences—for example, *The Merry Wives of Windsor*, 4.1) suggests that he did. We also lack generally accepted documentation about Shakespeare's life after his schooling ended and his professional life in London began. His marriage in 1582 (at age eighteen) to Anne Hathaway and the subsequent births of his daughter Susanna (1583) and the twins Judith and Hamnet (1585) are recorded, but how he supported himself and where he lived are not known. Nor do we know when and why he left Stratford for the London theatrical world, nor how he rose to be the important figure in that world that he had become by the early 1590s.

We do know that by 1592 he had achieved some prominence in London as both an actor and a playwright. In that year was published a book by the playwright Robert Greene attacking an actor who had the audacity to write blank-verse drama and who was "in his own conceit [i.e., opinion] the only Shake-scene in a country." Since Greene's attack includes a parody of a line from one of Shakespeare's early plays, there is little doubt that it is Shakespeare to whom he refers, a "Shake-scene" who had aroused Greene's fury by successfully competing with university-educated dramatists like Greene himself. It was in 1593 that Shakespeare became a published poet. In that year he published his long narrative poem *Venus and Adonis*; in 1594, he followed it with *The Rape of Lucrece*. Both poems were dedicated to the young earl of Southampton (Henry Wriothesley), who may have become Shakespeare's patron.

It seems no coincidence that Shakespeare wrote these narrative poems at a time when the theaters were closed because of the plague, a contagious epidemic disease that devastated the population of London. When the theaters reopened in 1594, Shakespeare apparently resumed his double career of actor and playwright and began his long (and seemingly profitable) service as an acting-company shareholder. Records for December of 1594 show him to be a leading member of the Lord Chamberlain's Men. It was this company of actors, later named the King's Men, for whom he would be a principal actor, dramatist, and shareholder for the rest of his career.

So far as we can tell, that career spanned about twenty years. In the 1590s, he wrote his plays on English history as well as several comedies and at least two tragedies (*Titus Andronicus* and *Romeo and Juliet*). These histories, comedies, and tragedies are the plays credited to him in 1598 in a work, *Palladis Tamia*, that in one chapter compares English writers with "Greek, Latin, and Italian Poets." There the author, Francis Meres, claims that Shakespeare is comparable to the Latin dramatists Seneca for tragedy and Plautus for comedy, and calls him "the most excellent in both kinds for the stage." He also names him "Mellifluous and honey-tongued Shakespeare": "I say," writes Meres, "that the Muses would speak with Shakespeare's fine filed phrase, if they would speak English." Since Meres also mentions Shakespeare's "sugared sonnets among his private friends," it is assumed that many of Shakespeare's sonnets (not published until 1609) were also written in the 1590s.

In 1599, Shakespeare's company built a theater for themselves across the river from London, naming it the Globe. The plays that are considered by many to be Shakespeare's major tragedies (*Hamlet, Othello, King Lear,* and *Macbeth*) were written while the company was resident in this theater, as were such comedies as *Twelfth Night* and *Measure for Measure.* Many of Shakespeare's plays were performed at court (both for Queen Elizabeth I and, after her death in 1603, for King James I), some were presented at the Inns of Court (the residences of London's legal societies), and some were doubtless performed in other towns, at the universities, and at great houses when the King's Men went on tour; otherwise, his plays from 1599 to 1608 were, so far as we know, performed only at the Globe. Between 1608 and 1612, Shakespeare wrote several plays—among them *The Winter's Tale* and *The Tempest*—presumably for the company's new indoor Blackfriars theater, though the plays were performed also at the Globe and at court. Surviving documents describe a performance of *The Winter's Tale* in 1611 at the Globe, for example, and performances of *The Tempest* in 1611 and 1613 at the royal palace of Whitehall.

Shakespeare seems to have written very little after 1612, the year in which he probably wrote *King Henry VIII.* (It was at a performance of *Henry VIII* in 1613 that the Globe caught fire and burned to the ground.) Sometime between 1610 and 1613, according to many biographers, he returned to live in Stratford-upon-Avon, where he owned a large house and considerable prop-

Ptolemaic universe.
From Marcus Manilius, *The sphere of* . . . (1675).

erty, and where his wife and his two daughters lived. (His son Hamnet had died in 1596.) However, other biographers suggest that Shakespeare did not leave London for good until much closer to the time of his death. During his professional years in London, Shakespeare had presumably derived income from the acting company's profits as well as from his own career as an actor, from the sale of his play manuscripts to the acting company, and, after 1599, from his shares as an owner of the Globe. It was presumably that income, carefully invested in land and other property, that made him the wealthy man that surviving documents show him to have become. It is also assumed that William Shakespeare's growing wealth and reputation played some part in inclining the Crown, in 1596, to grant John Shakespeare, William's father, the coat of arms that he had so long sought. William Shakespeare died in Stratford on April 23, 1616 (according to the epitaph carved under his bust in Holy Trinity Church) and was buried on April 25. Seven years after his death, his collected plays were published as *Mr. William Shakespeares Comedies, Histories, & Tragedies* (the work now known as the First Folio).

The years in which Shakespeare wrote were among the most exciting in English history. Intellectually, the discovery, translation, and printing of Greek and Roman classics were making available a set of works and worldviews that interacted complexly with Christian texts and beliefs. The result was a questioning, a vital intellectual ferment, that provided energy for the period's amazing dramatic and literary output and that fed directly into Shakespeare's plays. The Ghost in *Hamlet*, for example, is wonderfully complicated in part because he is a figure from Roman tragedy—the spirit of the dead returning to seek revenge—who at the same time inhabits a Christian hell (or purgatory); Hamlet's description of humankind reflects at one moment the Neoplatonic wonderment at mankind ("What a piece of work is a man!") and, at the next, the Christian view of the human condition ("And yet, to me, what is this quintessence of dust?").

As intellectual horizons expanded, so also did geographical and cosmological horizons. New worlds— both North and South America—were explored, and in them were found human beings who lived and worshiped in ways radically different from those of Renaissance Europeans and Englishmen. The universe during these years also seemed to shift and expand. Copernicus had earlier theorized that the Earth was not the center of the cosmos but revolved as a planet around the sun. Galileo's telescope, created in 1609, allowed scientists to see that Copernicus had been correct: the universe was not organized with the Earth at the center, nor was it so nicely circumscribed as people had, until that time, thought. In terms of expanding horizons, the impact of these discoveries on people's beliefs— religious, scientific, and philosophical—cannot be overstated.

London, too, rapidly expanded and changed during the years that Shakespeare lived there. London—the center of England's government, its economy, its royal court, its overseas trade—was, during these years, becoming an exciting metropolis, drawing to it thousands of new citizens every year. Troubled by overcrowding, by poverty, by recurring epidemics of the plague, London was also a mecca for the wealthy and the aristocratic, and for those who sought advancement at court, or power in government or finance or trade. One hears in Shakespeare's plays the voices of London—the struggles for power, the fear of venereal disease, the language of buying and selling. One hears as well the voices of Stratford-upon-Avon—references to the nearby Forest of Arden, to sheepherding, to small-town gossip, to village fairs and markets. Part of the richness of Shakespeare's work is the influence felt there of the various worlds in which he lived: the world of metropolitan London, the world of small-town and rural England, the world of the theater, and the worlds of craftsmen and shepherds.

That Shakespeare inhabited such worlds we know from surviving London and Stratford documents, as well as from the evidence of the plays and poems themselves. From such records we can sketch the dramatist's life. We know from his works that he was a voracious reader. We know from legal and business documents that he was a multifaceted theater man who became a wealthy landowner. We know a bit about his family life and a fair amount about his legal and financial dealings. Most scholars today depend upon such evidence as they draw their picture of the world's greatest playwright. Such, however, has not always been the case. Until the late eighteenth century, the William Shakespeare who lived in most biographies was the creation of legend and tradition. This was the Shakespeare who was supposedly caught poaching deer at Charlecote, the estate of Sir Thomas Lucy close by Stratford; this was the Shakespeare who fled from Sir Thomas's vengeance and made his way in London by taking care of horses outside a playhouse; this was the Shakespeare who reportedly could barely read, but whose natural gifts were extraordinary, whose father was a butcher who allowed his gifted son sometimes to help in the butcher shop, where William supposedly killed calves "in a high style," making a speech for the occasion. It was this legendary William Shakespeare whose Falstaff (in *1* and *2 Henry IV*) so pleased Queen Elizabeth that she demanded a play about Falstaff in love, and demanded that it be written in fourteen days (hence the existence of *The Merry Wives of Windsor*). It was this legendary Shakespeare who reached the top of his acting career in the roles of the Ghost in *Hamlet* and old Adam in *As You Like It*—and who died of a fever contracted by drinking too hard at "a merry meeting" with the poets Michael Drayton and Ben Jonson. This legendary Shakespeare is a rambunctious, undisciplined man, as attractively "wild" as his plays were seen by earlier generations to be. Unfortunately, there is no trace of evidence to support these wonderful stories.

Perhaps in response to the disreputable Shakespeare of legend—or perhaps in response to the fragmentary and, for some, all-too-ordinary Shakespeare documented by surviving records—some people since the mid-nineteenth century have argued that William Shakespeare could not have written the plays that bear his name. These persons have put forward some dozen names as more likely authors, among them Queen Elizabeth, Sir Francis Bacon, Edward de Vere (earl of Oxford), and Christopher Marlowe. Such attempts to find what for these people is a more believable author of the plays is a tribute to the regard in which the plays are held. Unfortunately for their claims, the documents that exist that provide evidence for the facts of Shakespeare's life tie him inextricably to the body of plays and poems that bear his name. Unlikely as it seems to those who want the works to have been written by an aristocrat, a university graduate, or an "important" person, the plays and poems seem clearly to have been produced by a man from Stratford-upon-Avon with a very good "grammar-school" education and a life of experience in London and in the world of the London theater. How this particular man produced the works that dominate the cultures of much of the world almost four hundred years after his death is one of life's mysteries—and one that will continue to tease our imaginations as we continue to delight in his plays and poems.

## Shakespeare's Theater

The actors of Shakespeare's time are known to have performed plays in a great variety of locations. They played at court (that is, in the great halls of such royal residences as Whitehall, Hampton Court, and Greenwich); they played in halls at the universities of Oxford and Cambridge, and at the Inns of Court (the residences in London of the legal societies); and they also played in the private houses of great lords and civic officials. Sometimes acting companies went on tour from London into the provinces, often (but not only) when outbreaks of bubonic plague in the capital forced the closing of theaters to reduce the possibility of contagion in crowded audiences. In the provinces the actors usually staged their plays in churches (until around 1600) or in guildhalls. While surviving records show only a handful of occasions when actors played at inns while on tour, London inns were important playing places up until the 1590s.

The building of theaters in London had begun only shortly before Shakespeare wrote his first plays in the 1590s. These theaters were of two kinds: outdoor or public playhouses that could accommodate large numbers of playgoers, and indoor or private theaters for much smaller audiences. What is usually regarded as the first London outdoor public playhouse was called simply the Theatre. James Burbage—the father of Richard Burbage, who was perhaps the most famous actor

A stylized representation of the Globe theater.
From Claes Jansz Visscher, *Londinum florentissima Britanniae urbs* . . . [c. 1625].

in Shakespeare's company—built it in 1576 in an area north of the city of London called Shoreditch. Among the more famous of the other public playhouses that capitalized on the new fashion were the Curtain and the Fortune (both also built north of the city), the Rose, the Swan, the Globe, and the Hope (all located on the Bankside, a region just across the Thames south of the city of London). All these playhouses had to be built outside the jurisdiction of the city of London because many civic officials were hostile to the performance of drama and repeatedly petitioned the royal council to abolish it.

The theaters erected on the Bankside (a region under the authority of the Church of England, whose head was the monarch) shared the neighborhood with houses of prostitution and with the Paris Garden, where the blood sports of bearbaiting and bullbaiting were carried on. There may have been no clear distinction between playhouses and buildings for such sports, for we know that the Hope was used for both plays and baiting and that Philip Henslowe, owner of the Rose and, later, partner in the ownership of the Fortune, was also a partner in a monopoly on baiting. All these forms of entertainment were easily accessible to Londoners by boat across the Thames or over London Bridge.

Evidently Shakespeare's company prospered on the Bankside. They moved there in 1599. Threatened by difficulties in renewing the lease on the land where their first theater (the Theatre) had been built, Shakespeare's company took advantage of the Christmas holiday in 1598 to dismantle the Theatre and transport its timbers across the Thames to the Bankside, where, in 1599, these timbers were used in the building of the Globe. The weather in late December 1598 is recorded as having been especially harsh. It was so cold that the Thames was "nigh [nearly] frozen," and there was heavy snow. Perhaps the weather aided Shakespeare's company in eluding their landlord, the snow hiding their activity and the freezing of the Thames allowing them to slide the timbers across to the Bankside without paying tolls for repeated trips over London Bridge. Attractive as this narrative is, it remains just as likely that the heavy snow hampered transport of the timbers in wagons through the London streets to the river. It also must be remembered that the Thames was, according to report, only "nigh frozen," and therefore did not necessarily provide solid footing. Whatever the precise circumstances of this fascinating event in English theater history, Shakespeare's company was able to begin playing at their new Globe theater on the Bankside in 1599. After this theater burned down in 1613 during the staging of Shakespeare's *Henry VIII* (its thatch roof was set alight by cannon fire called for in performance), Shakespeare's company immediately rebuilt on the same location. The second Globe seems to have been a grander structure than its predecessor. It remained in use until the beginning of the English Civil War in 1642, when Parliament officially closed the theaters. Soon thereafter it was pulled down.

The public theaters of Shakespeare's time were very different buildings from our theaters today. First of all, they were open-air playhouses. As recent excavations of the Rose and the Globe confirm, some were polygonal or roughly circular in shape; the Fortune, however, was square. The most recent estimates of their size put the diameter of these buildings at 72 feet (the Rose) to 100 feet (the Globe), but we know that they held vast audiences of two or three thousand, who must have been squeezed together quite tightly. Some of these spectators paid extra to sit or stand in the two or three levels of roofed galleries that extended, on the upper levels, all the way around the theater and surrounded an open space. In this space were the stage and, perhaps, the tiring house (what we would call dressing rooms), as well as the so-called yard. In the yard stood the spectators who chose to pay less, the ones whom Hamlet contemptuously called "groundlings." For a roof they had only the sky, and so they were exposed to all kinds of weather. They stood on a floor that was sometimes made of mortar and sometimes of ash mixed with the shells of hazelnuts, which, it has recently been discovered, were standard flooring material in the period.

Unlike the yard, the stage itself was covered by a roof. Its ceiling, called "the heavens," is thought to have been elaborately painted to depict the sun, moon, stars, and planets. The exact size of the stage remains hard to determine. We have a single sketch of part of the interior of the Swan. A Dutchman named Johannes de Witt visited this theater around 1596 and sent a sketch of it back to his friend, Arend van Buchel. Because van Buchel found de Witt's letter and sketch of interest, he copied both into a book. It is van Buchel's copy, adapted, it seems, to the shape and size of the page in his book, that survives. In this sketch, the stage appears to be a large rectangular platform that thrusts far out into the yard, perhaps even as far as the center of the circle formed by the surrounding galleries. This drawing, combined with the specifications for the size of the stage in the building contract for the Fortune, has led scholars to conjecture that the stage on which Shakespeare's plays were performed must have measured approximately 43 feet in width and 27 feet in depth, a vast acting area. But the digging up of a large part of the Rose by late-twentieth-century archaeologists has provided evidence of a quite different stage design. The Rose stage was a platform tapered at the corners and much shallower than what seems to be depicted in the van Buchel sketch. Indeed, its measurements seem to be about 37.5 feet across at its widest point and only 15.5 feet deep. Because the surviving indications of stage size and design differ from each other so much, it is possible that the stages in other theaters, like the Theatre, the Curtain, and the Globe (the outdoor playhouses where we know that Shakespeare's plays were performed), were different from those at both the Swan and the Rose.

After about 1608 Shakespeare's plays were staged not only at the Globe but also at an indoor or private playhouse in Blackfriars. This theater had been constructed in 1596 by James Burbage in an upper hall of a former Dominican priory or monastic house. Although Henry VIII had dissolved all English monasteries in the 1530s (shortly after he had founded the Church of England), the area remained under church, rather than hostile civic, control. The hall that Burbage had purchased and renovated was a large one in which Parliament had once met. In the private theater that he constructed, the stage, lit by candles, was built across the narrow end of the hall, with boxes flanking it. The rest of the hall offered seating room only. Because there was no provision for standing room, the largest audience it could hold was less than a thousand, or about a quarter of what the Globe could accommodate. Admission to Blackfriars was correspondingly more expensive. Instead of a penny to stand in the yard at the Globe, it cost a minimum of sixpence to get into Blackfriars. The best seats at the Globe (in the Lords' Room in the gallery above and behind the stage) cost sixpence; but the boxes flanking the stage at Blackfriars were half a crown, or five times sixpence. Some spectators who were particularly interested in displaying themselves paid even more to sit on stools on the Blackfriars stage.

Whether in the outdoor or indoor playhouses, the

stages of Shakespeare's time were different from ours. They were not separated from the audience by the dropping of a curtain between acts and scenes. Therefore the playwrights of the time had to find other ways of signaling to the audience that one scene (to be imagined as occurring in one location at a given time) had ended and the next (to be imagined at perhaps a different location at a later time) had begun. The customary way used by Shakespeare and many of his contemporaries was to have everyone on stage exit at the end of one scene and have one or more different characters enter to begin the next. In a few cases, where characters remain onstage from one scene to another, the dialogue or stage action makes the change of location clear, and the characters are generally to be imagined as having moved from one place to another. For example, in *Romeo and Juliet*, Romeo and his friends remain onstage in Act 1 from scene 4 to scene 5, but they are represented as having moved between scenes from the street that leads to Capulet's house into Capulet's house itself. The new location is signaled in part by the appearance onstage of Capulet's servingmen carrying table napkins, something they would not take into the streets. Playwrights had to be quite resourceful in the use of hand properties, like the napkin, or in the use of dialogue to specify where the action was taking place in their plays because, in contrast to most of today's theaters, the playhouses of Shakespeare's time did not fill the stage with scenery to make the setting precise. A consequence of this difference was that the playwrights of Shakespeare's time did not have to specify exactly where the action of their plays was set when they did not choose to do so, and much of the action of their plays is tied to no specific place.

Usually Shakespeare's stage is referred to as a "bare stage," to distinguish it from the stages of the past two or three centuries with their elaborate sets. But the stage in Shakespeare's time was not completely bare. Philip Henslowe, owner of the Rose, lists in his inventory of stage properties a rock, three tombs, and two mossy banks. Stage directions in plays of the time also call for such things as thrones (or "states"), banquets (presumably tables with plaster replicas of food on them), and beds and tombs to be pushed onto the stage. Thus the stage often held more than the actors.

The actors did not limit their performing to the stage alone. Occasionally they went beneath the stage, as the Ghost appears to do in the first act of *Hamlet*. From there they could emerge onto the stage through a trapdoor. They could retire behind the hangings across the back of the stage, as, for example, the actor playing Polonius does when he hides behind the arras. Sometimes the hangings could be drawn back during a performance to "discover" one or more actors behind them. When performance required that an actor appear "above," as when Juliet is imagined to stand at the window of her chamber in the famous and misnamed "balcony scene," then the actor probably climbed the stairs to the gallery over the back of the stage and temporarily shared it with some of the spectators. The stage was also provided with ropes and winches so that actors could descend from, and reascend to, the "heavens."

Perhaps the greatest difference between dramatic performances in Shakespeare's time and ours was that in Shakespeare's England the roles of women were played by boys. (Some of these boys grew up to take male roles in their maturity.) There were no women in the acting companies. It was not so in Europe, and it had not always been so in the history of the English stage. There are records of women on English stages in the thirteenth and fourteenth centuries, two hundred years before Shakespeare's plays were performed. After the accession of James I in 1603, the queen of England and her ladies took part in entertainments at court called masques, and with the reopening of the theaters in 1660 at the restoration of Charles II, women again took their place on the public stage.

The chief competitors of such acting companies as the one to which Shakespeare belonged and for which he wrote were companies of exclusively boy actors. The competition was most intense in the early 1600s. There were then two principal children's companies: the Children of Paul's (the choirboys from St. Paul's Cathedral, whose private playhouse was near the cathedral); and the Children of the Chapel Royal (the choirboys from the monarch's private chapel, who performed at the Blackfriars theater built by Burbage in 1596). In *Hamlet* Shakespeare writes of "an aerie [nest] of children, little eyases [hawks], that cry out on the top of question and are most tyrannically clapped for 't. These are now the fashion and . . . berattle the common stages [attack the public theaters]." In the long run, the adult actors prevailed. The Children of Paul's dissolved around 1606. By about 1608 the Children of the Chapel Royal had been forced to stop playing at the Blackfriars theater, which was then taken over by the King's Men, Shakespeare's own troupe.

Acting companies and theaters of Shakespeare's time seem to have been organized in various ways. For example, with the building of the Globe, Shakespeare's company apparently managed itself, with the principal actors, Shakespeare among them, having the status of "sharers" and the right to a share in the takings, as well as the responsibility for a part of the expenses. Five of the sharers, including Shakespeare, owned the Globe. As actor, as sharer in an acting company and in ownership of theaters, and as playwright, Shakespeare was about as involved in the theatrical industry as one could imagine. Although Shakespeare and his fellows prospered, their status under the law was conditional upon the protection of powerful patrons. "Common players"—those who did not have patrons or masters—were classed in the language of the law with "vagabonds and sturdy beggars." So the actors had to secure for themselves the official rank of servants of patrons. Among the patrons under whose protection Shakespeare's company worked were the lord chamberlain and, after the accession of King James in 1603, the king himself.

In the early 1990s we began to learn a great deal more about the theaters in which Shakespeare and his contemporaries performed—or, at least, began to open up new questions about them. At that time about 70 percent of the Rose had been excavated, as had about 10 percent of the second Globe, the one built in 1614. Excavation was halted at that point, but London has come to value the sites of its early playhouses, and takes what opportunities it can to explore them more deeply, both on the Bankside and in Shoreditch. Information about the playhouses of Shakespeare's London is therefore a constantly changing resource.

# The Publication of Shakespeare's Plays

Eighteen of Shakespeare's plays found their way into print during the playwright's lifetime, but there is nothing to suggest that he took any interest in their publication. These eighteen appeared separately in editions in quarto or, in the case of *Henry VI, Part 3*, octavo format. The quarto pages are not much larger than a modern mass-market paperback book, and the octavo pages are even smaller; these little books were sold unbound for a few pence. The earliest of the quartos that still survive were printed in 1594, the year that both *Titus Andronicus* and a version of the play now called *Henry VI, Part 2* became available. While almost every one of these early quartos displays on its title page the name of the acting company that performed the play, only about half provide the name of the playwright, Shakespeare. The first quarto edition to bear the name Shakespeare on its title page is *Love's Labor's Lost* of 1598. A few of the quartos were popular with the book-buying public of Shakespeare's lifetime; for example, quarto *Richard II* went through five editions between 1597 and 1615. But most of the quartos were far from best sellers; *Love's Labor's Lost* (1598), for instance, was not reprinted in quarto until 1631. After Shakespeare's death, two more of his plays appeared in quarto format: *Othello* in 1622 and *The Two Noble Kinsmen*, coauthored with John Fletcher, in 1634.

In 1623, seven years after Shakespeare's death, *Mr. William Shakespeares Comedies, Histories, & Tragedies* was published. This printing offered readers in a single book thirty-six of the thirty-eight plays now thought to have been written by Shakespeare, including eighteen that had never been printed before. And it offered them in a style that was then reserved for serious literature and scholarship. The plays were arranged in double columns on pages nearly a foot high. This large page size is called "folio," as opposed to the smaller "quarto," and the 1623 volume is usually called the Shakespeare First Folio. It is reputed to have sold for the lordly price of a pound. (One copy at the Folger Shakespeare Library is marked fifteen shillings—that is, three-quarters of a pound.)

In a preface to the First Folio entitled "To the great

Variety of Readers," two of Shakespeare's former fellow actors in the King's Men, John Heminge and Henry Condell, wrote that they themselves had collected their dead companion's plays. They suggested that they had seen his own papers: "we have scarce received from him a blot in his papers." The title page of the Folio declared that the plays within it had been printed "according to the True Original Copies." Comparing the Folio to the quartos, Heminge and Condell disparaged the quartos, advising their readers that "before you were abused with divers stolen and surreptitious copies, maimed, and deformed by the frauds and stealths of injurious impostors." Many Shakespeareans of the eighteenth and nineteenth centuries believed Heminge and Condell and regarded the Folio plays as superior to anything in the quartos.

Once we begin to examine the Folio plays in detail, it becomes less easy to take at face value the word of Heminge and Condell about the superiority of the Folio texts. For example, of the first nine plays in the Folio (one-quarter of the entire collection), four were essentially reprinted from earlier quarto printings that Heminge and Condell had disparaged, and four have now been identified as printed from copies written in the hand of a professional scribe of the 1620s named Ralph Crane; the ninth, *The Comedy of Errors*, was apparently also printed from a manuscript, but one whose origin cannot be readily identified. Evidently, then, eight of the first nine plays in the First Folio were not printed, in spite of what the Folio title page announces, "according to the True Original Copies," or Shakespeare's own papers, and the source of the ninth is unknown. Since today's editors have been forced to treat Heminge and Condell's pronouncements with skepticism, they must choose whether to base their own editions upon quartos or the Folio on grounds other than Heminge and Condell's story of where the quarto and Folio versions originated.

Editors have often fashioned their own narratives to explain what lies behind the quartos and Folio. They have said that Heminge and Condell meant to criticize only a few of the early quartos, the ones that offer much shorter and sometimes quite different, often garbled, versions of plays. Among the examples of these are the 1600 quarto of *Henry V* (the Folio offers a much fuller version) or the 1603 *Hamlet* quarto. (In 1604 a different, much longer form of the play got into print as a quarto.) Early twentieth-century editors speculated that these questionable texts were produced when someone in the audience took notes from the plays' dialogue during performances and then employed "hack poets" to fill out the notes. The poor results were then sold to a publisher and presented in print as Shakespeare's plays. More recently this story has given way to another in which the shorter versions are said to be re-creations from memory of Shakespeare's plays by actors who wanted to stage them in the provinces but lacked manuscript copies. Most of the quartos offer much better texts than these so-called bad quartos. Indeed, in most of the quartos we find texts that are at least equal to or better than what is printed in the Folio. Many Shakespeare enthusiasts persuaded themselves that most of the quartos were set into type directly from Shakespeare's own papers, although there is nothing on which to base this conclusion except the desire for it to be true. Thus speculation continues about how the Shakespeare plays got to be printed. All that we have are the printed texts.

The book collector who was most successful in bringing together copies of the quartos and the First Folio was Henry Clay Folger, founder of the Folger Shakespeare Library in Washington, D.C. While it is estimated that there survive around the world only about 230 copies of the First Folio, Mr. Folger was able to acquire more than seventy-five copies, as well as a large number of fragments, for the library that bears his name. He also amassed a substantial number of quartos. For example, only fourteen copies of the First Quarto of *Love's Labor's Lost* are known to exist, and three are at the Folger Shakespeare Library. As a consequence of Mr. Folger's labors, scholars visiting the Folger Shakespeare Library have been able to learn a great deal about sixteenth- and seventeenth-century printing and, particularly, about the printing of Shakespeare's plays. And Mr. Folger did not stop at the First Folio, but collected many copies of later editions of Shakespeare, beginning with the Second Folio (1632), the Third (1663–64), and the Fourth (1685). Each of these later folios was based on its immediate predecessor and was edited anonymously. The first editor of Shakespeare whose name we know was Nicholas Rowe, whose first edition came out in 1709. Mr. Folger collected this edition and many, many more by Rowe's successors, and the collecting and scholarship continue.

# An Introduction to This Text

The play we call *King Lear* was printed in two different versions in the first quarter of the seventeenth century.

In 1608 appeared *M. William Shak-speare: His True Chronicle Historie of the life and death of King Lear and his three Daughters. With the vnfortunate life of Edgar, sonne and heire to the Earle of Gloster, and his sullen and assumed humor of Tom of Bedlam.* This printing was a quarto or pocket-size book known today as "Q1." It is remarkable among early printed Shakespeare plays for its hundreds of lines of verse that are either erroneously divided or set as prose; in addition, some of its prose is set as verse. As Q1 was going through the press, it was extensively corrected; thus different copies of its pages contain different readings. Sometimes the correction appears to be competent; at other times, however, it is better called "miscorrection." (In 1619 appeared a second quarto printing of the play ["Q2"]. It was, for the most part, simply a reprint of Q1, but it contained many corrections [as well as new errors] and changes, especially in the lining of verse in the last scene or so of Act 4 and in Act 5. This second printing had exactly the same title as Q1, and it even retained on its title page the 1608 date of Q1; the true date of Q2's printing [1619] was not discovered until early in the twentieth century.)

The second version to see print is found in the First Folio of Shakespeare's plays, published in 1623 ("F"). Entitled simply *The Tragedie of King Lear*, F contains over 100 lines that are not in Q1; at the same time F lacks about 300 lines (including a whole scene, 4.3) that are present in Q1. Many of the lines unique to Q1 or to F cluster together in quite extensive passages. The Q1 and F versions also differ from each other in their readings of over 800 words. In spite of the wide differences between the quarto and Folio printings, there is, nevertheless, such close agreement in punctuation between Q2 and F on some pages that the suspicion arises that the F typesetters may have referred to Q2 even if their copy was a manuscript. Thus when F agrees with Q2 against Q1, editors sometimes suspect that F may have been led into error by Q2 (see, for example, in the textual notes 1.4.32, 141; 2.1.141; 2.2.165; 4.2.74, 96; 4.6.299; 4.7.68; 5.3.186). In other cases, however, F

# M. William Shak-speare:

## HIS
### True Chronicle Historie of the life and death of King LEAR and his three Daughters.

*With the vnfortunate life of* Edgar, *sonne* and heire to the Earle of Gloster, and his sullen and assumed humor of TOM of Bedlam:

*As it was played before the Kings Maiestie at Whitehall vpon* S. Stephans *night in Christmas Hollidayes.*

By his Maiesties seruants playing vsually at the Gloabe on the Bancke-side.

LONDON,
Printed for *Nathaniel Butter,* and are to be sold at his shop in *Pauls* Church-yard at the signe of the Pide Bull neere S<sup>t</sup>. *Austins* Gate. 1608

Title page of the First Quarto of *King Lear,* 1608 (facsimile).

# THE TRAGEDIE OF
## KING LEAR.

### *Actus Primus. Scœna Prima.*

*Enter Kent, Gloucester, and Edmond.*

*Kent.*

Thought the King had more affected the Duke of *Albany*, then *Cornwall.*

*Glou.* It did alwayes feeme fo to vs : But now in the diuifion of the Kingdome, it appeares not which of the Dukes hee valewes moft, for qualities are fo weigh'd, that curiofity in neither, can make choife of eithers moity.

*Kent.* Is not this your Son, my Lord?

*Glou.* His breeding Sir, hath bin at my charge. I haue fo often bluth'd to acknowledge him, that now I am braz'd too't.

*Kent.* I cannot conceiue you.

*Glou.* Sir, this yong Fellowes mother could ; whervpon fhe grew round womb'd, and had indeede (Sir) a Sonne for her Cradle, ere fhe had a husband for her bed. Do you fmell a fault?

*Kent.* I cannot wifh the fault vndone, the iffue of it, being fo proper.

*Glou.* But I haue a Sonne, Sir, by order of Law, fome yeere elder then this ; who, yet is no deerer in my account, though this Knaue came fomthing fawcily to the world before he was fent for : yet was his Mother fayre, there was good fport at his making, and the horfon muft be acknowledged. Doe you know this Noble Gentleman, *Edmond*?

*Edm.* No, my Lord.

*Glou.* My Lord of Kent : Remember him heereafter, as my Honourable Friend.

*Edm.* My feruices to your Lordfhip.

*Kent.* I muft loue you, and fue to know you better.

*Edm.* Sir, I fhall ftudy deferuing.

*Glou.* He hath bin out nine yeares, and away he fhall againe. The King is comming.

*Sonnet. Enter King Lear, Cornwall, Albany, Gonerill, Regan, Cordelia, and attendants.*

*Lear.* Attend the Lords of France & Burgundy, Glofter.

*Glou.* I fhall, my Lord. *Exit.*

*Lear.* Meane time we fhal expreffe our darker purpofe. Giue me the Map there. Know, that we haue diuided In three our Kingdome : and 'tis our faft intent, To fhake all Cares and Bufineffe from our Age, Conferring them on yonger ftrengths, while we Vnburthen'd crawle toward death. Our fon of *Cornwal*, And you our no leffe louing Sonne of *Albany*,

We haue this houre a conftant will to publifh Our daughters feuerall Dowers, that future ftrife May be preuented now. The Princes, *France* & *Burgundy*, Great Riuals in our yongeft daughters loue, Long in our Court, haue made their amorous foiourne, And heere are to be anfwer'd. Tell me my daughters (Since now we will diueft vs both of Rule, Intereft of Territory, Cares of State) Which of you fhall we fay doth loue vs moft, That we, our largeft bountie may extend Where Nature doth with merit challenge. *Gonerill*, Our eldeft borne, fpeake firft.

*Gon.* Sir, I loue you more then word can weild y matter, Deerer then eye-fight, fpace, and libertie, Beyond what can be valewed, rich or rare, No leffe then life, with grace, health, beauty, honor : As much as Childe ere lou'd, or Father found. A loue that makes breath poore, and fpeech vnable, Beyond all manner of fo much I loue you.

*Cor.* What fhall *Cordelia* fpeake? Loue, and be filent.

*Lear.* Of all thefe bounds euen from this Line, to this, With fhadowie Forrefts, and with Champains rich'd With plenteous Riuers, and wide-skirted Meades We make thee Lady. To thine and *Albanies* iffues Be this perpetuall. What fayes our fecond Daughter? Our deereft *Regan*, wife of *Cornwall*?

*Reg.* I am made of that felfe-mettle as my Sifter, And prize me at her worth. I finde the names my very deede of loue : Onely fhe comes too fhort, that I profeffe My felfe an enemy to all other ioyes, Which the moft precious fquare of fenfe profeffes, And finde I am alone felicitate In your deere Highneffe loue.

*Cor.* Then poore *Cordelia*, And yet not fo, fince I am fure my loue's More ponderous then my tongue.

*Lear.* To thee, and thine hereditarie euer, Remaine this ample third of our faire Kingdome, No leffe in fpace, validitie, and pleafure Then that conferr'd on *Gonerill*. Now our Ioy, Although our laft and leaft ; to whofe yong loue, The Vines of France, and Milke of Burgundie, Striue to be intereft. What can you fay, to draw A third, more opilent then your Sifters? fpeake.

*Cor.* Nothing my Lord.

*Lear.* Nothing?

qq 2    Cor.

---

From the 1623 First Folio.
(Copy 54 in the Folger Shakespeare Library collection.)

agrees with Q2 in the correction of obvious (or nearly obvious) errors in Q1 (see, for example, in the textual notes 1.1.163; 1.4.327; 1.5.8; 2.1.13SD, 63; 2.2.98, 152, 163, 171; 2.4.121; 186, 246; 3.3.3; 3.7.90; 4.1.10; 4.2.18; 4.4.30; 4.5.8; 4.6.49, 53, 85, 100, 127, 286; 5.1.63; 5.2.5SD; 5.3.30SD, 365, 370).

Since early in the eighteenth century, editors have combined Q1 and F to produce what is termed a "conflated text." But it is impossible in any edition to combine the whole of the two versions, because they often provide alternative readings that are mutually exclusive; for example, when Q1 has the earl of Gloucester in his first speech refer to Lear's planned "division of the kingdoms," the Folio prints the singular "kingdom." In such cases (and there are a great many such cases), editors must choose whether to be guided by Q1 or by F in selecting what to print.

Twentieth-century editors of Shakespeare made the decision about which version of *King Lear* to prefer according to their theories about the origins of the early printed texts. For the greater part of the century, editors preferred F to Q1 in the belief that the Q1 text originated either in a shorthand transcription of a performance or in a reconstruction of the play by actors who depended on their memories of their parts. On the other hand, the F text was believed to have come down to us without the intervention of shorthand or memorial reconstruction. In the past few decades, however, Q1 has found more favor with some editors according to a theory that it was printed directly from Shakespeare's own manuscript and that F was set into type from a version of the play that had been rehandled by another dramatist after Shakespeare's retirement from the theater. This second theory is today in competition with yet a third theory that holds that Q1 and F are distinct, independent Shakespearean versions of the play that ought never to be combined with each other in an edition. Those who hold this third theory think that Q1 was printed from Shakespeare's own manuscript, but they also think that the F text is the product of a revision of the play by Shakespeare after the printing of Q1. Nevertheless, as scholars reexamine all such narratives about the origins of the printed texts, we discover that the evidence upon which they are based is questionable, and we become more skeptical about ever identifying with any certainty how the play assumed the forms in which it was printed.

The present edition is based upon a fresh examination of the early printed texts rather than upon any modern edition.* It offers its readers the Folio printing of *King Lear.*** But it offers an *edition* of the Folio because it prints such Q1 readings and such later editorial emendations as are, in the editors' judgments, necessary to repair what may be errors and deficiencies in the Folio. Furthermore, the present edition also offers its readers all the passages and a number of the words that are to be found only in Q1 (and not in F), marking them as such (see below).

Q1 words are *added* when their omission seems to leave a gap in our text. For example, in the first scene of the play, a speech of Cordelia's concludes in F with

---

*We have also consulted a computerized text of the First Folio provided by the Text Archive of the Oxford University Computing Centre, to which we are grateful. Also of great value was Michael Warren's *The Complete King Lear* (Berkeley: University of California Press, 1989).

**We choose F not because we believe that it stands in closer relation to Shakespeare than Q1 (we do not think it possible to establish which of Q1 or F is closer to the historical figure Shakespeare) but because F is a "better" text than Q1 in that it requires an editor to make fewer changes to its line division and wording than an editor must make to Q1.

the line "Sure I shall never marry like my sisters"—without specifying the respect in which her marriage will differ from theirs. Q1 alone provides the required specification with an additional half-line, "To love my father all," and we include Q1's half-line in our text. (For similar additions, see 1.1.49, 75, 175, 246, 335; 1.2.140–41; 1.3.29; 1.4.195, 267–68, 321; 2.2.29; 3.2.85; 3.4.51, 52, 122, 143; 4.1.48; 4.5.43; 4.6.299; 4.7.28, 67; 5.1.20; 5.3.54. In a number of these cases the Q1 word or words are added to fill out short [and metrically deficient] lines in F.) We also add an oath from Q1 ("Fut," 1.2.138) that may have been removed from the F text through censorship. However, when F lacks Q1 words that appear to add nothing of significance, we do not add these words to our text. For example, Q1 adds the word "attire" to the end of Lear's statement to Edgar, "I do not like the fashion of your garments. You will say they are Persian" (3.6.83–85). Here the Q1 word "attire" seems a mere repetition of the earlier "garments." (Compare, among many instances, Q1 additions not included in our text—words that are sometimes needless, sometimes superfluous—listed in the textual notes at 1.1.60; 2.4.266; 3.6.83; 3.7.66, 68; 4.6.298.)

Sometimes Q1 readings are *substituted* for F words when a word in F is unintelligible (i.e., not a word) or is incorrect according to the standards of that time for acceptable grammar, rhetoric, idiom, or usage, and Q1 provides an intelligible and acceptable word. Examples of such substitutions are Q1's "fathers" (modernized to "father's") for F's "Farhers" (1.2.18), Q1's "your" for F's "yout" (2.1.122), Q1's "possesses" for F's "professes" (1.1.82), or Q1's "panting" for F's "painting" when Oswald is referred to as "half breathless, ⟨panting⟩" (2.4.36). (Compare substitutions from Q1 at 1.1.5, 72, 176, 259; 1.4.1, 51, 164, 182, 203; 2.1.2, 61, 80, 92, 101–2, 144; 2.2.0SD, 23, 82, 83, 131, 141, 166, 187; 2.3.4, 18, 19; 2.4.8, 12, 39, 65, 82, 144, 146, 212; 3.2.3;

3.4.12, 51, 56, 57, 97, 123; 3.5.26; 3.6.73; 4.1.65; 4.2.91; 4.4.3, 12SP, 20; 4.6.22, 77, 102, 180, 300; 4.7.0SP, 15SP; 5.1.52, 55; 5.3.82SP, 99, 101, 118, 160, 163, 177, 308.) We recognize that our understanding of what was acceptable in Shakespeare's time is to some extent inevitably based upon reading others' editions of *King Lear*, but it is also based on reading other writing from the period and on historical dictionaries and studies of Shakespeare's grammar.

Finally, we print a word from Q1 rather than from F when a word in F seems at odds with the story that the play tells and Q1 supplies a word that coheres with the story. For example, when Lear enters at the beginning of 2.4 he wonders, in F, why Cornwall and Regan did "not send back my Messengers." But, as far as we know, Lear has sent only a single messenger (Kent) to Cornwall and Regan. Therefore, like most other editors, we print Q1's "messenger" for F's "Messengers." (Compare 1.1.214 and 5.3.193.) Because we rarely substitute Q1 words for F's, our edition is closer to F than are most other editions of the play available today.

In order to enable its readers to tell the difference between the F and Q1 versions, the present edition uses a variety of signals:

(1) All the words in this edition that are printed only in the First Quarto but not in the Folio appear in pointed brackets (⟨ ⟩).

(2) All full lines that are found only in the Folio and not in the First Quarto are printed in brackets ([ ]).

(3) Sometimes neither the Folio nor the First Quarto seems to offer a satisfactory reading, and it is necessary to print a word different from what is offered by either. Such words (called "emendations" by editors) are printed within half-brackets (⌜ ⌝).

In this edition, whenever we change the wording of the Folio or add anything to its stage directions, we mark the change. We want our readers to be immediately aware when we have intervened. (Only when we correct an obvious typographical error in the First Quarto or Folio does the change not get marked in our text.) Whenever we change the Folio or Quarto's wording or change their punctuation so that meaning is changed, we list the change in the textual notes at the back of the book. Those who wish to find the Quarto's alternatives to the Folio's readings will be able to find these also in the textual notes.

For the convenience of the reader, we have modernized the punctuation and the spelling of both the Folio and the First Quarto. Thus, for example, our text supplies the modern standard spelling "father's" for the Quarto's spelling "fathers" (quoted above). Sometimes we go so far as to modernize certain old forms of words; for example, when *a* means "he," we change it to *he;* we change *mo* to *more* and *ye* to *you.* But it is not our practice in editing any of the plays to modernize forms of words that sound distinctly different from modern forms. For example, when the early printed texts read *sith* or *apricocks* or *porpentine,* we have not modernized to *since, apricots, porcupine.* When the forms *an, and,* or *and if* appear instead of the modern form *if,* we have reduced *and* to *an* but have not changed any of these forms to their modern equivalent, *if.* We also modernize and, where necessary, correct passages in foreign languages, unless an error in the early printed text can be reasonably explained as a joke.

We correct or regularize a number of the proper names, as is the usual practice in editions of the play. For example, the Folio's spellings "Gloster" and "Burgundie" are changed to the familiar "Gloucester" and "Burgundy"; and there are a number of other comparable adjustments in the names.

This edition differs from many earlier ones in its efforts to aid the reader in imagining the play as a performance rather than as a series of historical events. Thus stage directions are written with reference to the stage. For example, in 1.2 Edmund is represented in the dialogue and in the fiction of the play as putting a letter in his pocket. On the stage this letter would, however, be represented by a piece of paper. Thus the present edition reads *"He puts a paper in his pocket"* rather than "a letter."

Whenever it is reasonably certain, in our view, that a speech is accompanied by a particular action, we provide a stage direction describing the action. (Occasional exceptions to this rule occur when the action is so obvious that to add a stage direction would insult the reader.) Stage directions for the entrance of characters in mid-scene are, with rare exceptions, placed so that they immediately precede the characters' participation in the scene, even though these entrances may appear somewhat earlier in the early printed texts. Whenever we move a stage direction, we record this change in the textual notes. Latin stage directions (e.g., *Exeunt*) are translated into English (e.g., *They exit*).

We expand the often severely abbreviated forms of names used as speech headings in early printed texts into the full names of the characters. We also regularize the speakers' names in speech headings, using only a single designation for each character, even though the early printed texts sometimes use a variety of designations. Variations in the speech headings of the early printed texts are recorded in the textual notes.

In the present edition, as well, we mark with a dash any change of address within a speech, unless a stage direction intervenes. When the *-ed* ending of a word is to be pronounced, we mark it with an accent.

Like editors for the last two centuries, we print metrically linked lines in the following way:

LEAR
  Mak'st thou this shame thy pastime?
KENT                                    No, my lord.

However, when there are a number of short verse lines that can be linked in more than one way, we do not, with rare exceptions, indent any of them.

## The Explanatory Notes

The notes that appear on the pages facing the text are designed to provide readers with the help that they may need to enjoy the play. Whenever the meaning of a word in the text is not readily accessible in a good contemporary dictionary, we offer the meaning in a note. Sometimes we provide a note even when the relevant meaning is to be found in the dictionary but when the word has acquired since Shakespeare's time other potentially confusing meanings. In our notes, we try to offer modern synonyms for Shakespeare's words. We also try to indicate to the reader the connection between the word in the play and the modern synonym. For example, Shakespeare sometimes uses the word *head* to mean "source," but, for modern readers, there may be no connection evident between these two words. We provide the connection by explaining Shakespeare's usage as follows: "**head:** fountainhead, source." On some occasions, a whole phrase or clause needs explanation. Then, when space allows, we rephrase in our own words the difficult passage, and add at the end synonyms for individual words in the passage. When scholars have been unable to determine the meaning of a word or phrase, we acknowledge the uncertainty. Biblical quotations are from the Geneva Bible (1560), with the spelling and punctuation modernized.

*The Tragedy of*

# KING LEAR

# Characters in the Play

LEAR, king of Britain

GONERIL, Lear's eldest daughter
DUKE OF ALBANY, her husband
OSWALD, her steward

REGAN, Lear's second daughter
DUKE OF CORNWALL, her husband

CORDELIA, Lear's youngest daughter
KING OF FRANCE, her suitor and then husband
DUKE OF BURGUNDY, her suitor

EARL OF KENT

FOOL

EARL OF GLOUCESTER
EDGAR, his elder son
EDMUND, his younger and illegitimate son
CURAN, gentleman of Gloucester's household
OLD MAN, a tenant of Gloucester's

KNIGHT, serving Lear
GENTLEMEN
Three SERVANTS
MESSENGERS
DOCTOR
CAPTAINS
HERALD

Knights in Lear's train, Servants, Officers, Soldiers, Attendants, Gentlemen

3

*The Tragedy of*

# KING LEAR

---

ACT 1

**1.1** King Lear, intending to divide his power and kingdom among his three daughters, demands public professions of their love. His youngest daughter, Cordelia, refuses. Lear strips her of her dowry, divides the kingdom between his two other daughters, and then banishes the earl of Kent, who has protested against Lear's rash actions. The king of France, one of Cordelia's suitors, chooses to marry her despite her father's casting her away. Lear tells his daughters Goneril and Regan that they and their husbands should divide his powers and revenues; he himself will keep a hundred knights and will live with Goneril and Regan by turns.

---

1. **more affected:** been more partial to
5–7. **equalities . . . moiety:** i.e., the equal portions (of the divided kingdom awarded by Lear to the dukes) are so balanced that the most minute examination of either can find no difference between their shares   **moiety:** share, portion
9–10. **breeding . . . charge:** (1) upbringing has been at my expense; (2) parentage has been imputed to me
11. **brazed:** hardened (like brass)
12. **conceive:** understand (with sexual wordplay in line 13)
15. **ere:** before
16. **fault:** misdeed
17. **issue:** (1) result; (2) offspring, child
18. **proper:** (1) appropriate, fitting; (2) handsome
19. **a son . . . law:** i.e., **a** legitimate **son**

*(continued)*

# *ACT 1*

## Scene 1
*Enter Kent, Gloucester, and Edmund.*

KENT  I thought the King had more affected the Duke
of Albany than Cornwall.

GLOUCESTER  It did always seem so to us, but now in
the division of the kingdom, it appears not which
of the dukes he values most, for ⟨equalities⟩ are so   5
weighed that curiosity in neither can make choice
of either's moiety.

KENT  Is not this your son, my lord?

GLOUCESTER  His breeding, sir, hath been at my
charge. I have so often blushed to acknowledge   10
him that now I am brazed to 't.

KENT  I cannot conceive you.

GLOUCESTER  Sir, this young fellow's mother could,
whereupon she grew round-wombed and had in-
deed, sir, a son for her cradle ere she had a husband   15
for her bed. Do you smell a fault?

KENT  I cannot wish the fault undone, the issue of it
being so proper.

GLOUCESTER  But I have a son, sir, by order of law,
some year elder than this, who yet is no dearer in   20
my account. Though this knave came something
saucily to the world before he was sent for, yet was
his mother fair, there was good sport at his making,

7

20. **some year:** i.e., a **year** or so

20–21. **dearer . . . account:** (1) more loved by me; (2) more valuable in my assessment

21. **this knave:** i.e., Edmund, the illegitimate son (The word **knave** meant "boy" or "fellow," but was also a term for a servant, a sense playfully continued by Gloucester in "came something saucily . . . before he was sent for," as if he were an impudent servant who intrudes before he is summoned.) **something:** somewhat

22. **saucily:** (1) impudently; (2) bawdily

23. **fair:** beautiful

24. **whoreson:** bastard (here used affectionately)

24–25. **Do . . . Edmund:** It is possible that Edmund does not hear the conversation until this point.

29. **services:** respects (a courtly term)

30. **sue:** beg, entreat

31. **study deserving:** strive to deserve (your acquaintance)

32. **He:** i.e., Edmund; **out:** i.e., away

33 SD. **Sennet:** trumpets announcing an approach

34. **Attend:** escort (to the king's presence)

37. **we:** i.e., I (the royal "we," which continues in the lines that follow)

40. **fast:** firm

43. **son:** i.e., son-in-law

46. **constant will:** firm intention; **publish:** make public

47. **several:** separate, particular; **dowers:** i.e., inheritances, legacies (Only Cordelia's portion would have been an actual dowry.)

and the whoreson must be acknowledged.—Do you
know this noble gentleman, Edmund?                          25
EDMUND  No, my lord.
GLOUCESTER  My lord of Kent. Remember him here-
after as my honorable friend.
EDMUND  My services to your Lordship.
KENT  I must love you and sue to know you better.          30
EDMUND  Sir, I shall study deserving.
GLOUCESTER  He hath been out nine years, and away he
shall again. (*Sennet.*) The King is coming.

*Enter King Lear, Cornwall, Albany, Goneril, Regan,*
*Cordelia, and Attendants.*

LEAR
Attend the lords of France and Burgundy,
Gloucester.                                                35
GLOUCESTER  I shall, my lord.              *He exits.*
LEAR
Meantime we shall express our darker purpose.—
Give me the map there.        ⌈*He is handed a map.*⌉
                Know that we have divided
In three our kingdom, and 'tis our fast intent            40
To shake all cares and business from our age,
Conferring them on younger strengths, [while we
Unburdened crawl toward death. Our son of
    Cornwall
And you, our no less loving son of Albany,                 45
We have this hour a constant will to publish
Our daughters' several dowers, that future strife
May be prevented now.]
The ⟨two great⟩ princes, France and Burgundy,
Great rivals in our youngest daughter's love,             50
Long in our court have made their amorous sojourn
And here are to be answered. Tell me, my
    daughters—
[Since now we will divest us both of rule,

55. **Interest of:** claim or title to

58. **Where nature ... challenge:** i.e., **where merit** and natural affection lay claim to it (i.e., to Lear's **largest bounty**)

60–61. **wield the matter:** express the substance (of her love)

63. **valued:** estimated, appraised

65. **found:** i.e., **found** himself to be loved

66. **breath:** voice; **unable:** unequal to the task

69. **these bounds:** i.e., the lands within these boundaries

70. **shadowy:** shady; **champains riched:** i.e., rich plains

71. **wide-skirted meads:** broad meadows

72. **issue:** descendants

76. **self:** same; **mettle:** (1) temperament; (2) metal

77. **prize:** esteem, value (with a secondary sense of "price")

78. **my ... love:** i.e., **my love** exactly

79. **that:** i.e., in that

81. **square of sense:** No satisfactory explanation of these words has been found. Among the possible meanings of **square** are (1) area; (2) measure (i.e., carpenter's square); (3) perfection.

83. **felicitate:** made happy

87. **More ponderous:** weightier (and therefore more significant)

Interest of territory, cares of state—]                    55
Which of you shall we say doth love us most,
That we our largest bounty may extend
Where nature doth with merit challenge. Goneril,
Our eldest born, speak first.

GONERIL
Sir, I love you more than word can wield the       60
   matter,
Dearer than eyesight, space, and liberty,
Beyond what can be valued, rich or rare,
No less than life, with grace, health, beauty, honor;
As much as child e'er loved, or father found;     65
A love that makes breath poor, and speech unable.
Beyond all manner of so much I love you.

CORDELIA, ⌐aside⌐
What shall Cordelia speak? Love, and be silent.

LEAR, ⌐*pointing to the map*⌐
Of all these bounds, even from this line to this,
With shadowy forests [and with champains riched,    70
With plenteous rivers] and wide-skirted meads,
We make thee lady. To thine and Albany's ⟨issue⟩
Be this perpetual.—What says our second
   daughter,
Our dearest Regan, wife of Cornwall? ⟨Speak.⟩    75

REGAN
I am made of that self mettle as my sister
And prize me at her worth. In my true heart
I find she names my very deed of love;
Only she comes too short, that I profess
Myself an enemy to all other joys                 80
Which the most precious square of sense
   ⟨possesses,⟩
And find I am alone felicitate
In your dear Highness' love.

CORDELIA, ⌐aside⌐            Then poor Cordelia!   85
And yet not so, since I am sure my love's
More ponderous than my tongue.

90. **validity:** value

93. **vines:** i.e., vineyards; **milk:** i.e., pastures

94. **to be interessed:** (1) to have a right or share; (2) to be closely connected; **draw:** gain

99. **Nothing . . . nothing:** proverbial

102. **bond:** duty or obligation (of child to father)

106. **bred me:** educated me, brought me up

107. **right fit:** fitting, appropriate

110. **Haply:** perchance, perhaps

111. **must take my plight:** will receive my vow or pledge

"He that makes his generation messes." (1.1.130)
From Bauern-praktik, *Bawren Practica, odder Wetterbüchlin* . . . (1555).

LEAR
To thee and thine hereditary ever
Remain this ample third of our fair kingdom,
No less in space, validity, and pleasure                    90
Than that conferred on Goneril.—Now, our joy,
Although our last and least, to whose young love
[The vines of France and milk of Burgundy
Strive to be interessed,] what can you say to draw
A third more opulent than your sisters'? Speak.            95
CORDELIA  Nothing, my lord.
[LEAR  Nothing?
CORDELIA  Nothing.]
LEAR
Nothing will come of nothing. Speak again.
CORDELIA
Unhappy that I am, I cannot heave                          100
My heart into my mouth. I love your Majesty
According to my bond, no more nor less.
LEAR
How, how, Cordelia? Mend your speech a little,
Lest you may mar your fortunes.
CORDELIA                              Good my lord,         105
You have begot me, bred me, loved me.
I return those duties back as are right fit:
Obey you, love you, and most honor you.
Why have my sisters husbands if they say
They love you all? Haply, when I shall wed,                110
That lord whose hand must take my plight shall
    carry
Half my love with him, half my care and duty.
Sure I shall never marry like my sisters,
⟨To love my father all.⟩                                  115
LEAR  But goes thy heart with this?
CORDELIA  Ay, my good lord.
LEAR  So young and so untender?
CORDELIA  So young, my lord, and true.

122. **mysteries:** secret rites; **Hecate:** goddess of witchcraft and of the moon. (Her name, in Shakespeare, is pronounced as a two-syllable word.)
123–24. **operation . . . be:** i.e., influence of the planets that govern human life and death
126. **Propinquity . . . blood:** kinship
127–28. **as . . . this:** i.e., consider you **a stranger from this** moment
129. **Scythian:** member of a tribe noted in classical literature for savagery (See picture, page 22.)
130. **makes . . . messes:** eats his own offspring (See picture, page 12.)
132. **well neighbored:** closely placed; **relieved:** helped in distress
133. **sometime:** former
137–38. **thought . . . nursery:** i.e., expected to commit myself entirely to her loving care   **set my rest:** venture everything (The term is from the card game of primero.) **nursery:** i.e., caretaking
140. **So . . . as:** i.e., as I hope to rest in **peace** in **my grave**
141. **France:** i.e., the king of **France; Who stirs?:** an impatient outburst: "Does no one move?"
144. **digest the third:** i.e., absorb what was to be Cordelia's dowry
145. **plainness:** plain-speaking, frankness; **marry her:** i.e., get her a husband
146. **invest:** endow; clothe
147–48. **large effects . . . majesty:** i.e., considerable signs (of power), or splendid shows, that are associated with rulership
148. **Ourself:** the royal "we"; **by monthly course:** i.e., a month at a time

*(continued)*

*14*

LEAR

    Let it be so. Thy truth, then, be thy dower,     120
For by the sacred radiance of the sun,
The ⌜mysteries⌝ of Hecate and the night,
By all the operation of the orbs
From whom we do exist and cease to be,
Here I disclaim all my paternal care,     125
Propinquity, and property of blood,
And as a stranger to my heart and me
Hold thee from this forever. The barbarous
    Scythian,
Or he that makes his generation messes     130
To gorge his appetite, shall to my bosom
Be as well neighbored, pitied, and relieved
As thou my sometime daughter.

KENT                   Good my liege—

LEAR   Peace, Kent.     135
Come not between the dragon and his wrath.
I loved her most and thought to set my rest
On her kind nursery. ⌜*To Cordelia.*⌝ Hence and avoid
    my sight!—
So be my grave my peace as here I give     140
Her father's heart from her.—Call France. Who stirs?
Call Burgundy. ⌜*An Attendant exits.*⌝ Cornwall and
    Albany,
With my two daughters' dowers digest the third.
Let pride, which she calls plainness, marry her.     145
I do invest you jointly with my power,
Preeminence, and all the large effects
That troop with majesty. Ourself by monthly course,
With reservation of an hundred knights
By you to be sustained, shall our abode     150
Make with you by due turn. Only we shall retain
The name and all th' addition to a king.
The sway, revenue, execution of the rest,

149. **With reservation of:** i.e., reserving for myself
150. **sustained:** provided for
152. **addition to:** titles of
153. **revenue:** accent on second syllable; **execution:** carrying out, performance; **rest:** i.e., everything else associated with kingship
160. **Make . . . shaft:** get out of the way of the arrow
161. **fork:** forked arrowhead
165–66. **To plainness . . . bound:** i.e., honor obliges one to speak bluntly
167. **Reserve thy state:** keep your power
168. **in . . . consideration:** i.e., by pausing for reflection; **check:** stop
169–70. **Answer . . . judgment:** i.e., I will bet **my life** on the truth of my opinion that
172–73. **those . . . hollowness:** Proverbial: "Empty vessels have the loudest sounds."
175. **pawn:** (1) something to be set at risk; (2) chess piece of least value
176. **wage:** (1) wager, bet; (2) risk in warfare
178. **motive:** i.e., my reason for acting
181. **blank:** white bull's eye in the center of a target (See picture, page 26.)
182. **Apollo:** god of the sun
185. **vassal:** slave; **Miscreant:** misbeliever; villain

Belovèd sons, be yours, which to confirm,
This coronet part between you.                               155
KENT                          Royal Lear,
   Whom I have ever honored as my king,
   Loved as my father, as my master followed,
   As my great patron thought on in my prayers—
LEAR
   The bow is bent and drawn. Make from the shaft.    160
KENT
   Let it fall rather, though the fork invade
   The region of my heart. Be Kent unmannerly
   When Lear is mad. What wouldst thou do, old man?
   Think'st thou that duty shall have dread to speak
   When power to flattery bows? To plainness honor's   165
      bound
   When majesty falls to folly. Reserve thy state,
   And in thy best consideration check
   This hideous rashness. Answer my life my
      judgment,                                        170
   Thy youngest daughter does not love thee least,
   Nor are those empty-hearted whose low sounds
   Reverb no hollowness.
LEAR                          Kent, on thy life, no more.
KENT
   My life I never held but as ⟨a⟩ pawn                175
   To wage against thine enemies, ⟨nor⟩ fear to lose
      it,
   Thy safety being motive.
LEAR                          Out of my sight!
KENT
   See better, Lear, and let me still remain           180
   The true blank of thine eye.
LEAR   Now, by Apollo—
KENT   Now, by Apollo, king,
   Thou swear'st thy gods in vain.
LEAR   O vassal! Miscreant!                             185

191. **recreant:** traitor
192. **That:** i.e., in that
193. **strained:** excessive
194. **our sentence:** my statement of condemnation, my judgment
195. **nor ... nor:** neither ... nor; **place:** position as king
196. **Our ... good:** i.e., with my power put into effect
201. **trunk:** i.e., body
202. **Jupiter:** king of the Roman gods
204. **Sith:** since
205. **hence:** elsewhere, away from here
209–10. **your large ... approve:** i.e., may your actions fulfill your grand expressions (of love)
211. **effects:** results, i.e., **deeds** (line 210)

[ALBANY/CORNWALL  Dear sir, forbear.]

KENT
Kill thy physician, and thy fee bestow
Upon the foul disease. Revoke thy gift,
Or whilst I can vent clamor from my throat,
I'll tell thee thou dost evil.                                   190

LEAR
Hear me, recreant; on thine allegiance, hear me!
That thou hast sought to make us break our vows—
Which we durst never yet—and with strained pride
To come betwixt our sentence and our power,
Which nor our nature nor our place can bear,      195
Our potency made good, take thy reward:
Five days we do allot thee for provision
To shield thee from disasters of the world,
And on the sixth to turn thy hated back
Upon our kingdom. If on the tenth day following   200
Thy banished trunk be found in our dominions,
The moment is thy death. Away! By Jupiter,
This shall not be revoked.

KENT
Fare thee well, king. Sith thus thou wilt appear,
Freedom lives hence, and banishment is here.       205
⌜To Cordelia.⌝ The gods to their dear shelter take
    thee, maid,
That justly think'st and hast most rightly said.
⌜To Goneril and Regan.⌝ And your large speeches
    may your deeds approve,                                  210
That good effects may spring from words of love.—
Thus Kent, O princes, bids you all adieu.
He'll shape his old course in a country new.
                                        *He exits.*

*Flourish. Enter Gloucester with France, and Burgundy,*
            ⌜*and*⌝ *Attendants.*

⟨GLOUCESTER⟩
Here's France and Burgundy, my noble lord.

216. **We . . . address:** i.e., I . . . **address** myself
217. **rivaled:** competed
218. **in present . . . her:** i.e., as her immediate (or available) dowry
222. **tender:** offer
224. **so:** i.e., **dear,** precious
226. **aught:** anything; **little seeming substance:** This dismissive reference to Cordelia may allude to her stature, her manners, or her monetary worth.
227. **pieced:** added, joined to it
228. **fitly:** suitably; **like:** please
231. **infirmities:** imperfections; **owes:** owns
233. **strangered with:** made a stranger to me by
237. **Election . . . conditions:** i.e., choice is not possible on such terms
239. **tell:** (1) describe for you; (2) count up for you; **For:** i.e., as for
240. **make . . . stray:** stray so much
241. **To:** as to; **match:** marry; **beseech:** i.e., I beseech
242. **avert:** turn
246–47. **best object:** dearest **object** of your love
248. **argument:** subject

LEAR   My lord of Burgundy,        215
  We first address toward you, who with this king
  Hath rivaled for our daughter. What in the least
  Will you require in present dower with her,
  Or cease your quest of love?
BURGUNDY           Most royal Majesty,   220
  I crave no more than hath your Highness offered,
  Nor will you tender less.
LEAR          Right noble Burgundy,
  When she was dear to us, we did hold her so,
  But now her price is fallen. Sir, there she stands.   225
  If aught within that little seeming substance,
  Or all of it, with our displeasure pieced
  And nothing more, may fitly like your Grace,
  She's there, and she is yours.
BURGUNDY          I know no answer.   230
LEAR
  Will you, with those infirmities she owes,
  Unfriended, new-adopted to our hate,
  Dowered with our curse and strangered with our
     oath,
  Take her or leave her?        235
BURGUNDY        Pardon me, royal sir,
  Election makes not up in such conditions.
LEAR
  Then leave her, sir, for by the power that made me
  I tell you all her wealth.—For you, great king,
  I would not from your love make such a stray   240
  To match you where I hate. Therefore beseech you
  T' avert your liking a more worthier way
  Than on a wretch whom Nature is ashamed
  Almost t' acknowledge hers.
FRANCE          This is most strange,   245
  That she whom even but now was your ⟨best⟩
     object,
  The argument of your praise, balm of your age,

250–51. **to dismantle . . . favor:** i.e., as to strip away the mantle of your goodwill

253. **That monsters it:** i.e., that makes it monstrous or hideous

253–54. **or . . . taint:** or else your hitherto professed love must now appear tainted (blemished, stained)

254. **which:** referring back to Cordelia's **offense** (line 251)

256. **Should:** i.e., could

258. **for I want:** because I do not have

259. **speak and purpose not:** i.e., say things that I do not intend to do

265. **for which:** i.e., **for** lacking **which**

266. **still-soliciting:** always begging or enticing

272. **tardiness in nature:** natural reserve

273. **leaves . . . unspoke:** does not tell the story

276. **regards:** considerations

276–77. **stands . . . from:** i.e., are irrelevant to

"The barbarous Scythian." (1.1.128–29)
From Conrad Lycosthenes, *Prodigiorum* . . . (1557).

The best, the dearest, should in this trice of time
Commit a thing so monstrous to dismantle　　　　　250
So many folds of favor. Sure her offense
Must be of such unnatural degree
That monsters it, or your forevouched affection
Fall into taint; which to believe of her
Must be a faith that reason without miracle　　　255
Should never plant in me.

CORDELIA, ⌈*to Lear*⌉　I yet beseech your Majesty—
If for I want that glib and oily art
To speak and purpose not, since what I ⟨well⟩
　　intend　　　　　260
I'll do 't before I speak—that you make known
It is no vicious blot, murder, or foulness,
No unchaste action or dishonored step
That hath deprived me of your grace and favor,
But even for want of that for which I am richer:　265
A still-soliciting eye and such a tongue
That I am glad I have not, though not to have it
Hath lost me in your liking.

LEAR　　　　　　　Better thou
Hadst not been born than not t' have pleased me　270
　　better.

FRANCE
Is it but this—a tardiness in nature
Which often leaves the history unspoke
That it intends to do?—My lord of Burgundy,
What say you to the lady? Love's not love　　275
When it is mingled with regards that stands
Aloof from th' entire point. Will you have her?
She is herself a dowry.

BURGUNDY, ⌈*to Lear*⌉　　Royal king,
Give but that portion which yourself proposed,　280
And here I take Cordelia by the hand,
Duchess of Burgundy.

LEAR
Nothing. I have sworn. I am firm.

286. **Peace be with:** a phrase usually used as a greeting, but used here as a farewell

288. **respect and fortunes:** i.e., mercenary considerations (Many editors print the First Quarto's reading "respects of fortune," which also means considerations of wealth.)

293. **Be it lawful:** i.e., if **it be lawful** that

298. **chance:** lot, fortune, fate

300. **wat'rish Burgundy:** (1) the river-filled duchy of **Burgundy;** (2) the weak and vapid duke of **Burgundy** (transferred epithet)

301. **unprized:** unvalued

302. **though unkind:** i.e., though they are (1) unnatural, (2) lacking kindness

303. **here:** i.e., this place; **where:** i.e., place

308. **benison:** blessing

311. **The:** i.e., you, who are the; **washed:** i.e., tear-filled

312. **what:** i.e., for **what**

313. **like a sister:** i.e., because I am your **sister**

BURGUNDY, ⌜*to Cordelia*⌝
I am sorry, then, you have so lost a father
That you must lose a husband.                              285
CORDELIA                              Peace be with
    Burgundy.
Since that respect and fortunes are his love,
I shall not be his wife.
FRANCE
Fairest Cordelia, that art most rich being poor;          290
Most choice, forsaken; and most loved, despised,
Thee and thy virtues here I seize upon,
Be it lawful I take up what's cast away.
Gods, gods! 'Tis strange that from their cold'st
    neglect                                               295
My love should kindle to enflamed respect.—
Thy dowerless daughter, king, thrown to my
    chance,
Is queen of us, of ours, and our fair France.
Not all the dukes of wat'rish Burgundy                    300
Can buy this unprized precious maid of me.—
Bid them farewell, Cordelia, though unkind.
Thou losest here a better where to find.
LEAR
Thou hast her, France. Let her be thine, for we
Have no such daughter, nor shall ever see                 305
That face of hers again. ⌜*To Cordelia.*⌝ Therefore
    begone
Without our grace, our love, our benison.—
Come, noble Burgundy.
            *Flourish.* ⌜*All but France, Cordelia, Goneril,*
                        *and Regan*⌝ *exit.*
FRANCE   Bid farewell to your sisters.                    310
CORDELIA
The jewels of our father, with washed eyes
Cordelia leaves you. I know you what you are,
And like a sister am most loath to call

314. **as they are named:** by their proper names
316. **professèd bosoms:** i.e., publicly proclaimed love
318. **prefer him:** recommend him
323. **At Fortune's alms:** i.e., as a charity donation from Fortune; **scanted:** withheld, begrudged
324. **are . . . wanted:** i.e., deserve to be deprived as you deprived (your father)
325. **unfold:** reveal; unpleat; **plighted:** pleated, folded
326. **Who . . . derides:** perhaps, **Time,** which **covers faults,** eventually **derides** them (The line is often emended.)
330. **appertains to:** pertains to, concerns
334. **changes:** changefulness, fickleness
338. **grossly:** obviously
341. **best . . . time:** i.e., prime of his life
342. **but rash:** i.e., completely hotheaded, over-hasty
343–44. **of . . . condition:** i.e., firmly embedded in his character
344. **therewithal:** together with them; i.e., also

Aiming at "the . . . blank." (1.1.181)
From Gilles Corrozet, *Hecatongraphie* . . . (1543).

Your faults as they are named. Love well our
    father.                       315
To your professèd bosoms I commit him;
But yet, alas, stood I within his grace,
I would prefer him to a better place.
So farewell to you both.
REGAN
Prescribe not us our duty.          320
GONERIL         Let your study
Be to content your lord, who hath received you
At Fortune's alms. You have obedience scanted
And well are worth the want that you have wanted.
CORDELIA
  Time shall unfold what plighted cunning hides,  325
Who covers faults at last with shame derides.
Well may you prosper.
FRANCE        Come, my fair Cordelia.
           *France and Cordelia exit.*
GONERIL  Sister, it is not little I have to say of what
most nearly appertains to us both. I think our  330
father will hence tonight.
REGAN  That's most certain, and with you; next month
with us.
GONERIL  You see how full of changes his age is; the
observation we have made of it hath ⟨not⟩ been  335
little. He always loved our sister most, and with
what poor judgment he hath now cast her off
appears too grossly.
REGAN  'Tis the infirmity of his age. Yet he hath ever
but slenderly known himself.  340
GONERIL  The best and soundest of his time hath been
but rash. Then must we look from his age to
receive not alone the imperfections of long-en-
graffed condition, but therewithal the unruly way-
wardness that infirm and choleric years bring with  345
them.

347. **unconstant starts:** i.e., abrupt fits or outbursts; **like:** i.e., likely
349. **compliment:** ceremony
350. **sit:** take counsel
352. **last surrender of his:** i.e., recent **surrender of** the kingdom
355. **i' th' heat:** Compare the proverb, "Strike while the iron is hot."

---

**1.2** Edmund, the earl of Gloucester's illegitimate son, plots to displace his legitimate brother, Edgar, as Gloucester's heir by turning Gloucester against Edgar. He tricks Gloucester into thinking Edgar seeks Gloucester's life.

---

1. **Nature:** i.e., that which is natural, as opposed to spiritual or social
2. **Wherefore:** why
3. **Stand in . . . custom:** i.e., be exposed to the evil of a social convention (by which the elder—and legitimate—son will inherit everything)
4. **curiosity of nations:** i.e., elaborate legal or social distinctions
5. **For that:** because; **moonshines:** months
6. **Lag of:** lagging behind (in birth); younger than; **base:** (1) base-born; illegitimate; (2) inferior
7. **compact:** compacted, put together
8. **generous:** noble, courageous; **true:** proper
9. **honest . . . issue:** the child of a legally married woman  **honest:** chaste

*(continued)*

REGAN  Such unconstant starts are we like to have
 from him as this of Kent's banishment.
GONERIL  There is further compliment of leave-taking
 between France and him. Pray you, let us sit  350
 together. If our father carry authority with such
 disposition as he bears, this last surrender of his will
 but offend us.
REGAN  We shall further think of it.
GONERIL  We must do something, and i' th' heat.   355
*They exit.*

Scene 2
*Enter ⌜Edmund, the⌝ Bastard.*

EDMUND
 Thou, Nature, art my goddess. To thy law
 My services are bound. Wherefore should I
 Stand in the plague of custom, and permit
 The curiosity of nations to deprive me
 For that I am some twelve or fourteen moonshines  5
 Lag of a brother? Why "bastard"? Wherefore "base,"
 When my dimensions are as well compact,
 My mind as generous and my shape as true
 As honest madam's issue? Why brand they us
 With "base," with "baseness," "bastardy," "base,"  10
  "base,"
 Who, in the lusty stealth of nature, take
 More composition and fierce quality
 Than doth within a dull, stale, tired bed
 Go to th' creating a whole tribe of fops  15
 Got 'tween asleep and wake? Well then,
 Legitimate Edgar, I must have your land.
 Our father's love is to the bastard Edmund
 As to th' legitimate. Fine word, "legitimate."
 Well, my legitimate, if this letter speed  20

13. **More . . . quality:** i.e., a stronger constitution and more energy

15. **fops:** fools

16. **Got:** begotten, conceived

17. **your land:** i.e., the **land** you are to inherit

20. **speed:** prove successful

21. **invention:** inventiveness; or, plot, scheme

24. **choler:** anger; **parted:** departed

25. **tonight:** i.e., last night; **prescribed his power:** i.e., told how much power he retains

26. **Confined to exhibition:** restricted to an allowance

27. **Upon the gad:** i.e., on a sudden impulse   **gad:** goad, spur; **how now:** an interjection, here used as a greeting meaning, roughly, "**how** are you **now?**"

29. **put up:** i.e., **put** away

34. **terrible:** frightened

34–35. **dispatch:** putting away

35. **quality:** nature

40–41. **for . . . o'erlooking:** i.e., for you to read

44–45. **to blame:** blameworthy, deserving rebuke

48. **essay or taste:** test

49. **This policy . . . age:** i.e., **this policy of** reverencing the aged

50. **the best . . . times:** the prime of our lives

And my invention thrive, Edmund the base
Shall ⌜top⌝ th' legitimate. I grow, I prosper.
Now, gods, stand up for bastards!

> · *Enter Gloucester.*

GLOUCESTER
  Kent banished thus? And France in choler parted?
  And the King gone tonight, prescribed his power,          25
  Confined to exhibition? All this done
  Upon the gad?—Edmund, how now? What news?
EDMUND  So please your Lordship, none. ⌜*He puts a*
  *paper in his pocket.*⌝
GLOUCESTER  Why so earnestly seek you to put up that
  letter?                                                   30
EDMUND  I know no news, my lord.
GLOUCESTER  What paper were you reading?
EDMUND  Nothing, my lord.
GLOUCESTER  No? What needed then that terrible dis-
  patch of it into your pocket? The quality of nothing      35
  hath not such need to hide itself. Let's see. Come, if
  it be nothing, I shall not need spectacles.
EDMUND  I beseech you, sir, pardon me. It is a letter
  from my brother that I have not all o'erread; and
  for so much as I have perused, I find it not fit for      40
  your o'erlooking.
GLOUCESTER  Give me the letter, sir.
EDMUND  I shall offend either to detain or give it. The
  contents, as in part I understand them, are to
  blame.                                                    45
GLOUCESTER  Let's see, let's see.

> ⌜*Edmund gives him the paper.*⌝

EDMUND  I hope, for my brother's justification, he
  wrote this but as an essay or taste of my virtue.
GLOUCESTER  (*reads*)  *This policy and reverence of age*
  *makes the world bitter to the best of our times, keeps*  50
  *our fortunes from us till our oldness cannot relish*

52. **idle and fond:** silly and foolish
53. **who sways:** which rules
54. **suffered:** allowed, tolerated
64. **closet:** private room
65. **character:** handwriting
67. **matter:** i.e., subject **matter**
68. **in respect of that:** i.e., considering the contents
69. **fain:** gladly
73. **sounded:** i.e., questioned
76. **fit:** fitting, appropriate; **at perfect age:** i.e., fully grown
77. **declined:** i.e., in decline, or failing in vigor; **ward:** one legally placed under the protection of a guardian
80. **Abhorred:** abhorrent; **detested:** detestable
81. **sirrah:** term of address that shows the speaker's position of authority
87. **run ... course:** i.e., act with certainty; **where:** i.e., whereas

*them. I begin to find an idle and fond bondage in the*
*oppression of aged tyranny, who sways not as it hath*
*power but as it is suffered. Come to me, that of this I*
*may speak more. If our father would sleep till I waked* 55
*him, you should enjoy half his revenue forever and*
*live the beloved of your brother.*       *Edgar.*
Hum? Conspiracy? "Sleep till I wake him, you
should enjoy half his revenue." My son Edgar! Had
he a hand to write this? A heart and brain to breed it 60
in?—When came you to this? Who brought it?

EDMUND   It was not brought me, my lord; there's the
cunning of it. I found it thrown in at the casement
of my closet.

GLOUCESTER   You know the character to be your 65
brother's?

EDMUND   If the matter were good, my lord, I durst
swear it were his; but in respect of that, I would
fain think it were not.

GLOUCESTER   It is his. 70

EDMUND   It is his hand, my lord, but I hope his heart is
not in the contents.

GLOUCESTER   Has he never before sounded you in this
business?

EDMUND   Never, my lord. But I have heard him oft 75
maintain it to be fit that, sons at perfect age and
fathers declined, the father should be as ward to the
son, and the son manage his revenue.

GLOUCESTER   O villain, villain! His very opinion in the
letter. Abhorred villain! Unnatural, detested, brut- 80
ish villain! Worse than brutish!—Go, sirrah, seek
him. I'll apprehend him.—Abominable villain!—
Where is he?

EDMUND   I do not well know, my lord. If it shall please
you to suspend your indignation against my brother 85
till you can derive from him better testimony of his
intent, you should run a certain course; where, if

91. **pawn down:** stake, bet

92. **feel:** test

93. **pretense of danger:** dangerous purpose

95. **meet:** fitting, proper

97. **auricular:** perceived by the ear; **have your satisfaction:** i.e., convince yourself

103. **wind me into him:** i.e., for my sake, insinuate yourself into his confidence; **Frame:** manage

104. **after . . . wisdom:** as you judge wise

104–5. **unstate . . . resolution:** i.e., give up my rank and fortune if only I could resolve my doubts

106. **presently:** immediately; **convey:** conduct

108. **withal:** i.e., with what happens

109. **late:** recent

110–11. **the wisdom of nature:** i.e., the study of nature, "natural philosophy" (what we would now call "science")

111. **nature:** i.e., human nature

112. **scourged:** afflicted; **sequent effects:** disasters that follow (the **eclipses** [line 109])

113–14. **mutinies:** riots

116. **prediction:** portent, omen

117. **bias of nature:** natural inclination (In the game of bowls, the **bias** is the curve that brings the ball to the desired point. See picture, page 44.)

120. **disquietly:** in a disturbing manner

you violently proceed against him, mistaking his
purpose, it would make a great gap in your own
honor and shake in pieces the heart of his obedi-        90
ence. I dare pawn down my life for him that he hath
writ this to feel my affection to your Honor, and to
no other pretense of danger.

GLOUCESTER   Think you so?

EDMUND   If your Honor judge it meet, I will place you        95
where you shall hear us confer of this, and by an
auricular assurance have your satisfaction, and that
without any further delay than this very evening.

GLOUCESTER   He cannot be such a monster.

⟨EDMUND   Nor is not, sure.        100

GLOUCESTER   To his father, that so tenderly and entirely loves him! Heaven and Earth!⟩ Edmund, seek him
out; wind me into him, I pray you. Frame the
business after your own wisdom. I would unstate
myself to be in a due resolution.        105

EDMUND   I will seek him, sir, presently, convey the
business as I shall find means, and acquaint you
withal.

GLOUCESTER   These late eclipses in the sun and moon
portend no good to us. Though the wisdom of        110
nature can reason it thus and thus, yet nature finds
itself scourged by the sequent effects. Love cools,
friendship falls off, brothers divide; in cities, mutinies; in countries, discord; in palaces, treason; and
the bond cracked 'twixt son and father. [This villain        115
of mine comes under the prediction: there's son
against father. The King falls from bias of nature:
there's father against child. We have seen the best of
our time. Machinations, hollowness, treachery, and
all ruinous disorders follow us disquietly to our        120
graves.]—Find out this villain, Edmund. It shall
lose thee nothing. Do it carefully.—And the noble
and true-hearted Kent banished! His offense, honesty! 'Tis strange.        *He exits.*

125. **foppery:** foolishness
126. **surfeits:** sicknesses caused by intemperance
127–28. **guilty . . . stars:** Edmund here places his father's talk about omens within the larger context of belief in astrology, where the position of the stars, moon, and planets at the moment of one's birth are thought to control one's life. (See picture, page 74.)
129. **on:** by
130. **treachers:** deceivers, traitors; **by spherical predominance:** i.e., through the influence of the celestial spheres (According to Ptolemaic astronomy heavenly bodies were carried around the Earth in crystalline spheres. See picture, page xxxiv.)
133. **divine thrusting on:** supernatural incitement
134–35. **lay . . . star:** blame his lecherousness on **a star**
136. **compounded with:** i.e., had sex with (literally, contracted with, made terms with)
136–37. **under the Dragon's tail:** perhaps, when the constellation Draco was in the ascendant; or, perhaps, while the moon was at the southward node of its orbit
137. **Ursa Major:** the constellation called the Great Bear
138. **rough:** violent, harsh, rude; **Fut:** i.e., 'sfoot, or Christ's foot (a strong oath)
139. **that:** that which; **maidenliest:** i.e., chastest
140. **twinkled . . . bastardizing:** in astrological terms, "been in the ascendant at the moment I was conceived (as a bastard)"
141. **pat:** at exactly the right moment; **catastrophe:** conclusion, winding up

*(continued)*
36

EDMUND   This is the excellent foppery of the world, that   125
when we are sick in fortune (often the surfeits of
our own behavior) we make guilty of our disasters
the sun, the moon, and stars, as if we were villains
on necessity; fools by heavenly compulsion; knaves,
thieves, and treachers by spherical predominance;   130
drunkards, liars, and adulterers by an enforced
obedience of planetary influence; and all that we
are evil in, by a divine thrusting on. An admirable
evasion of whoremaster man, to lay his goatish
disposition on the charge of a star! My father   135
compounded with my mother under the Dragon's
tail, and my nativity was under Ursa Major, so that it
follows I am rough and lecherous. ⟨Fut,⟩ I should
have been that I am, had the maidenliest star in the
firmament twinkled on my bastardizing. ⟨Edgar⟩—   140

*Enter Edgar.*

⟨and⟩ pat he comes like the catastrophe of the old
comedy. My cue is villainous melancholy, with a
sigh like Tom o' Bedlam.—O, these eclipses do
portend these divisions. *Fa, sol, la, mi.*
EDGAR   How now, brother Edmund, what serious con-   145
templation are you in?
EDMUND   I am thinking, brother, of a prediction I read
this other day, what should follow these eclipses.
EDGAR   Do you busy yourself with that?
EDMUND   I promise you, the effects he writes of suc-   150
ceed unhappily, ⟨as of unnaturalness between the
child and the parent, death, dearth, dissolutions of
ancient amities, divisions in state, menaces and
maledictions against king and nobles, needless diffidences, banishment of friends, dissipation of co-   155
horts, nuptial breaches, and I know not what.
EDGAR   How long have you been a sectary astronomical?

143. **Tom o' Bedlam:** a beggar who has escaped or been discharged from Bedlam (London's Bethlehem Hospital for the insane) or who pretends to be so in order to make people give him money

144. **Fa, sol, la, mi:** The notes of the musical scale were sung to the syllables *do, re, mi, fa, sol, la,* and *ti.* Presumably Edmund sings these four syllables.

148. **this:** i.e., the

150–51. **succeed:** follow, turn out

154–55. **diffidences:** distrust

155–56. **dissipation of cohorts:** (perhaps mutinous) disbanding of troops of soldiers

157–58. **sectary astronomical:** believer in astrology

163. **in:** on

164. **countenance:** manner

166. **Bethink yourself:** recollect

167–68. **forbear his presence:** i.e., avoid him

168. **qualified:** reduced

170. **with . . . person:** i.e., even physical harm to you

171. **allay:** calm, assuage

173–74. **have . . . forbearance:** i.e., restrain yourself patiently (Both **continent** and **forbearance** connote self-restraint.)

176. **fitly:** at a convenient time

181. **meaning:** intention

183. **image and horror:** i.e., horrible **image**

185. **anon:** soon

190. **practices ride easy:** i.e., plots easily succeed; **the business:** i.e., how to proceed

191. **wit:** cleverness

192. **meet:** i.e., welcome (literally, appropriate); **fashion fit:** i.e., shape to my own ends

EDMUND   Come, come,⟩ when saw you my father last?
EDGAR   The night gone by.                                            160
EDMUND   Spake you with him?
EDGAR   Ay, two hours together.
EDMUND   Parted you in good terms? Found you no
displeasure in him by word nor countenance?
EDGAR   None at all.                                                  165
EDMUND   Bethink yourself wherein you may have of-
fended him, and at my entreaty forbear his presence until some little time hath qualified the heat
of his displeasure, which at this instant so rageth in
him that with the mischief of your person it would   170
scarcely allay.
EDGAR   Some villain hath done me wrong.
EDMUND   That's my fear. [I pray you have a continent
forbearance till the speed of his rage goes slower;
and, as I say, retire with me to my lodging, from   175
whence I will fitly bring you to hear my lord speak.
Pray you go. There's my key. If you do stir abroad,
go armed.
EDGAR   Armed, brother?]
EDMUND   Brother, I advise you to the best. I am no   180
honest man if there be any good meaning toward
you. I have told you what I have seen and heard, but
faintly, nothing like the image and horror of it. Pray
you, away.
EDGAR   Shall I hear from you anon?                             185
EDMUND   I do serve you in this business.   *Edgar exits.*
A credulous father and a brother noble,
Whose nature is so far from doing harms
That he suspects none; on whose foolish honesty
My practices ride easy. I see the business.             190
Let me, if not by birth, have lands by wit.
All with me's meet that I can fashion fit.
                                              *He exits.*

**1.3** Goneril, with whom Lear has gone to live, expresses her anger at Lear and his knights. She orders her steward, Oswald, to inform Lear that she will not see him and to treat Lear coldly.

---

5. **crime:** offense
10. **come slack:** fall short
11. **answer:** i.e., **answer** for
14. **to question:** into dispute
15. **distaste:** dislike; **let him:** i.e., **let him** go
17. **Idle:** silly, useless
18. **authorities:** powers
21–22. **checks . . . abused:** reprimands in place of (or, perhaps, as well as) flattering words, **when they** (old men) **are seen** to be misguided
27. **would . . . occasions:** i.e., wish to create opportunities
28. **straight:** straightway, immediately
29. **hold . . . course:** i.e., follow exactly **my course** of action

"Old fools are babes again." (1.3.20)
From August Casimir Redel, *Apophtegmata symbolica* . . . (n.d.).

Scene 3
*Enter Goneril and* ⌐*Oswald, her*⌐ *Steward.*

GONERIL   Did my father strike my gentleman for chid-
ing of his Fool?
OSWALD   Ay, madam.
GONERIL
By day and night he wrongs me. Every hour
He flashes into one gross crime or other                              5
That sets us all at odds. I'll not endure it.
His knights grow riotous, and himself upbraids us
On every trifle. When he returns from hunting,
I will not speak with him. Say I am sick.
If you come slack of former services,                                10
You shall do well. The fault of it I'll answer.
OSWALD   He's coming, madam. I hear him.
GONERIL
Put on what weary negligence you please,
You and your fellows. I'd have it come to question.
If he distaste it, let him to my sister,                              15
Whose mind and mine I know in that are one,
⟨Not to be overruled. Idle old man
That still would manage those authorities
That he hath given away. Now, by my life,
Old fools are babes again and must be used                           20
With checks as flatteries, when they are seen
  abused.⟩
Remember what I have said.
OSWALD                                Well, madam.
GONERIL
And let his knights have colder looks among you.      25
What grows of it, no matter. Advise your fellows so.
⟨I would breed from hence occasions, and I shall,
That I may speak.⟩ I'll write straight to my sister
To hold my ⟨very⟩ course. Prepare for dinner.
*They exit* ⌐*in different directions.*⌐

**1.4** The earl of Kent returns in disguise, offers his services to Lear, and is accepted as one of Lear's followers. Goneril rebukes Lear for his knights' rowdiness and demands he dismiss half of them. After attacking her verbally for her ingratitude, he prepares to leave for Regan's.

---

1–4. **If . . . likeness:** i.e., **if I can** disguise my way of speaking as well as I have my appearance, then I may be able fully to carry out my plan **diffuse:** disorder, and thereby disguise **razed:** erased; shaved off **likeness:** outward appearance

5–6. **where . . . condemned:** i.e., in Lear's presence

7. **come:** i.e., happen that

8 SD. **Horns:** i.e., the sound of hunting **horns; within:** offstage

9. **stay:** wait

12. **What . . . profess?:** What is your trade or calling?

14. **profess to be:** assert that I am

15. **put . . . trust:** i.e., trust me, have confidence in me

16. **honest:** honorable; **converse:** associate

17. **fear judgment:** i.e., fear coming before a judge, either divine or human

17–18. **cannot choose:** i.e., have no choice

18. **eat no fish:** This seems to be a joke, though its meaning is unclear. It may mean "I am a Protestant" or "I eat meat and am therefore manly."

23. **What wouldst thou?:** i.e., what do you want?

29. **fain:** gladly

Scene 4
*Enter Kent ⌜in disguise.⌝*

KENT
If but as ⟨well⟩ I other accents borrow
That can my speech diffuse, my good intent
May carry through itself to that full issue
For which I razed my likeness. Now, banished Kent,
If thou canst serve where thou dost stand                    5
   condemned,
So may it come thy master, whom thou lov'st,
Shall find thee full of labors.

*Horns within. Enter Lear, ⌜Knights,⌝ and Attendants.*

LEAR    Let me not stay a jot for dinner. Go get it ready.
                                          *⌜An Attendant exits.⌝*
How now, what art thou?                                      10
KENT    A man, sir.
LEAR    What dost thou profess? What wouldst thou with
   us?
KENT    I do profess to be no less than I seem, to serve
   him truly that will put me in trust, to love him that    15
   is honest, to converse with him that is wise and says
   little, to fear judgment, to fight when I cannot
   choose, and to eat no fish.
LEAR    What art thou?
KENT    A very honest-hearted fellow, and as poor as the    20
   King.
LEAR    If thou be'st as poor for a subject as he's for a
   king, thou art poor enough. What wouldst thou?
KENT    Service.
LEAR    Who wouldst thou serve?                             25
KENT    You.
LEAR    Dost thou know me, fellow?
KENT    No, sir, but you have that in your countenance
   which I would fain call master.

**33. keep . . . counsel: keep** honorable secrets; or, perhaps, honestly **keep** secrets

**34. curious:** elaborate

**38. to love:** i.e., as **to love**

**43. knave:** boy; servant

**44. Fool:** A professional **Fool** made his living by entertaining his aristocratic patron. He was both allowed and encouraged to speak the truth, thus countering the flattery of the other attendants surrounding the monarch or nobleman.

**47. clotpole:** blockhead

**52. slave:** rascal, menial servant

**54. roundest:** rudest

**58. entertained:** treated

**59. were wont:** i.e., used to be

A game of bowls. (1.2.117)
From *Le centre de l'amour . . .* (1650?).

LEAR  What's that?  30
KENT  Authority.
LEAR  What services canst do?
KENT  I can keep honest counsel, ride, run, mar a
curious tale in telling it, and deliver a plain mes-
sage bluntly. That which ordinary men are fit for I  35
am qualified in, and the best of me is diligence.
LEAR  How old art thou?
KENT  Not so young, sir, to love a woman for singing,
nor so old to dote on her for anything. I have years
on my back forty-eight.  40
LEAR  Follow me. Thou shalt serve me—if I like thee
no worse after dinner. I will not part from thee
yet.—Dinner, ho, dinner!—Where's my knave, my
Fool? Go you and call my Fool hither.
⌜*An Attendant exits.*⌝

*Enter* ⌜*Oswald, the*⌝ *Steward.*

You, you, sirrah, where's my daughter?  45
OSWALD  So please you—  *He exits.*
LEAR  What says the fellow there? Call the clotpole
back. ⌜*A Knight exits.*⌝ Where's my Fool? Ho! I think
the world's asleep.

⌜*Enter Knight again.*⌝

How now? Where's that mongrel?  50
KNIGHT  He says, my lord, your ⟨daughter⟩ is not well.
LEAR  Why came not the slave back to me when I
called him?
KNIGHT  Sir, he answered me in the roundest manner,
he would not.  55
LEAR  He would not?
KNIGHT  My lord, I know not what the matter is, but to
my judgment your Highness is not entertained
with that ceremonious affection as you were wont.
There's a great abatement of kindness appears as  60

61. **the . . . dependents:** i.e., all the servants
67. **but remembrest:** only remind
67–68. **conception:** idea, thought
68. **faint neglect:** i.e., unenthusiastic service
69–70. **blamed . . . curiosity:** charged to my own oversensitivity
70. **very pretense:** actual intention
72. **this:** i.e., these
84. **bandy:** exchange (literally, hit back and forth like a tennis ball)
85. **strucken:** struck
86. **base:** low, inferior
91. **differences:** perhaps, **differences** in rank
91–92. **measure . . . length:** i.e., be tripped   **lubber's:** clumsy oaf's

Football players. (1.4.87)
From Henry Peacham, *Minerua Britanna* . . . (1612).

well in the general dependents as in the Duke
himself also, and your daughter.
LEAR  Ha? Sayst thou so?
KNIGHT  I beseech you pardon me, my lord, if I be
mistaken, for my duty cannot be silent when I think     65
your Highness wronged.
LEAR  Thou but remembrest me of mine own conception. I have perceived a most faint neglect of late,
which I have rather blamed as mine own jealous
curiosity than as a very pretense and purpose of     70
unkindness. I will look further into 't. But where's
my Fool? I have not seen him this two days.
KNIGHT  Since my young lady's going into France, sir,
the Fool hath much pined away.
LEAR  No more of that. I have noted it well.—Go you     75
and tell my daughter I would speak with her. ⌜An
Attendant exits.⌝ Go you call hither my Fool.
⌜*Another exits.*⌝

Enter ⌜*Oswald, the*⌝ *Steward.*

O you, sir, you, come you hither, sir. Who am I, sir?
OSWALD  My lady's father.
LEAR  "My lady's father"? My lord's knave! You whore-     80
son dog, you slave, you cur!
OSWALD  I am none of these, my lord, I beseech your
pardon.
LEAR  Do you bandy looks with me, you rascal?
⌜*Lear strikes him.*⌝
OSWALD  I'll not be strucken, my lord.     85
KENT, ⌜*tripping him*⌝ Nor tripped neither, you base
football player?
LEAR  I thank thee, fellow. Thou serv'st me, and I'll
love thee.
KENT, ⌜*to Oswald*⌝ Come, sir, arise. Away. I'll teach you     90
differences. Away, away. If you will measure your
lubber's length again, tarry. But away. Go to. Have
you wisdom? So.     ⌜*Oswald exits.*⌝

94. **knave:** servant

95. **earnest:** a small payment that promises a greater reward to come

97. **coxcomb:** fool's cap (See picture, page 52.)

99. **were best:** had better

103–4. **an . . . sits:** i.e., if you cannot adjust to shifts in power **an:** i.e., if **as the wind sits:** in the direction **the wind** blows

105. **on 's:** i.e., of his

108. **nuncle:** i.e., mine uncle, the Fool's familiar way of addressing Lear

111. **living:** property

115–17. **Truth's . . . stink:** perhaps, truth-telling is **whipped out** of the house while flattery is rewarded (This meaning depends on the traditional symbolic link between flattery and dogs.) **Brach:** bitch-hound

118. **gall:** painful sore; or, vexation

121. **Mark:** pay attention to, listen to

124. **owest:** own

125. **goest:** walk

126. **trowest:** believe

127. **Set . . . throwest:** bet less than you win throwing dice

LEAR  Now, my friendly knave, I thank thee. There's
earnest of thy service.  ⌜*He gives Kent a purse.*⌝  95

*Enter Fool.*

FOOL  Let me hire him too. ⌜*To Kent.*⌝ Here's my
coxcomb.  ⌜*He offers Kent his cap.*⌝
LEAR  How now, my pretty knave, how dost thou?
FOOL, ⌜*to Kent*⌝  Sirrah, you were best take my coxcomb.  100
LEAR  Why, my boy?
FOOL  Why? For taking one's part that's out of favor.
⌜*To Kent.*⌝ Nay, an thou canst not smile as the
wind sits, thou'lt catch cold shortly. There, take my
coxcomb. Why, this fellow has banished two on 's  105
daughters and did the third a blessing against his
will. If thou follow him, thou must needs wear my
coxcomb.—How now, nuncle? Would I had two
coxcombs and two daughters.
LEAR  Why, my boy?  110
FOOL  If I gave them all my living, I'd keep my coxcombs myself. There's mine. Beg another of thy
daughters.
LEAR  Take heed, sirrah—the whip.
FOOL  Truth's a dog must to kennel; he must be  115
whipped out, when the Lady Brach may stand by th'
fire and stink.
LEAR  A pestilent gall to me!
FOOL  Sirrah, I'll teach thee a speech.
LEAR  Do.  120
FOOL  Mark it, nuncle:
     Have more than thou showest,
     Speak less than thou knowest,
     Lend less than thou owest,
     Ride more than thou goest,  125
     Learn more than thou trowest,
     Set less than thou throwest;

131. **a score:** twenty

133. **unfee'd:** unpaid (Proverbial: "A **lawyer** will not plead without a fee.")

140. **bitter:** harsh, cutting

147. **Do . . . stand:** i.e., you **stand** in his place

149. **presently:** immediately

150. **motley:** the multicolored costume of the professional fool

155. **altogether fool:** i.e., just fooling (The Fool's reply assumes that "altogether fool" means "all the folly that there is.")

156. **let me:** i.e., allow me to monopolize foolishness

157. **on 't:** i.e., of it

162–63. **eat . . . meat:** i.e., eaten up the edible part

"And ladies too . . . they'll be snatching." (1.4.158–59)
From Theodor de Bry, *Emblemata . . .* (1593).

Leave thy drink and thy whore
And keep in-a-door,
And thou shalt have more                    130
Than two tens to a score.
KENT   This is nothing, Fool.
FOOL   Then 'tis like the breath of an unfee'd lawyer.
You gave me nothing for 't.—Can you make no use
of nothing, nuncle?                          135
LEAR   Why no, boy. Nothing can be made out of
nothing.
FOOL, ⌈*to Kent*⌉   Prithee tell him, so much the rent of his
land comes to. He will not believe a Fool.
LEAR   A bitter Fool!                        140
FOOL   Dost know the difference, my boy, between a
bitter fool and a sweet one?
LEAR   No, lad, teach me.
FOOL         ⟨That lord that counseled thee
To give away thy land,                       145
Come place him here by me;
Do thou for him stand.
The sweet and bitter fool
Will presently appear.
The one in motley here,                       150
The other found out there.
LEAR   Dost thou call me "fool," boy?
FOOL   All thy other titles thou hast given away. That
thou wast born with.
KENT   This is not altogether fool, my lord.  155
FOOL   No, faith, lords and great men will not let me. If
I had a monopoly out, they would have part on 't.
And ladies too, they will not let me have all the fool
to myself; they'll be snatching.⟩—Nuncle, give me
an egg, and I'll give thee two crowns.        160
LEAR   What two crowns shall they be?
FOOL   Why, after I have cut the egg i' th' middle and eat
up the meat, the two crowns of the egg. When thou

164. **clovest:** split
165. **bor'st ... ass:** i.e., carried your donkey
168. **like myself:** i.e., like a fool
170. **grace:** favor
171. **foppish:** foolish
172. **wear:** possess and enjoy as their own
173. **apish:** foolishly imitative
176. **used it:** made it my practice
178. **put'st down ... breeches:** i.e., volunteered to be whipped
181. **bo-peep:** a child's game
194. **frontlet:** i.e., frown

"Here's my coxcomb." (1.4.96–97)
From Sebastian Brant, *Stultifera nauis* (1570).

clovest thy ⟨crown⟩ i' th' middle and gav'st away
both parts, thou bor'st thine ass on thy back o'er    165
the dirt. Thou hadst little wit in thy bald crown
when thou gav'st thy golden one away. If I speak
like myself in this, let him be whipped that first
finds it so. ⌈*Sings.*⌉

    Fools had ne'er less grace in a year,    170
      For wise men are grown foppish
    And know not how their wits to wear,
      Their manners are so apish.

LEAR  When were you wont to be so full of songs,
sirrah?    175
FOOL  I have used it, nuncle, e'er since thou mad'st thy
daughters thy mothers. For when thou gav'st them
the rod and put'st down thine own breeches,
⌈*Sings.*⌉

    Then they for sudden joy did weep,
      And I for sorrow sung,    180
    That such a king should play bo-peep
      And go the ⟨fools⟩ among.

Prithee, nuncle, keep a schoolmaster that can teach
thy Fool to lie. I would fain learn to lie.
LEAR  An you lie, sirrah, we'll have you whipped.    185
FOOL  I marvel what kin thou and thy daughters are.
They'll have me whipped for speaking true, thou'lt
have me whipped for lying, and sometimes I am
whipped for holding my peace. I had rather be any
kind o' thing than a Fool. And yet I would not be    190
thee, nuncle. Thou hast pared thy wit o' both sides
and left nothing i' th' middle. Here comes one o' the
parings.

           *Enter Goneril.*

LEAR
How now, daughter? What makes that frontlet on?
⟨Methinks⟩ you are too much of late i' th' frown.    195

197–98. **an O without a figure:** a zero with no number before it (to give it a numerical value)
204. **want:** need
205. **shelled peascod:** an empty pea pod
206. **all-licensed Fool:** i.e., servant who, as **Fool,** may do whatever he pleases
208. **carp:** (1) find fault; (2) talk noisily
209. **rank:** gross, excessive
211. **a . . . redress:** a sure remedy
212. **yourself too late:** you all too recently
213. **put it on:** encourage it
214. **allowance:** approval
214–19. **which . . . proceeding:** Goneril's speech becomes much less intelligible as she begins to threaten Lear, but her general sense is clear: **if you** continue to encourage your knights' riotous behavior, I will move against them for the general good even if I offend and embarrass you; and I will be thought right to do so.
215. **censure:** blame; **redresses:** remedies
216. **tender . . . weal:** regard for the general good
217. **working:** implementation
218. **else were:** otherwise would be seen as; **shame:** shameful; **necessity:** the obvious need
221–22. **The hedge . . . young:** This couplet offers a nature story: **the cuckoo** lays its egg in the sparrow's nest, and the sparrow feeds the young cuckoo until it gets so big it kills the sparrow. **it's:** i.e., it has; **it:** i.e., its
223. **darkling:** (1) in the dark; (2) confused
225. **I would:** I wish
226. **fraught:** filled
227. **dispositions:** (1) inclinations; (2) temperaments

FOOL   Thou wast a pretty fellow when thou hadst no
need to care for her frowning. Now thou art an O
without a figure. I am better than thou art now. I
am a Fool. Thou art nothing. ⌈*To Goneril.*⌉ Yes,
forsooth, I will hold my tongue. So your face bids   200
me, though you say nothing.
        Mum, mum,
        He that keeps nor crust ⟨nor⟩ crumb,
        Weary of all, shall want some.
                                ⌈*He points at Lear.*⌉
That's a shelled peascod.                             205
GONERIL
Not only, sir, this your all-licensed Fool,
But other of your insolent retinue
Do hourly carp and quarrel, breaking forth
In rank and not-to-be-endurèd riots. Sir,
I had thought by making this well known unto you   210
To have found a safe redress, but now grow fearful,
By what yourself too late have spoke and done,
That you protect this course and put it on
By your allowance; which if you should, the fault
Would not 'scape censure, nor the redresses sleep   215
Which in the tender of a wholesome weal
Might in their working do you that offense,
Which else were shame, that then necessity
Will call discreet proceeding.
FOOL   For you know, nuncle,                          220
        The hedge-sparrow fed the cuckoo so long,
        That it's had it head bit off by it young.
So out went the candle, and we were left darkling.
LEAR   Are you our daughter?
GONERIL
I would you would make use of your good wisdom,    225
Whereof I know you are fraught, and put away
These dispositions which of late transport you
From what you rightly are.

230. **Jug:** a nickname for "Joan"
234. **notion:** mind; **discernings:** mental faculties
235. **lethargied:** asleep; **Waking?:** i.e., am I awake?
238–40. **marks . . . reason:** i.e., by the tokens that designate kingship (titles, dress, entourage), and **by knowledge and reason**
240. **false:** falsely
242. **Which:** i.e., whom
244. **admiration:** pretended amazement
244–45. **much o' th' savor / Of:** i.e., of a kind with
245. **other your:** i.e., others of your
247. **should:** i.e., you **should**
249. **disordered:** disorderly, unruly
251. **Shows:** looks; **Epicurism:** sensuality; or, gluttony
253. **graced:** honorable, dignified; **speak:** i.e., ask
254. **desired:** requested
255. **else:** otherwise
256. **disquantity:** lessen the number of; **train:** attendants
257. **remainders . . . depend:** i.e., those that remain as your dependents
258. **besort:** suit

FOOL   May not an ass know when the cart draws the
    horse? Whoop, Jug, I love thee!    230
LEAR
    Does any here know me? This is not Lear.
    Does Lear walk thus, speak thus? Where are his
        eyes?
    Either his notion weakens, his discernings
    Are lethargied—Ha! Waking? 'Tis not so.    235
    Who is it that can tell me who I am?
FOOL   Lear's shadow.
⟨LEAR   I would learn that, for, by the marks of
    sovereignty,
    Knowledge, and reason, I should be false persuaded  240
    I had daughters.
FOOL   Which they will make an obedient father.⟩
LEAR   Your name, fair gentlewoman?
GONERIL
    This admiration, sir, is much o' th' savor
    Of other your new pranks. I do beseech you    245
    To understand my purposes aright.
    As you are old and reverend, should be wise.
    Here do you keep a hundred knights and squires,
    Men so disordered, so debauched and bold,
    That this our court, infected with their manners,    250
    Shows like a riotous inn. Epicurism and lust
    Makes it more like a tavern or a brothel
    Than a graced palace. The shame itself doth speak
    For instant remedy. Be then desired,
    By her that else will take the thing she begs,    255
    A little to disquantity your train,
    And the remainders that shall still depend
    To be such men as may besort your age,
    Which know themselves and you.
LEAR                  Darkness and    260
    devils!—
    Saddle my horses. Call my train together.
                               ⌜*Some exit.*⌝

267. **Woe that:** i.e., **woe** to the one who
271. **thou show'st thee:** you reveal yourself
273. **patient:** calm
274. **kite:** vulture, vicious bird of prey (See picture, below.)
275. **train:** attendants; **parts:** qualities
277. **in . . . support:** i.e., maintain with precise observance (of their duty)
278. **worships:** honor
280–82. **Which . . . place:** i.e., which distorted, twisted, me away from what I should be (The image of these lines may be of a building [**frame**] dislodged from its foundation [**fixed place**].) **engine:** machine
285. **dear:** precious
287. **moved you:** aroused your feelings

A kite. (1.4.274)
From Konrad Gesner, *Historiae animalium* . . . (1585–1604).

Degenerate bastard, I'll not trouble thee.
Yet have I left a daughter.

GONERIL
You strike my people, and your disordered rabble    265
Make servants of their betters.

                       *Enter Albany.*

LEAR
Woe that too late repents!—⟨O, sir, are you
   come?⟩
Is it your will? Speak, sir.—Prepare my horses.
                           ⌜*Some exit.*⌝
Ingratitude, thou marble-hearted fiend,    270
More hideous when thou show'st thee in a child
Than the sea monster!
[ALBANY          Pray, sir, be patient.]
LEAR, ⌜*to Goneril*⌝  Detested kite, thou liest.
My train are men of choice and rarest parts,    275
That all particulars of duty know
And in the most exact regard support
The worships of their name. O most small fault,
How ugly didst thou in Cordelia show,
Which, like an engine, wrenched my frame of    280
   nature
From the fixed place, drew from my heart all love
And added to the gall! O Lear, Lear, Lear!
                  ⌜*He strikes his head.*⌝
Beat at this gate that let thy folly in
And thy dear judgment out. Go, go, my people.    285
                        ⌜*Some exit.*⌝

ALBANY
My lord, I am guiltless as I am ignorant
[Of what hath moved you.]
LEAR               It may be so, my lord.—
Hear, Nature, hear, dear goddess, hear!
Suspend thy purpose if thou didst intend    290

291. **this creature:** i.e., Goneril
293. **increase:** procreation
294. **derogate:** dishonored
295. **If . . . teem:** i.e., if it is her destiny to bear a child
296. **spleen:** spite, malice
297. **thwart:** perverse; **disnatured:** unnatural
299. **cadent:** falling; **fret:** wear
300. **her . . . benefits:** i.e., Goneril's motherly efforts and kindnesses
306. **disposition:** temperament
307. **As dotage:** i.e., that senility
308. **at a clap:** i.e., at one stroke
314. **perforce:** i.e., against my will
315. **Blasts and fogs:** sudden infections and foul (infectious) air
317. **untented woundings:** perhaps, wounds too deep to be probed (**A tent** was a probe used to cleanse a wound.)
318. **fond:** foolish
319. **Beweep . . . again:** i.e., (if you) weep **again** over **this** matter

To make this creature fruitful.
Into her womb convey sterility.
Dry up in her the organs of increase,
And from her derogate body never spring
A babe to honor her. If she must teem, 295
Create her child of spleen, that it may live
And be a thwart disnatured torment to her.
Let it stamp wrinkles in her brow of youth,
With cadent tears fret channels in her cheeks,
Turn all her mother's pains and benefits 300
To laughter and contempt, that she may feel
How sharper than a serpent's tooth it is
To have a thankless child.—Away, away!
⌜*Lear and the rest of his train*⌝ *exit.*

ALBANY
Now, gods that we adore, whereof comes this?

GONERIL
Never afflict yourself to know more of it, 305
But let his disposition have that scope
As dotage gives it.

*Enter Lear* ⌜*and the Fool.*⌝

LEAR
What, fifty of my followers at a clap?
Within a fortnight?

ALBANY What's the matter, sir? 310

LEAR
I'll tell thee. ⌜*To Goneril.*⌝ Life and death! I am
    ashamed
That thou hast power to shake my manhood thus,
That these hot tears, which break from me perforce,
Should make thee worth them. Blasts and fogs upon 315
    thee!
Th' untented woundings of a father's curse
Pierce every sense about thee! Old fond eyes,
Beweep this cause again, I'll pluck you out

320. **waters . . . loose:** i.e., tears **that you** shed
321. **temper:** moisten, soften
323. **comfortable:** comforting
325. **visage:** face
328. **mark:** hear
337. **Should . . . slaughter:** i.e., would certainly be sent to execution
338. **halter:** hangman's rope
342. **politic:** prudent (said sarcastically)
343. **At point:** armed
344–45. **dream, buzz, fancy:** All mean "whim," but **buzz** may also mean "whisper," "rumor."
346. **enguard:** i.e., guard, protect
347. **in mercy:** i.e., at his **mercy**
348. **too far:** i.e., unreasonably
350. **still take away:** always remove
351. **Not . . . taken:** i.e., rather than always **fear** being overtaken (by those **harms**)
354. **unfitness:** unsuitableness

"A tavern or a brothel." (1.4.252)
From *Le centre de l'amour . . .* (1650?).

And cast you, with the waters that you loose,     320
To temper clay. ⟨Yea, is 't come to this?⟩
Ha! Let it be so. I have another daughter
Who, I am sure, is kind and comfortable.
When she shall hear this of thee, with her nails
She'll flay thy wolvish visage. Thou shalt find     325
That I'll resume the shape which thou dost think
I have cast off forever.           *He exits.*
GONERIL         Do you mark that?
ALBANY
   I cannot be so partial, Goneril,
   To the great love I bear you—       330
GONERIL   Pray you, content.—What, Oswald, ho!—
   You, sir, more knave than Fool, after your master.
FOOL   Nuncle Lear, Nuncle Lear, tarry. Take the Fool
   with thee.
       A fox, when one has caught her,     335
       And such a daughter,
       Should sure to the slaughter,
       If my cap would buy a halter.
       So the Fool follows after.      *He exits.*
[GONERIL
   This man hath had good counsel. A hundred    340
     knights!
   'Tis politic and safe to let him keep
   At point a hundred knights! Yes, that on every
     dream,
   Each buzz, each fancy, each complaint, dislike,    345
   He may enguard his dotage with their powers
   And hold our lives in mercy.—Oswald, I say!
ALBANY    Well, you may fear too far.
GONERIL    Safer than trust too far.
   Let me still take away the harms I fear,     350
   Not fear still to be taken. I know his heart.
   What he hath uttered I have writ my sister.
   If she sustain him and his hundred knights
   When I have showed th' unfitness—

356. **What:** an interjection introducing a question
359. **full:** i.e., fully
361. **compact:** confirm
364. **milky ... course:** i.e., mild and gentle course
365. **under pardon:** i.e., if you will excuse me
366. **at task:** blamed; **want:** lack
371. **Well ... event:** perhaps a version of a proverb such as "time will tell" or "the end crowns all"

**1.5** Lear, setting out for Regan's with his Fool, sends the disguised Kent ahead with a letter to Regan.

---

1. **Gloucester:** presumably, the town (or county) of that name
1–2. **these letters:** i.e., this letter
3. **demand out of:** questions arising from
8. **in 's:** in his
9. **kibes:** chilblains (i.e., sores resulting from exposure to the cold)

*Enter ⌜Oswald, the⌝ Steward.*

How now, Oswald?]  355
What, have you writ that letter to my sister?
OSWALD   Ay, madam.
GONERIL
Take you some company and away to horse.
Inform her full of my particular fear,
And thereto add such reasons of your own        360
As may compact it more. Get you gone,
And hasten your return. ⌜*Oswald exits.*⌝ No, no, my
   lord,
This milky gentleness and course of yours,
Though I condemn not, yet, under pardon,         365
⌜You⌝ are much more at task for want of wisdom
Than praised for harmful mildness.
ALBANY
How far your eyes may pierce I cannot tell.
Striving to better, oft we mar what's well.
GONERIL   Nay, then—                              370
ALBANY   Well, well, th' event.

                                    *They exit.*


Scene 5
*Enter Lear, Kent ⌜in disguise,⌝ Gentleman, and Fool.*

LEAR, ⌜*to Kent*⌝   Go you before to Gloucester with these
   letters. Acquaint my daughter no further with anything you know than comes from her demand out of
   the letter. If your diligence be not speedy, I shall be
   there afore you.                               5
KENT   I will not sleep, my lord, till I have delivered
   your letter.                        *He exits.*
FOOL   If a man's brains were in 's heels, were 't not in
   danger of kibes?
LEAR   Ay, boy.                                   10

11–12. **go slipshod:** i.e., have to wear slippers (The Fool may be suggesting that Lear has no brains, or that his brains do not lie in his heels, since his heels are taking him on a senseless journey.)

14. **Shalt:** i.e., thou **shalt**

15. **this:** i.e., Goneril; **crab's:** i.e., crabapple is

20. **on 's:** of his

22. **of either side 's:** i.e., on **either side** of his

24. **her:** i.e., Cordelia

34. **gone about 'em:** i.e., getting them ready

35. **seven stars:** i.e., the star cluster known as the Pleiades

39. **perforce:** forcibly

45. **mad:** insane

46. **in temper:** i.e., steady, calm; **would not:** do not want to be

"The cart draws the horse." (1.4.229–30)
From Edmund W. Ashbee's 1871 reprint from John Taylor, *Mad fashions, od fashions . . .* (1642).

FOOL   Then, I prithee, be merry; thy wit shall not go
  slipshod.
LEAR   Ha, ha, ha!
FOOL   Shalt see thy other daughter will use thee kind-
  ly, for, though she's as like this as a crab's like an     15
  apple, yet I can tell what I can tell.
LEAR   What canst tell, boy?
FOOL   She will taste as like this as a crab does to a crab.
  Thou canst tell why one's nose stands i' th' middle
  on 's face?     20
LEAR   No.
FOOL   Why, to keep one's eyes of either side 's nose,
  that what a man cannot smell out he may spy into.
LEAR   I did her wrong.
FOOL   Canst tell how an oyster makes his shell?     25
LEAR   No.
FOOL   Nor I neither. But I can tell why a snail has a
  house.
LEAR   Why?
FOOL   Why, to put 's head in, not to give it away to his     30
  daughters and leave his horns without a case.
LEAR   I will forget my nature. So kind a father!—Be
  my horses ready?          ⌜*Gentleman exits.*⌝
FOOL   Thy asses are gone about 'em. The reason why
  the seven stars are no more than seven is a pretty     35
  reason.
LEAR   Because they are not eight.
FOOL   Yes, indeed. Thou wouldst make a good Fool.
LEAR   To take 't again perforce! Monster ingratitude!
FOOL   If thou wert my Fool, nuncle, I'd have thee     40
  beaten for being old before thy time.
LEAR   How's that?
FOOL   Thou shouldst not have been old till thou hadst
  been wise.
LEAR
  O, let me not be mad, not mad, sweet heaven!     45
  Keep me in temper. I would not be mad!

⌜*Enter Gentleman.*⌝

How now, are the horses ready?

GENTLEMAN  Ready, my lord.

LEAR  Come, boy.

FOOL
She that's a maid now and laughs at my departure,    50
Shall not be a maid long, unless things be cut
  shorter.
                                          *They exit.*

*The Tragedy of*

# KING LEAR

ACT 2

**2.1** Edmund tricks Edgar into fleeing from Gloucester's castle. After more of Edmund's lies, Gloucester condemns Edgar to death and makes Edmund his heir. Cornwall and Regan arrive at Gloucester's castle, hear the false stories about Edgar, and welcome Edmund into their service.

---

0 SD. **severally:** separately

1. **Save:** i.e., God **save** (an ordinary greeting)

5. **How comes that?:** i.e., how did this happen?

7. **abroad:** i.e., going around; **ones, they:** i.e., news (regarded as plural)

8. **ear-kissing:** i.e., barely heard because not yet widely known; **arguments:** topics of conversation

10. **toward:** about to happen

13. **do:** i.e., hear

14. **The better, best:** i.e., so much **the better**—in fact, the **best** that could happen

15. **perforce:** necessarily

17. **queasy question:** hazardous, uncertain nature

18. **Briefness:** i.e., quick action; **work:** succeed

20. **watches:** perhaps, has ordered that a watch be kept for you; or, perhaps, is on the lookout

# ACT 2

___

### Scene 1
*Enter ⌜Edmund, the⌝ Bastard and Curan, severally.*

EDMUND   Save thee, Curan.

CURAN   And ⟨you,⟩ sir. I have been with your father and
given him notice that the Duke of Cornwall and
Regan his duchess will be here with him this night.

EDMUND   How comes that?                                    5

CURAN   Nay, I know not. You have heard of the news
abroad?—I mean the whispered ones, for they are
yet but ear-kissing arguments.

EDMUND   Not I. Pray you, what are they?

CURAN   Have you heard of no likely wars toward 'twixt   10
the dukes of Cornwall and Albany?

EDMUND   Not a word.

CURAN   You may do, then, in time. Fare you well, sir.
                                                *He exits.*

EDMUND
The Duke be here tonight? The better, best.
This weaves itself perforce into my business.          15
My father hath set guard to take my brother,
And I have one thing of a queasy question
Which I must act. Briefness and fortune work!—
Brother, a word. Descend. Brother, I say!

*Enter Edgar.*

My father watches. O sir, fly this place!                20

73

21. **Intelligence is given:** i.e., information has been **given** out
24. **i' th' haste:** i.e., in **haste**
26. **Upon . . . Albany:** perhaps, against Cornwall's side in his dispute with Albany; or, perhaps, on Cornwall's behalf against the duke of Albany
27. **Advise yourself:** i.e., think about it
31. **Draw:** i.e., **draw** your sword; **quit you:** i.e., acquit yourself
33–35. **Yield . . . farewell:** Edmund alternates between hostile shouts and instructions uttered in a low voice.
36. **drawn on:** i.e., **drawn** from
36–37. **beget . . . endeavor:** i.e., create a belief that I fought fiercely
38. **in sport:** i.e., as a joke, for amusement
45. **stand:** i.e., **stand** in support of him as

Astrologers casting a baby's horoscope. (1.2.127–28)
From Jakob Rüff, *De conceptu et generatione hominis . . .* (1580).

Intelligence is given where you are hid.
You have now the good advantage of the night.
Have you not spoken 'gainst the Duke of Cornwall?
He's coming hither, now, i' th' night, i' th' haste,
And Regan with him. Have you nothing said          25
Upon his party 'gainst the Duke of Albany?
Advise yourself.
EDGAR          I am sure on 't, not a word.
EDMUND
I hear my father coming. Pardon me.
In cunning I must draw my sword upon you.          30
Draw. Seem to defend yourself. Now, quit you
well.                              ⌜*They draw.*⌝
Yield! Come before my father! Light, hoa, here!
⌜*Aside to Edgar.*⌝ Fly, brother.—Torches, torches!
—So, farewell.                    *Edgar exits.*    35
Some blood drawn on me would beget opinion
Of my more fierce endeavor. I have seen drunkards
Do more than this in sport.    ⌜*He wounds his arm.*⌝
                    Father, father!
Stop, stop! No help?                               40

    *Enter Gloucester, and Servants with torches.*

GLOUCESTER          Now, Edmund, where's the
    villain?
EDMUND
Here stood he in the dark, his sharp sword out,
Mumbling of wicked charms, conjuring the moon
To stand auspicious mistress.                      45
GLOUCESTER                    But where is he?
EDMUND    Look, sir, I bleed.
GLOUCESTER                    Where is the villain,
    Edmund?
EDMUND
Fled this way, sir, when by no means he could—     50

54. **that:** i.e., when
55. **thunder:** It was believed that **thunder** (also *thunderbolt, thunderstone*) was a tangible object that caused the damage associated with lightning strikes. **bend:** direct
56. **Spoke with:** i.e., and when I **spoke** of
57. **in fine:** in conclusion
58. **how . . . stood:** i.e., with what loathing I opposed
59. **fell motion:** fierce attack
60. **preparèd:** i.e., already drawn; **charges home:** impetuously and effectively attacks
61. **unprovided:** defenseless
62. **best alarumed spirits:** i.e., **best** courage aroused by the alarum (call to arms)
63. **quarrel's right:** i.e., in the rightness of my cause
64. **ghasted:** aghast, frightened
65. **Full:** very
66. **Let . . . far:** perhaps, "he'd better flee a long way if he hopes to escape me"
68. **dispatch:** i.e., let him be killed
69. **arch and patron:** i.e., archpatron, chief **patron**
71. **he which finds him:** i.e., whoever finds Edgar
72. **stake:** place of execution
75. **pight:** determined (obsolete form of "pitched"); **curst:** angry
76. **discover:** expose
77. **unpossessing:** i.e., without property (Illegitimate children could not inherit.)
77–80. **dost . . . faithed:** i.e., if **I** contradicted you, do you **think** anyone would believe you, or repose in you the **trust, virtue, or worth** necessary to credit your words? **faithed:** credited, believed

GLOUCESTER
Pursue him, ho! Go after. ⌐*Servants exit.*⌐ By no
  means what?

EDMUND
  Persuade me to the murder of your Lordship,
  But that I told him the revenging gods
  'Gainst parricides did all the thunder bend,       55
  Spoke with how manifold and strong a bond
  The child was bound to th' father—sir, in fine,
  Seeing how loathly opposite I stood
  To his unnatural purpose, in fell motion
  With his preparèd sword he charges home      60
  My unprovided body, ⟨lanced⟩ mine arm;
  And when he saw my best alarumed spirits,
  Bold in the quarrel's right, roused to th' encounter,
  Or whether ghasted by the noise I made,
  Full suddenly he fled.               65
GLOUCESTER          Let him fly far!
  Not in this land shall he remain uncaught,
  And found—dispatch. The noble duke my master,
  My worthy arch and patron, comes tonight.
  By his authority I will proclaim it      70
  That he which finds him shall deserve our thanks,
  Bringing the murderous coward to the stake;
  He that conceals him, death.

EDMUND
  When I dissuaded him from his intent
  And found him pight to do it, with curst speech  75
  I threatened to discover him. He replied
  "Thou unpossessing bastard, dost thou think
  If I would stand against thee, would the reposal
  Of any trust, virtue, or worth in thee
  Make thy words faithed? No. What ⟨I should⟩  80
    deny—
  As this I would, though thou didst produce

83. **My very character:** i.e., evidence against me written in my own handwriting

83–84. **turn . . . To:** i.e., make it all appear to be

84. **suggestion:** tempting; **practice:** treachery

85–88. **thou must . . . seek it:** i.e., you must think **the world** is stupid **if** you think people would not be aware that the benefits for you, should I die, are powerful incitements to you to seek **my death pregnant and potential:** obvious and powerful

89. **strange and fastened:** unnatural and confirmed

91. **got:** begot, fathered

91 SD. **Tucket:** trumpet signal

94. **ports:** sea harbors

98. **natural:** i.e., showing **natural** affection (but the word also had the meaning of "illegitimate," as well as of "legitimate")

99. **capable:** i.e., legally **capable** of inheriting (in spite of illegitimacy)

101. **Which . . . now:** i.e., **which** was only just **now**

111. **tended upon:** i.e., attended

My very character—I'd turn it all
To thy suggestion, plot, and damnèd practice.
And thou must make a dullard of the world          85
If they not thought the profits of my death
Were very pregnant and potential ⟨spurs⟩
To make thee seek it."
GLOUCESTER          O strange and fastened villain!
Would he deny his letter, said he?                 90
⟨I never got him.⟩          *Tucket within.*
Hark, the Duke's trumpets. I know not ⟨why⟩ he
   comes.
All ports I'll bar. The villain shall not 'scape.
The Duke must grant me that. Besides, his picture   95
I will send far and near, that all the kingdom
May have due note of him. And of my land,
Loyal and natural boy, I'll work the means
To make thee capable.

          *Enter Cornwall, Regan, and Attendants.*

CORNWALL
How now, my noble friend? Since I came hither,     100
Which I can call but now, I have heard strange
   ⟨news.⟩
REGAN
If it be true, all vengeance comes too short
Which can pursue th' offender. How dost, my
   lord?                                           105
GLOUCESTER
O madam, my old heart is cracked; it's cracked.
REGAN
What, did my father's godson seek your life?
He whom my father named, your Edgar?
GLOUCESTER
O lady, lady, shame would have it hid!
REGAN
Was he not companion with the riotous knights      110
That tended upon my father?

113. **consort:** company
114. **though:** i.e., if; **ill affected:** evilly inclined
115. **put him on:** i.e., incited him to attempt
116. **expense:** spending; **revenues:** accent on second syllable
123. **childlike office:** service appropriate to a son
125. **He . . . practice:** i.e., Edmund exposed Edgar's plot
130–31. **Make . . . please:** i.e., use my power (against Edgar) however you like
131. **For:** i.e., as for
137. **however else:** i.e., at least
140. **Thus out of season:** i.e., at such an inopportune time

A snail. (1.5.27)
From Thomas Trevelyon's pictorial commonplace book (1608).

GLOUCESTER
I know not, madam. 'Tis too bad, too bad.
EDMUND
Yes, madam, he was of that consort.
REGAN
No marvel, then, though he were ill affected.
'Tis they have put him on the old man's death,          115
To have th' expense and waste of his revenues.
I have this present evening from my sister
Been well informed of them, and with such cautions
That if they come to sojourn at my house
I'll not be there.                                                    120
CORNWALL                Nor I, assure thee, Regan.—
Edmund, I hear that you have shown your father
A childlike office.
EDMUND                It was my duty, sir.
GLOUCESTER
He did bewray his practice, and received          125
This hurt you see striving to apprehend him.
CORNWALL   Is he pursued?
GLOUCESTER   Ay, my good lord.
CORNWALL
If he be taken, he shall never more
Be feared of doing harm. Make your own purpose,          130
How in my strength you please.—For you, Edmund,
Whose virtue and obedience doth this instant
So much commend itself, you shall be ours.
Natures of such deep trust we shall much need.
You we first seize on.                                              135
EDMUND                I shall serve you, sir,
Truly, however else.
GLOUCESTER   For him I thank your Grace.
CORNWALL
You know not why we came to visit you—
REGAN
Thus out of season, threading dark-eyed night.          140

141. **poise:** weight
144. **which:** i.e., the letters
145. **from:** while away from; **several:** various
146. **attend dispatch:** are waiting to be dismissed
148. **needful:** necessary
149. **the instant use:** i.e., immediate action

**2.2** Kent meets Oswald at Gloucester's castle (where both await answers to the letters they have brought Regan) and challenges Oswald to fight. The disturbance and Kent's explanations provoke Cornwall into putting Kent into the stocks for punishment.

---

6. **if thou lov'st me:** i.e., please
9. **in Lipsbury pinfold:** A **pinfold** is a pound for animals. Since no such place as **Lipsbury** is known, editors have guessed that Kent means "between my teeth."
14. **broken meats:** i.e., leftover food
15. **base:** low; **three-suited:** For the earl of Kent, a man who owned three suits would be a pitiful creature.
15–16. **hundred-pound:** perhaps, in total worth; or, perhaps, in annual salary
16. **worsted:** woolen, rather than the preferred silk
16–17. **lily-livered:** cowardly (i.e., with a liver, supposedly the seat of courage, pale from lack of blood)

*(continued)*

Occasions, noble Gloucester, of some ⟨poise,⟩
Wherein we must have use of your advice.
Our father he hath writ, so hath our sister,
Of differences, which I best ⟨thought⟩ it fit
To answer from our home. The several messengers          145
From hence attend dispatch. Our good old friend,
Lay comforts to your bosom and bestow
Your needful counsel to our businesses,
Which craves the instant use.
GLOUCESTER                    I serve you, madam.          150
Your Graces are right welcome.
                              *Flourish. They exit.*


                    Scene 2
*Enter Kent ⌜in disguise⌝ and ⌜Oswald, the⌝ Steward,*
                    *severally.*

OSWALD  Good dawning to thee, friend. Art of this
    house?
KENT  Ay.
OSWALD  Where may we set our horses?
KENT  I' th' mire.                                        5
OSWALD  Prithee, if thou lov'st me, tell me.
KENT  I love thee not.
OSWALD  Why then, I care not for thee.
KENT  If I had thee in Lipsbury pinfold, I would make
    thee care for me.                                     10
OSWALD  Why dost thou use me thus? I know thee not.
KENT  Fellow, I know thee.
OSWALD  What dost thou know me for?
KENT  A knave, a rascal, an eater of broken meats; a
    base, proud, shallow, beggarly, three-suited, hun-   15
    dred-pound, filthy worsted-stocking knave; a lily-
    livered, action-taking, whoreson, glass-gazing, su-
    perserviceable, finical rogue; one-trunk-inheriting

17. **action-taking:** i.e., settling disputes in court, rather than fighting; **glass-gazing:** i.e., fond of admiring himself in a mirror

17–18. **superserviceable:** perhaps, overeager to be of service

18. **finical:** over-particular; **one-trunk-inheriting:** i.e., possessing no more than will fit in a single trunk

19–20. **wouldst . . . service:** would, in order to give **good service,** play pimp or pander

20. **composition:** combination

24. **addition:** title (i.e., the one that I just gave you)

26. **of:** i.e., to

28. **varlet:** rascal

32–33. **make . . . you:** perhaps, fill you so full of holes that you soak up moonlight (**A sop** is a piece of bread soaked in liquid.)

33–34. **cullionly barbermonger:** despicable fop

37. **Vanity the puppet:** probably his name for Goneril (The phrase may mean a figure who personifies the sin of vanity or an actor who plays the allegorical figure Vanity.)

39. **carbonado:** slice up (like meat before it is broiled)

39–40. **Come your ways:** i.e., come on

42. **Stand:** Kent's repetition of this command suggests that Oswald keeps trying to run away.

42–43. **neat slave:** perhaps, elegant rascal

46. **With you:** an offer to fight; **goodman:** a form of address to a man below the rank of gentleman, insulting to Edmund

47. **flesh you:** initiate you into fighting

slave; one that wouldst be a bawd in way of good
service, and art nothing but the composition of a    20
knave, beggar, coward, pander, and the son and heir
of a mongrel bitch; one whom I will beat into
⟨clamorous⟩ whining if thou deny'st the least syllable
of thy addition.

OSWALD  Why, what a monstrous fellow art thou thus    25
to rail on one that is neither known of thee nor
knows thee!

KENT  What a brazen-faced varlet art thou to deny thou
knowest me! Is it two days ⟨ago⟩ since I tripped up
thy heels and beat thee before the King? ⌜*He draws*    30
*his sword.* ⌝ Draw, you rogue, for though it be night,
yet the moon shines. I'll make a sop o' th' moon-
shine of you, you whoreson, cullionly barbermonger. Draw!

OSWALD  Away! I have nothing to do with thee.    35

KENT  Draw, you rascal! You come with letters against
the King and take Vanity the puppet's part against
the royalty of her father. Draw, you rogue, or I'll so
carbonado your shanks! Draw, you rascal! Come
your ways.    40

OSWALD  Help, ho! Murder! Help!

KENT  Strike, you slave! Stand, rogue! Stand, you neat
slave! Strike!                          ⌜*He beats Oswald.*⌝

OSWALD  Help, ho! Murder, murder!

*Enter Bastard ⟨Edmund, with his rapier drawn,⟩*
*Cornwall, Regan, Gloucester, Servants.*

EDMUND  How now, what's the matter? Part!    45

KENT  With you, goodman boy, if you please. Come, I'll
flesh you. Come on, young master.

GLOUCESTER
Weapons? Arms? What's the matter here?

CORNWALL  Keep peace, upon your lives! He dies that
strikes again. What is the matter?    50

52. **your difference:** i.e., the cause of your quarrel
55. **disclaims in:** refuses to acknowledge
59. **stonecutter:** sculptor
60. **ill:** badly
61. **o':** i.e., in
64. **at suit of:** i.e., moved to mercy by
65. **zed:** the letter *z*; **unnecessary:** i.e., not included in the Latin alphabet
67. **unbolted:** unsifted or lumpy; **daub:** plaster
68. **jakes:** outhouse
69. **wagtail:** a bird so-called because of its constantly wagging tail
74–75. **should . . . honesty:** i.e., **should wear** the symbol of manhood without being honorable
77–78. **oft . . . unloose:** This seems to allude to the Gordian knot, which could not be untied because it was so intricately knotted. (It was cut apart by Alexander the Great.) The **holy cords** may, therefore, refer to marriage bonds, since the Gordian knot often symbolized marriage.   **atwain:** in two   **intrinse:** intricately tied
78–83. **smooth . . . masters:** i.e., encourage every rebelliously overpowering emotion of their lords by catering to it either through denial or affirmation, changing with every change in their master **smooth:** encourage   **Renege:** deny   **halcyon:** kingfisher, whose dead body, if hung up, was believed to turn in the direction of the wind   **vary:** variation, change

REGAN
   The messengers from our sister and the King.
CORNWALL   What is your difference? Speak.
OSWALD   I am scarce in breath, my lord.
KENT   No marvel, you have so bestirred your valor.
   You cowardly rascal, nature disclaims in thee; a          55
   tailor made thee.
CORNWALL   Thou art a strange fellow. A tailor make a
   man?
KENT   A tailor, sir. A stonecutter or a painter could not
   have made him so ill, though they had been but two          60
   years o' th' trade.
CORNWALL   Speak yet, how grew your quarrel?
OSWALD   This ancient ruffian, sir, whose life I have
   spared at suit of his gray beard—
KENT   Thou whoreson zed, thou unnecessary letter!          65
   —My lord, if you will give me leave, I will tread
   this unbolted villain into mortar and daub the wall
   of a jakes with him.—Spare my gray beard, you
   wagtail?
CORNWALL   Peace, sirrah!          70
   You beastly knave, know you no reverence?
KENT
   Yes, sir, but anger hath a privilege.
CORNWALL   Why art thou angry?
KENT
   That such a slave as this should wear a sword,
   Who wears no honesty. Such smiling rogues as          75
      these,
   Like rats, oft bite the holy cords atwain
   Which are ⟨too⟩ intrinse t' unloose; smooth every
      passion
   That in the natures of their lords rebel—          80
   Being oil to fire, snow to the colder moods—
   ⟨Renege,⟩ affirm, and turn their halcyon beaks
   With every ⟨gale⟩ and vary of their masters,

85. **epileptic:** i.e., distorted
86. **Smile . . . as:** i.e., do **you smile** . . . **as** if
87. **Sarum plain:** Salisbury plain (a very large open expanse just north of Salisbury, and, in prehistoric England, the location of the city of Old **Sarum**)
88. **Camelot:** in the Arthurian legends, the place where King Arthur's court was located (It has been variously placed in Winchester, in Somersetshire, and in Wales.)
94. **likes:** pleases
96. **occupation:** custom, habit; **plain:** i.e., plain-spoken, blunt
101-3. **doth . . . nature:** i.e., pretends to be plain-spoken, and thus twists plain speech away from its own nature (that is, truth)  **saucy:** insolent  **garb:** appearance, manner  **his:** its
105. **An they:** i.e., if they; **so:** i.e., fine
109. **silly-ducking observants:** ridiculously bowing sycophants
110. **stretch . . . nicely:** strain to carry out **their duties** punctiliously
111-14. **Sir . . . front:** Kent here abandons plain speaking and mocks elaborate courtly language. **allowance:** approval  **aspect:** (1) look; (2) astrological position (Kent flatteringly associates Cornwall with a heavenly body.)  **Phoebus' front:** the sun's forehead

Knowing naught, like dogs, but following.—
A plague upon your epileptic visage!                              85
⌜Smile⌝ you my speeches, as I were a fool?
Goose, if I had you upon Sarum plain,
I'd drive you cackling home to Camelot.
CORNWALL   What, art thou mad, old fellow?
GLOUCESTER   How fell you out? Say that.                          90
KENT
No contraries hold more antipathy
Than I and such a knave.
CORNWALL
Why dost thou call him "knave"? What is his fault?
KENT   His countenance likes me not.
CORNWALL
No more, perchance, does mine, nor his, nor hers.                 95
KENT
Sir, 'tis my occupation to be plain:
I have seen better faces in my time
Than stands on any shoulder that I see
Before me at this instant.
CORNWALL                     This is some fellow                  100
Who, having been praised for bluntness, doth affect
A saucy roughness and constrains the garb
Quite from his nature. He cannot flatter, he.
An honest mind and plain, he must speak truth!
An they will take it, so; if not, he's plain.                    105
These kind of knaves I know, which in this
     plainness
Harbor more craft and more corrupter ends
Than twenty silly-ducking observants
That stretch their duties nicely.                                110
KENT
Sir, in good faith, in sincere verity,
Under th' allowance of your great aspect,
Whose influence, like the wreath of radiant fire
On ⌜flick'ring⌝ Phoebus' front—

116. **dialect:** i.e., plainspokenness; **discommend:** disapprove

117–18. **He . . . knave:** i.e., whoever it was who used plain speaking to deceive you was an out-and-out villain

119–20. **though . . . to 't:** perhaps, even **though** I may displease you (by refusing to be plain) when you ask me to be

124. **late:** recently

125. **upon his misconstruction:** i.e., because of the king's misunderstanding me

126. **he, compact:** i.e., Kent, joined in a compact (with the king); **his:** i.e., the king's

127. **being down, insulted:** i.e., I **being down,** he **insulted**

128–30. **put . . . self-subdued:** acted like such a courageous man that he made himself appear worthy and won praise from the king by attacking one (namely Oswald) who had already chosen to give up **man:** courage  **worthied:** got a reputation for  **For him attempting:** for attacking someone

131. **fleshment:** excitement arising from a first success

134. **Ajax:** in Greek mythology and in Shakespeare's *Troilus and Cressida*, a dull-witted, blustering Greek warrior in the Trojan War

135. **stocks:** an instrument of punishment that imprisoned the ankles in a wooden frame (See picture, page 92.)

136. **reverent:** i.e., reverend (worthy of respect because old)

142. **malice:** ill will

143. **grace:** i.e., royal honor

CORNWALL                    What mean'st by this?    115
KENT   To go out of my dialect, which you discommend
so much. I know, sir, I am no flatterer. He that
beguiled you in a plain accent was a plain knave,
which for my part I will not be, though I should
win your displeasure to entreat me to 't.    120
CORNWALL, ⌐*to Oswald*⌐   What was th' offense you gave
him?
OSWALD   I never gave him any.
It pleased the King his master very late
To strike at me, upon his misconstruction;    125
When he, compact, and flattering his displeasure,
Tripped me behind; being down, insulted, railed,
And put upon him such a deal of man
That worthied him, got praises of the King
For him attempting who was self-subdued;    130
And in the fleshment of this ⟨dread⟩ exploit,
Drew on me here again.
KENT   None of these rogues and cowards
But Ajax is their fool.
CORNWALL                    Fetch forth the stocks.—    135
You stubborn ancient knave, you reverent braggart,
We'll teach you.
KENT                    Sir, I am too old to learn.
Call not your stocks for me. I serve the King,
On whose employment I was sent to you.    140
You shall do small ⟨respect,⟩ show too bold
malice
Against the grace and person of my master,
Stocking his messenger.
CORNWALL
Fetch forth the stocks.—As I have life and honor,    145
There shall he sit till noon.
REGAN
Till noon? Till night, my lord, and all night, too.

149. **should:** i.e., would
150. **knave:** (1) servant; (2) villain
151. **color:** nature
152. **sister:** sister-in-law; **away:** i.e., in
155. **check:** rebuke; **Your purposed low correction:** the ignoble punishment you intend
156. **contemned'st:** most despised
161. **answer:** i.e., be accountable for
169. **rubbed:** hindered
170. **watched:** gone without sleep
172. **A . . . heels:** i.e., even good men can have bad luck **grow . . . heels:** decay, like stockings worn through at the heel
173. **Give:** i.e., God **give**

A man in the stocks. (2.2.135)
From August Casimir Redel, *Apophtegmata symbolica* . . . (n.d.).

KENT
  Why, madam, if I were your father's dog,
  You should not use me so.
REGAN   Sir, being his knave, I will.        150
CORNWALL
  This is a fellow of the selfsame color
  Our sister speaks of.—Come, bring away the stocks.
                              *Stocks brought out.*
GLOUCESTER
  Let me beseech your Grace not to do so.
  ⟨His fault is much, and the good king his master
  Will check him for 't. Your purposed low correction        155
  Is such as basest and ⌜contemned'st⌝ wretches
  For pilf'rings and most common trespasses
  Are punished with.⟩ The King must take it ill
  That he, so slightly valued in his messenger,
  Should have him thus restrained.        160
CORNWALL                      I'll answer that.
REGAN
  My sister may receive it much more worse
  To have her gentleman abused, assaulted
  ⟨For following her affairs.—Put in his legs.⟩
                      ⌜*Kent is put in the stocks.*⌝
CORNWALL   Come, my ⟨good⟩ lord, away.        165
                  ⌜*All but Gloucester and Kent*⌝ *exit.*
GLOUCESTER
  I am sorry for thee, friend. 'Tis the ⟨Duke's⟩
    pleasure,
  Whose disposition all the world well knows
  Will not be rubbed nor stopped. I'll entreat for thee.
KENT
  Pray, do not, sir. I have watched and traveled hard.        170
  Some time I shall sleep out; the rest I'll whistle.
  A good man's fortune may grow out at heels.
  Give you good morrow.

175. **king:** i.e., Lear; **approve:** confirm; **saw:** proverb

176–77. **out . . . sun:** This proverb ("Out of God's blessing into **the warm** [i.e., hot] **sun**") meant "to go from good to bad."

179. **comfortable:** cheering, helpful

183. **obscurèd course:** i.e., actions in disguise

183–85. **shall . . . remedies:** These lines are difficult to interpret, and many editors suspect textual corruption. In stage productions, they are often read as if fragments from Cordelia's letter.

185. **o'erwatched:** tired out from lack of sleep

186. **vantage:** advantage (of your fatigue)

188–89. **turn thy wheel:** i.e., change my luck (**Fortune** is often depicted turning a wheel on which mortals rise and fall. See pictures, pages 172 and 252.)


**2.3** Edgar disguises himself as a madman-beggar to escape his death sentence. (Although Kent remains onstage, a new scene begins because the locale shifts away from Gloucester's castle, from which Edgar has fled.)

---

1. **proclaimed:** i.e., as an outlaw

2. **happy . . . tree:** i.e., fortunate presence **of a** hollow **tree**

5. **attend . . . taking:** i.e., look out for my capture

6. **bethought:** resolved

8. **in contempt of:** i.e., **in** its **contempt** for

9. **grime:** begrime, blacken

10. **elf:** twist into elflocks (i.e., mat)

11. **presented:** displayed, offered; **outface:** defy

94

GLOUCESTER
  The Duke's to blame in this. 'Twill be ill taken.

                                *He exits.*

KENT
  Good king, that must approve the common saw,     175
  Thou out of heaven's benediction com'st
  To the warm sun.       ⌜*He takes out a paper.*⌝
  Approach, thou beacon to this under globe,
  That by thy comfortable beams I may
  Peruse this letter. Nothing almost sees miracles     180
  But misery. I know 'tis from Cordelia,
  Who hath most fortunately been informed
  Of my obscurèd course, and shall find time
  From this enormous state, seeking to give
  Losses their remedies. All weary and o'erwatched,     185
  Take vantage, heavy eyes, not to behold
  This shameful lodging.
  Fortune, good night. Smile once more; turn thy
    wheel.

                                  ⟨*Sleeps.*⟩


### Scene 3
*Enter Edgar.*

EDGAR   I heard myself proclaimed,
  And by the happy hollow of a tree
  Escaped the hunt. No port is free; no place
  That guard and most unusual vigilance
  Does not attend my taking. Whiles I may 'scape,     5
  I will preserve myself, and am bethought
  To take the basest and most poorest shape
  That ever penury in contempt of man
  Brought near to beast. My face I'll grime with filth,
  Blanket my loins, elf all my hairs in knots,     10
  And with presented nakedness outface

13. **proof:** example
14. **Bedlam beggars:** See note to 1.2.143 and picture, page 166.
15. **mortifièd:** deadened
16. **pricks:** skewers
17. **object:** spectacle
17–20. **from low farms . . . charity:** i.e., force country people to give them food **low:** lowly **pelting:** paltry **bans:** curses
20. **Turlygod:** The meaning of this word (unrecorded elsewhere) is unknown. **Poor Tom:** for the name *Tom o' Bedlam*, see note to 1.2.143.
21. **"Edgar" . . . am:** i.e., as **"Edgar,"** I am nothing

**2.4** At Gloucester's castle, Lear is angered that his messenger has been stocked and further angered that Regan and Cornwall refuse to see him. When Goneril arrives, Lear quarrels bitterly with her and with Regan, who claim that he needs no attendants of his own. When each daughter says that he may stay with her only if he dismisses all his knights, he rushes, enraged, out into a storm. Cornwall, Regan, and Goneril shut Gloucester's castle against Lear.

1. **they:** i.e., Regan and Cornwall
5. **remove:** change of residence
10. **cruel:** painful (with a pun on "crewel," thin woolen yarn)
12. **by th' loins:** i.e., around the waist

*(continued)*

The winds and persecutions of the sky.
The country gives me proof and precedent
Of Bedlam beggars who with roaring voices
Strike in their numbed and mortifièd arms                    15
Pins, wooden pricks, nails, sprigs of rosemary,
And, with this horrible object, from low farms,
Poor pelting villages, sheepcotes, and mills,
Sometime with lunatic bans, sometime with prayers,
Enforce their charity. "Poor Turlygod! Poor Tom!"            20
That's something yet. "Edgar" I nothing am.
                                        *He exits.*


### Scene 4
*Enter Lear, Fool, and Gentleman.*

LEAR
  'Tis strange that they should so depart from home
  And not send back my ⟨messenger.⟩
GENTLEMAN                        As I learned,
  The night before there was no purpose in them
  Of this remove.                                             5
KENT, ⌜*waking*⌝  Hail to thee, noble master.
LEAR  Ha?
  Mak'st thou this shame thy pastime?
[KENT                            No, my lord.]
FOOL  Ha, ha, he wears cruel garters. Horses are tied        10
  by the heads, dogs and bears by th' neck, monkeys
  by th' loins, and men by th' legs. When a ⟨man's⟩
  overlusty at legs, then he wears wooden nether-
  stocks.
LEAR
  What's he that hath so much thy place mistook            15
  To set thee here?
KENT                    It is both he and she,
  Your son and daughter.

**12–14. When . . . netherstocks:** Vagabonds were punished by being put in the stocks. **overlusty at legs:** i.e., too eager to wander **netherstocks:** stockings

**15–16. What's . . . To:** i.e., who **so mistook** your position as **to**

**18. son:** i.e., son-in-law

**23. Jupiter:** king of the Roman gods, also called Jove (See picture, page 112.)

**24. Juno:** queen of the Roman gods, often at odds with Jupiter

**28. upon respect:** i.e., against the king, whose messenger should be respected

**29. Resolve:** inform; **modest:** moderate

**30. usage:** treatment

**31. us:** i.e., me

**33. commend:** deliver

**34–35. Ere . . . kneeling:** i.e., before I could get up from where I knelt to show **my duty**

**35–36. reeking . . . haste:** i.e., a messenger hot and soaked (with the sweat from his hurried journey)

**38. spite of intermission:** i.e., although he interrupted me

**39. presently:** immediately; **on:** i.e., as a result of

**40. meiny:** train, retinue; **straight:** straightway, immediately

**44. meeting:** i.e., I, **meeting**

**47. Displayed so saucily:** i.e., put on such an impudent display

**48. more . . . wit:** more courage than intelligence

**52–53. that way:** i.e., south, the direction geese fly as winter approaches (The sense is that things are going to become still worse.)

LEAR   No.
KENT   Yes.                                                    20
LEAR   No, I say.
KENT   I say yea.
LEAR   By Jupiter, I swear no.
[KENT   By Juno, I swear ay.
LEAR]                          They durst not do 't.           25
   They could not, would not do 't. 'Tis worse than
      murder
   To do upon respect such violent outrage.
   Resolve me with all modest haste which way
   Thou might'st deserve or they impose this usage,           30
   Coming from us.
KENT                  My lord, when at their home
   I did commend your Highness' letters to them,
   Ere I was risen from the place that showed
   My duty kneeling, came there a reeking post,               35
   Stewed in his haste, half breathless, ⟨panting⟩ forth
   From Goneril his mistress salutations;
   Delivered letters, spite of intermission,
   Which presently they read; on ⟨whose⟩ contents
   They summoned up their meiny, straight took               40
      horse,
   Commanded me to follow and attend
   The leisure of their answer, gave me cold looks;
   And meeting here the other messenger,
   Whose welcome, I perceived, had poisoned mine,            45
   Being the very fellow which of late
   Displayed so saucily against your Highness,
   Having more man than wit about me, drew.
   He raised the house with loud and coward cries.
   Your son and daughter found this trespass worth          50
   The shame which here it suffers.
[FOOL   Winter's not gone yet if the wild geese fly that
   way.

55. **blind:** i.e., neglectful of their fathers
56. **bags:** i.e., **bags** of gold
58. **Fortune . . . whore:** The goddess Fortuna is called a **whore** because her favors are so fickle.
59. **turns the key to:** i.e., opens the door for
60. **dolors for:** sorrows on account of (with a possible pun on "dollars in exchange for")
61. **tell:** (1) count; (2) relate
62–64. **O, how . . . below:** "The **mother**" was the name given to hysteria, one symptom of which is the suffocation that Lear is represented as feeling in his rage and grief. (Its medical name is **hysterica passio.**) The disease was thought to be caused by a wandering womb (*hystera*), which belonged **below**, not up near the **heart.**
68. **but:** i.e., other than
70. **chance:** i.e., chances it that
74–81. **We'll . . . after:** The Fool explains the desertion of Lear's knights three ways, all of them emphasizing Lear's decline into adversity: Lear is in his **winter** (an unprofitable time for ants, just as following Lear is now unprofitable); Lear stinks with misfortune (so that even a blind man can smell his decay); Lear is like a **great wheel** going downhill, destroying everything attached to it.
84. **sir:** gentleman
85. **follows . . . form:** serves a master only in outward behavior
86. **pack:** hurry off

    Fathers that wear rags
      Do make their children blind,       55
    But fathers that bear bags
      Shall see their children kind.
    Fortune, that arrant whore,
    Ne'er turns the key to th' poor.
But, for all this, thou shalt have as many dolors for    60
thy daughters as thou canst tell in a year.]
LEAR
O, how this mother swells up toward my heart!
⌐Hysterica⌐ passio, down, thou climbing sorrow!
Thy element's below.—Where is this daughter?
KENT   With the Earl, sir, here within.      '      65
LEAR, ⌐to Fool and Gentleman⌐ Follow me not. Stay
here.                                *He exits.*
GENTLEMAN
Made you no more offense but what you speak of?
KENT   None.
How chance the King comes with so small a number?    70
FOOL   An thou hadst been set i' th' stocks for that
question, thou'dst well deserved it.
KENT   Why, Fool?
FOOL   We'll set thee to school to an ant to teach thee
there's no laboring i' th' winter. All that follow    75
their noses are led by their eyes but blind men, and
there's not a nose among twenty but can smell him
that's stinking. Let go thy hold when a great wheel
runs down a hill lest it break thy neck with following; but the great one that goes upward, let him    80
draw thee after. When a wise man gives thee better
counsel, give me mine again. I would have none but
knaves follow it, since a Fool gives it.
    That sir which serves and seeks for gain,
      And follows but for form,            85
    Will pack when it begins to rain

90. **knave:** servant
91. **knave:** rascal; **perdie:** *par Dieu,* French for "by God"
96. **fetches:** dodges, tricks
97. **images:** signs
100. **quality:** disposition
101. **unremovable:** immovable
103. **confusion:** ruin
113. **tends:** awaits, expects
114. **service:** homage, fealty, obedience

And leave thee in the storm.
But I will tarry; the Fool will stay,
And let the wise man fly.
The knave turns fool that runs away;                    90
The Fool no knave, perdie.
KENT   Where learned you this, Fool?
FOOL   Not i' th' stocks, fool.

*Enter Lear and Gloucester.*

LEAR
Deny to speak with me? They are sick? They are
    weary?                                              95
They have traveled all the night? Mere fetches,
The images of revolt and flying off.
Fetch me a better answer.
GLOUCESTER                  My dear lord,
You know the fiery quality of the Duke,                 100
How unremovable and fixed he is
In his own course.
LEAR
Vengeance, plague, death, confusion!
"Fiery"? What "quality"? Why Gloucester,
    Gloucester,                                         105
I'd speak with the Duke of Cornwall and his wife.
[GLOUCESTER
Well, my good lord, I have informed them so.
LEAR
"Informed them"? Dost thou understand me,
    man?]
GLOUCESTER   Ay, my good lord.                          110
LEAR
The King would speak with Cornwall. The dear
    father
Would with his daughter speak, commands, tends
    service.
[Are they "informed" of this? My breath and          115
    blood!]

119–20. **still ... bound:** i.e., always fail in those duties required of us when in good **health   office:** duties

123. **am ... will:** i.e., **am** angry with **my more** impetuous temper

124. **To take:** i.e., in mistaking

125–26. **Death ... state:** a curse   **my state:** i.e., my royal power

126. **Wherefore:** why

127. **This act:** the stocking of Kent

128. **remotion:** i.e., keeping remote from me

129. **practice:** contrivance, deception; **Give ... forth:** release **my servant**

130. **and 's:** i.e., and his

131. **presently:** immediately

133. **cry ... death:** i.e., put an end **to sleep**

136. **cockney:** city dweller; squeamish or affected woman

137. **paste:** pastry; **knapped:** knocked

138. **coxcombs:** i.e., heads

139. **wantons:** playful animals (with a secondary sense of "lewd persons")

140. **his hay:** its **hay**

146. **divorce ... tomb:** perhaps, **divorce** your dead mother; or, perhaps, refuse to be buried beside her

"Fiery"? The "fiery" duke? Tell the hot duke that—
No, but not yet. Maybe he is not well.
Infirmity doth still neglect all office
Whereto our health is bound. We are not ourselves          120
When nature, being oppressed, commands the mind
To suffer with the body. I'll forbear,
And am fallen out with my more headier will,
To take the indisposed and sickly fit
For the sound man. ⌜*Noticing Kent again.*⌝ Death on          125
  my state! Wherefore
Should he sit here? This act persuades me
That this remotion of the Duke and her
Is practice only. Give me my servant forth.
Go tell the Duke and 's wife I'd speak with them.          130
Now, presently, bid them come forth and hear me,
Or at their chamber door I'll beat the drum
Till it cry sleep to death.
GLOUCESTER    I would have all well betwixt you.
                                        *He exits.*
LEAR
  O me, my heart, my rising heart! But down!          135
FOOL    Cry to it, nuncle, as the cockney did to the eels
    when she put 'em i' th' paste alive. She knapped
    'em o' th' coxcombs with a stick and cried "Down,
    wantons, down!" 'Twas her brother that in pure
    kindness to his horse buttered his hay.          140

      *Enter Cornwall, Regan, Gloucester, Servants.*

LEAR    Good morrow to you both.
CORNWALL    Hail to your Grace.
                          *Kent here set at liberty.*
REGAN    I am glad to see your Highness.
LEAR
  Regan, I think ⟨you⟩ are. I know what reason
  I have to think so: if thou shouldst not be glad,          145
  I would divorce me from thy ⟨mother's⟩ tomb,

147. **Sepulch'ring:** i.e., since it would be the tomb of (Lear says that if Regan is not glad to see him, she could not be his daughter. Her mother would therefore be an **adult'ress.**)

150. **naught:** (1) worthless; (2) wicked

153. **quality:** manner

154–56. **I have . . . duty:** i.e., I hope you undervalue her merit rather than that she failed in **her duty**

165. **Nature in you:** i.e., your life

165–66. **very verge . . . confine:** i.e., its limit

167. **some discretion that:** i.e., the **discretion** of someone who; **state:** condition

172. **mark:** see; **house:** i.e., dignity of the royal family

174. **Age is unnecessary:** i.e., no one needs old people

Sepulch'ring an adult'ress. ⌜*To Kent.*⌝ O, are you
  free?
Some other time for that.—Belovèd Regan,
Thy sister's naught. O Regan, she hath tied          150
Sharp-toothed unkindness, like a vulture, here.
I can scarce speak to thee. Thou'lt not believe
With how depraved a quality—O Regan!
REGAN
  I pray you, sir, take patience. I have hope
  You less know how to value her desert          155
  Than she to scant her duty.
[LEAR              Say? How is that?
REGAN
  I cannot think my sister in the least
  Would fail her obligation. If, sir, perchance
  She have restrained the riots of your followers,          160
  'Tis on such ground and to such wholesome end
  As clears her from all blame.]
LEAR  My curses on her.
REGAN  O sir, you are old.
  Nature in you stands on the very verge          165
  Of his confine. You should be ruled and led
  By some discretion that discerns your state
  Better than you yourself. Therefore, I pray you
  That to our sister you do make return.
  Say you have wronged her.          170
LEAR              Ask her forgiveness?
  Do you but mark how this becomes the house:
                       ⌜*He kneels.*⌝
  "Dear daughter, I confess that I am old.
  Age is unnecessary. On my knees I beg
  That you'll vouchsafe me raiment, bed, and food."          175
REGAN
  Good sir, no more. These are unsightly tricks.
  Return you to my sister.

179. **abated:** deprived
180. **black:** angrily
183. **top:** i.e., head
184. **taking:** infectious
188–89. **fen-sucked . . . blister:** vapors **drawn** up from marshes **by the sun to fall** on and **blister** her
193. **tender-hefted:** perhaps, moved (i.e., heaved, swayed) by tender emotions
198. **scant my sizes:** diminish my allowance (as if he were a poor university student)
199. **oppose the bolt:** i.e., lock the door
201. **offices of nature:** i.e., natural duties
202. **Effects:** actions
205. **to th' purpose:** i.e., come to the point

LEAR, ⌈*rising*⌉                    Never, Regan.
  She hath abated me of half my train,
  Looked black upon me, struck me with her tongue        180
  Most serpentlike upon the very heart.
  All the stored vengeances of heaven fall
  On her ingrateful top! Strike her young bones,
  You taking airs, with lameness!
CORNWALL                          Fie, sir, fie!          185
LEAR
  You nimble lightnings, dart your blinding flames
  Into her scornful eyes! Infect her beauty,
  You fen-sucked fogs drawn by the powerful sun
  To fall and blister!
REGAN
  O, the blest gods! So will you wish on me               190
  When the rash mood is on.
LEAR
  No, Regan, thou shalt never have my curse.
  Thy tender-hefted nature shall not give
  Thee o'er to harshness. Her eyes are fierce, but
      thine                                               195
  Do comfort and not burn. 'Tis not in thee
  To grudge my pleasures, to cut off my train,
  To bandy hasty words, to scant my sizes,
  And, in conclusion, to oppose the bolt
  Against my coming in. Thou better know'st              200
  The offices of nature, bond of childhood,
  Effects of courtesy, dues of gratitude.
  Thy half o' th' kingdom hast thou not forgot,
  Wherein I thee endowed.
REGAN                     Good sir, to th' purpose.      205
                          *Tucket within.*
LEAR
  Who put my man i' th' stocks?
CORNWALL                     What trumpet's that?

208. **approves:** confirms
212. **grace:** favor
213. **varlet:** rascal
216. **on 't:** i.e., of it
218-19. **sway / Allow:** government approves
225-26. **that . . . so:** i.e., that is thought so by those who lack judgment and that is named so by the senile
227. **sides:** i.e., **sides** of his body
231. **advancement:** preferment, promotion

REGAN
I know 't—my sister's. This approves her letter,
That she would soon be here.

*Enter ⌐Oswald, the¬ Steward.*

Is your lady come? 210
LEAR
This is a slave whose easy-borrowed pride
Dwells in the ⟨fickle⟩ grace of her he follows.—
Out, varlet, from my sight!
CORNWALL What means your Grace?
LEAR
Who stocked my servant? Regan, I have good hope 215
Thou didst not know on 't.

*Enter Goneril.*

Who comes here? O heavens,
If you do love old men, if your sweet sway
Allow obedience, if you yourselves are old,
Make it your cause. Send down and take my part. 220
⌐*To Goneril.*¬ Art not ashamed to look upon this
beard? ⌐*Regan takes Goneril's hand.*¬
O Regan, will you take her by the hand?
GONERIL
Why not by th' hand, sir? How have I offended?
All's not offense that indiscretion finds 225
And dotage terms so.
LEAR O sides, you are too tough!
Will you yet hold?—How came my man i' th'
stocks?
CORNWALL
I set him there, sir, but his own disorders 230
Deserved much less advancement.
LEAR You? Did you?
REGAN
I pray you, father, being weak, seem so.
If till the expiration of your month

237. **from home:** i.e., away from my **home**
238. **entertainment:** proper care
241. **wage:** contend, struggle
243. **Necessity's . . . pinch:** i.e., I choose the pains of poverty and distress
246. **knee:** i.e., kneel before
248. **sumpter:** packhorse
249. **groom:** servant; or, stable hand
251. **mad:** insane
257. **embossèd carbuncle:** swollen, inflamed tumor
259. **call:** invoke
260. **thunder-bearer:** i.e., the king of Roman gods (called both **Jove** [line 261] and **Jupiter** [line 23])
267. **fit:** appropriate
268. **mingle . . . passion:** i.e., rationally assess your intemperate behavior

Jove, "the thunder-bearer." (2.4.260–61)
From Vincenzo Cartari, *Le vere e noue imagini* . . . (1615).

You will return and sojourn with my sister,                      235
Dismissing half your train, come then to me.
I am now from home and out of that provision
Which shall be needful for your entertainment.

LEAR
Return to her? And fifty men dismissed?
No! Rather I abjure all roofs, and choose                        240
To wage against the enmity o' th' air,
To be a comrade with the wolf and owl,
Necessity's sharp pinch. Return with her?
Why the hot-blooded France, that dowerless took
Our youngest born—I could as well be brought                    245
To knee his throne and, squire-like, pension beg
To keep base life afoot. Return with her?
Persuade me rather to be slave and sumpter
To this detested groom.          ⌜*He indicates Oswald.*⌝

GONERIL                       At your choice, sir.              250

LEAR
I prithee, daughter, do not make me mad.
I will not trouble thee, my child. Farewell.
We'll no more meet, no more see one another.
But yet thou art my flesh, my blood, my daughter,
Or, rather, a disease that's in my flesh,                       255
Which I must needs call mine. Thou art a boil,
A plague-sore or embossèd carbuncle
In my corrupted blood. But I'll not chide thee.
Let shame come when it will; I do not call it.
I do not bid the thunder-bearer shoot,                          260
Nor tell tales of thee to high-judging Jove.
Mend when thou canst. Be better at thy leisure.
I can be patient. I can stay with Regan,
I and my hundred knights.

REGAN       Not altogether so.                                  265
I looked not for you yet, nor am provided
For your fit welcome. Give ear, sir, to my sister,
For those that mingle reason with your passion

274. **sith that:** since; **charge:** expense
277. **Hold amity:** i.e., remain peaceful
280. **slack:** neglect (their duty to)
285. **notice:** acknowledgment
288. **depositaries:** trustees (of my power)
289. **kept a reservation:** i.e., reserved for myself the right
293. **well-favored:** attractive
295. **Stands . . . praise:** i.e., deserves a measure of praise

Must be content to think you old, and so—
But she knows what she does. 270

LEAR                    Is this well spoken?

REGAN
I dare avouch it, sir. What, fifty followers?
Is it not well? What should you need of more?
Yea, or so many, sith that both charge and danger
Speak 'gainst so great a number? How in one house 275
Should many people under two commands
Hold amity? 'Tis hard, almost impossible.

GONERIL
Why might not you, my lord, receive attendance
From those that she calls servants, or from mine?

REGAN
Why not, my lord? If then they chanced to slack 280
    you,
We could control them. If you will come to me
(For now I spy a danger), I entreat you
To bring but five-and-twenty. To no more
Will I give place or notice. 285

LEAR   I gave you all—

REGAN   And in good time you gave it.

LEAR
Made you my guardians, my depositaries,
But kept a reservation to be followed
With such a number. What, must I come to you 290
With five-and-twenty? Regan, said you so?

REGAN
And speak 't again, my lord. No more with me.

LEAR
Those wicked creatures yet do look well-favored
When others are more wicked. Not being the worst
Stands in some rank of praise. ⌜*To Goneril.*⌝ I'll go 295
   with thee.
Thy fifty yet doth double five-and-twenty,
And thou art twice her love.

GONERIL            Hear me, my lord.

301. **follow:** attend on you
304. **reason not:** i.e., do not argue in terms of
305. **Are . . . superfluous:** i.e., own something that exceeds what they actually need
306. **nature . . . nature:** i.e., humans . . . animals
308–10. **If . . . keeps thee warm:** i.e., if dressing warmly were the only gorgeousness a lady needed, then you would not need your **gorgeous** clothes, **which** hardly keep you **warm** anyway
316–17. **fool . . . To:** do not make me such a fool as to
326. **flaws:** fragments
327. **Or ere:** before
330. **bestowed:** accommodated

What need you five-and-twenty, ten, or five,                    300
To follow in a house where twice so many
Have a command to tend you?
REGAN                                    What need one?
LEAR
  O, reason not the need! Our basest beggars
  Are in the poorest thing superfluous.                         305
  Allow not nature more than nature needs,
  Man's life is cheap as beast's. Thou art a lady;
  If only to go warm were gorgeous,
  Why, nature needs not what thou gorgeous wear'st,
  Which scarcely keeps thee warm. But, for true               310
    need—
  You heavens, give me that patience, patience I need!
  You see me here, you gods, a poor old man
  As full of grief as age, wretched in both.
  If it be you that stirs these daughters' hearts              315
  Against their father, fool me not so much
  To bear it tamely. Touch me with noble anger,
  And let not women's weapons, water drops,
  Stain my man's cheeks.—No, you unnatural hags,
  I will have such revenges on you both                        320
  That all the world shall—I will do such things—
  What they are yet I know not, but they shall be
  The terrors of the Earth! You think I'll weep.
  No, I'll not weep.
  I have full cause of weeping, but this heart                 325
                              *Storm and tempest.*
  Shall break into a hundred thousand flaws
  Or ere I'll weep.—O Fool, I shall go mad!
                    ⟨*Lear, Kent, and Fool*⟩ *exit*
                ⌐*with Gloucester and the Gentleman.*⌐
CORNWALL   Let us withdraw. 'Twill be a storm.
REGAN
  This house is little. The old man and 's people
  Cannot be well bestowed.                                     330

331. **his ... himself:** i.e., **his** fault that has **put him**

332. **taste:** experience

333. **For his particular:** i.e., as for him in particular

340. **will:** i.e., **will** go

341. **give him way:** i.e., let **him** have his own **way; He leads himself:** i.e., he will take no one's advice

344. **sorely ruffle:** fiercely blow

349. **a desperate train:** i.e., a troop of violent supporters

350-51. **being ... abused:** i.e., being easily misled or deceived

GONERIL
'Tis his own blame hath put himself from rest,
And must needs taste his folly.
REGAN
For his particular, I'll receive him gladly,
But not one follower.
GONERIL
So am I purposed. Where is my lord of Gloucester?   335
CORNWALL
Followed the old man forth.

*Enter Gloucester.*

                    He is returned.
GLOUCESTER   The King is in high rage.
[CORNWALL   Whither is he going?
GLOUCESTER
He calls to horse,] but will I know not whither.   340
CORNWALL
'Tis best to give him way. He leads himself.
GONERIL, ⌐*to Gloucester*¬
My lord, entreat him by no means to stay.
GLOUCESTER
Alack, the night comes on, and the high winds
Do sorely ruffle. For many miles about
There's scarce a bush.   345
REGAN              O sir, to willful men
The injuries that they themselves procure
Must be their schoolmasters. Shut up your doors.
He is attended with a desperate train,
And what they may incense him to, being apt   350
To have his ear abused, wisdom bids fear.
CORNWALL
Shut up your doors, my lord. 'Tis a wild night.
My Regan counsels well. Come out o' th' storm.
                     *They exit.*

*The Tragedy of*

# KING LEAR

ACT 3

**3.1** Kent, searching for Lear, meets a Gentleman and learns that Lear and the Fool are alone in the storm. Kent tells the Gentleman that French forces are on their way to England.

---

0 SD. **Storm still:** i.e., **storm** sounds continue; **severally:** separately

5. **Bids:** i.e., he **bids**

6. **main:** mainland

10. **make nothing of:** i.e., treat irreverently; or, scatter and reduce to **nothing** as he **tears** it out

13. **cub-drawn:** i.e., ravenous, with her dugs sucked dry by her cubs

14. **couch:** i.e., stay in her den

17. **bids . . . take all:** The desperate gambler betting the last of his money cries "**Take all!**"

19–20. **outjest . . . injuries:** i.e., use jokes to relieve the **injuries** that have struck the king to the heart

# ACT 3

## Scene 1

*Storm still. Enter Kent ⌈in disguise,⌉ and a Gentleman, severally.*

KENT  Who's there, besides foul weather?

GENTLEMAN
One minded like the weather, most unquietly.

KENT  I know you. Where's the King?

GENTLEMAN
Contending with the fretful elements;
Bids the wind blow the earth into the sea        5
Or swell the curlèd waters 'bove the main,
That things might change or cease; ⟨tears his white
    hair,
Which the impetuous blasts with eyeless rage
Catch in their fury and make nothing of;        10
Strives in his little world of man to outscorn
The to-and-fro conflicting wind and rain.
This night, wherein the cub-drawn bear would
    couch,
The lion and the belly-pinchèd wolf             15
Keep their fur dry, unbonneted he runs
And bids what will take all.⟩

KENT                    But who is with him?

GENTLEMAN
None but the Fool, who labors to outjest
His heart-struck injuries.                      20

123

**21–46. Sir, I do know ... this office to you:** We combine the Folio and quarto versions of this speech in a new way designed to make Kent's words more intelligible. See "Appendix: 3.1.21–46" (pp. 287–91, below) and Richard Knowles, "Revision Awry" in Further Reading (p. 311, below).

22. **upon ... note:** i.e., justified by what I have observed in you

23. **Commend:** entrust, commit; **a dear:** an important, precious

26. **that ... stars:** i.e., whom the fates or destinies

27. **seem no less:** i.e., appear to be real servants

28. **spies, speculations:** Both words mean **spies.**

29. **Intelligent of:** giving information about

30. **a power:** an armed force

31. **scattered:** divided

32. **Wise in:** knowledgeable about; **feet:** i.e., footholds

33. **at point:** in readiness

34. **their open banner:** i.e., **their banner** openly

35. **credit:** credibility

37. **making just:** i.e., for **making** a true

38. **bemadding:** maddening

39. **plain:** complain about

40. **snuffs:** rages (against each other); **packings:** plots

43. **furnishings:** outer trappings

44. **blood:** noble birth

46. **office:** duty (i.e., to go to Dover)

50. **outwall:** outward appearance

54. **that fellow is:** i.e., who I am

KENT                                    Sir, I do know you
  And dare upon the warrant of my note
  Commend a dear thing to you. There is division,
  Although as yet the face of it is covered
  With mutual cunning, 'twixt Albany and Cornwall,          25
  [Who have—as who have not, that their great stars
  Throned and set high?—servants, who seem no less,
  Which are to France the spies and speculations
  Intelligent of our state.] ⟨From France there comes
      a power                                                30
  Into this scattered kingdom, who already,
  Wise in our negligence, have secret feet
  In some of our best ports and are at point
  To show their open banner. Now to you:
  If on my credit you dare build so far                      35
  To make your speed to Dover, you shall find
  Some that will thank you, making just report
  Of how unnatural and bemadding sorrow
  The King hath cause to plain:⟩ [what hath been seen,
  Either in snuffs and packings of the dukes,                40
  Or the hard rein which both of them hath borne
  Against the old kind king, or something deeper,
  Whereof perchance these are but furnishings.]
  ⟨I am a gentleman of blood and breeding,
  And from some knowledge and assurance offer                45
  This office to you.⟩
GENTLEMAN
  I will talk further with you.
KENT                              No, do not.
  For confirmation that I am much more
  Than my outwall, open this purse and take                  50
  What it contains.
                      ⌜*Kent hands him a purse and a ring.*⌝
                      If you shall see Cordelia
  (As fear not but you shall), show her this ring,
  And she will tell you who that fellow is

58. **to effect:** i.e., in their significance
59–61. **in . . . this:** i.e., **in which** effort, you seek
him **that way** while I go **this** way


**3.2** Lear rages against the elements while the Fool
begs him to return to his daughters for shelter; when
Kent finds them, he leads them toward a hovel.

---

1. **crack your cheeks:** On maps and illustrations
of the time, the winds are pictured as puffing out
their cheeks as they blow. (See picture, page 128.)
2. **cataracts and hurricanoes:** waterspouts, tor-
nadoes occurring over water
4. **cocks:** i.e., weathercocks, weathervanes (on
the top of **steeples**)
5. **thought-executing:** acting as quickly as
thought; or, destroying thought; **fires:** i.e., lightning
6. **Vaunt-couriers:** forerunners; **thunderbolts:**
See note to 2.1.55.
10. **Crack . . . molds:** destroy the **molds** in which
nature fashions life; **germens:** seeds; **spill:** destroy
12. **court holy water:** flattering speeches
18. **tax:** accuse

That yet you do not know. Fie on this storm!    55
I will go seek the King.

GENTLEMAN
Give me your hand. Have you no more to say?

KENT
Few words, but, to effect, more than all yet:
That when we have found the King—in which your
    pain    60
That way, I'll this—he that first lights on him
Holla the other.

*They exit ⌜separately.⌝*


Scene 2
*Storm still. Enter Lear and Fool.*

LEAR
Blow winds, and crack your cheeks! Rage, blow!
You cataracts and hurricanoes, spout
Till you have drenched our steeples, ⟨drowned⟩ the
    cocks.
You sulph'rous and thought-executing fires,    5
Vaunt-couriers of oak-cleaving thunderbolts,
Singe my white head. And thou, all-shaking
    thunder,
Strike flat the thick rotundity o' th' world.
Crack nature's molds, all germens spill at once    10
That makes ingrateful man.

FOOL   O nuncle, court holy water in a dry house is
better than this rainwater out o' door. Good nuncle, in. Ask thy daughters' blessing. Here's a night
pities neither wise men nor fools.    15

LEAR
Rumble thy bellyful! Spit, fire! Spout, rain!
Nor rain, wind, thunder, fire are my daughters.
I tax not you, you elements, with unkindness.

20. **subscription:** submission, allegiance

23. **ministers:** underlings, agents

25. **high-engendered battles:** heavenly battalions

28. **headpiece:** helmet; brain

29. **codpiece:** a showy appendage to the front of a man's breeches; here meaning the genitals themselves; **house:** lodge, take shelter (in sexual activity)

30. **any:** i.e., a house in which to live

31. **louse:** become infested with lice

37–38. **made mouths . . . glass:** i.e., **made** faces **in a** mirror

42. **Marry:** a mild oath (originally on the name of the Virgin Mary)

46. **Gallow:** frighten, terrify

47. **keep:** stay within

50. **carry:** endure

Wind swelling "the curlèd waters." (3.1.6; 3.2.1)
From Lodovico Dolce, *Imprese nobili . . .* (1583).

I never gave you kingdom, called you children;
You owe me no subscription. Then let fall          20
Your horrible pleasure. Here I stand your slave,
A poor, infirm, weak, and despised old man.
But yet I call you servile ministers,
That will with two pernicious daughters join
Your high-engendered battles 'gainst a head       25
So old and white as this. O, ho, 'tis foul!
FOOL   He that has a house to put 's head in has a good
   headpiece.
           The codpiece that will house
             Before the head has any,                30
           The head and he shall louse;
             So beggars marry many.
           The man that makes his toe
             What he his heart should make,
           Shall of a corn cry woe,                  35
             And turn his sleep to wake.
   For there was never yet fair woman but she made
   mouths in a glass.
LEAR
   No, I will be the pattern of all patience.
   I will say nothing.                               40

               *Enter Kent ⌜in disguise.⌝*

KENT   Who's there?
FOOL   Marry, here's grace and a codpiece; that's a
   wise man and a fool.
KENT
   Alas, sir, are you here? Things that love night
   Love not such nights as these. The wrathful skies  45
   Gallow the very wanderers of the dark
   And make them keep their caves. Since I was man,
   Such sheets of fire, such bursts of horrid thunder,
   Such groans of roaring wind and rain I never
   Remember to have heard. Man's nature cannot carry  50
   Th' affliction nor the fear.

53. **pudder:** pother, confusion
54. **Find out:** discover, expose
56. **of:** i.e., by
57. **perjured:** i.e., perjurer; **simular:** simulator, imitator
58. **Caitiff:** wretch, villain
59. **seeming:** deception
60. **practiced on:** plotted against; **Close pent-up:** hidden, confined
61. **Rive your concealing continents:** tear open that which contains and conceals you
61–62. **cry . . . grace:** i.e., **cry** for mercy from the elements—i.e., **these dreadful summoners (Summoners** were officers of church courts.)
66. **hard:** near
70–71. **Which . . . come in:** i.e., the residents of which forbade my entrance **demanding:** i.e., I asking
72. **scanted:** withheld; deficient
81–84. **He that . . . every day:** This song echoes the song that concludes Shakespeare's *Twelfth Night* (5.1.412–31).

LEAR                    Let the great gods
That keep this dreadful pudder o'er our heads
Find out their enemies now. Tremble, thou wretch,
That hast within thee undivulgèd crimes                    55
Unwhipped of justice. Hide thee, thou bloody hand,
Thou perjured, and thou simular of virtue
That art incestuous. Caitiff, to pieces shake,
That under covert and convenient seeming
Has practiced on man's life. Close pent-up guilts,        60
Rive your concealing continents and cry
These dreadful summoners grace. I am a man
More sinned against than sinning.
KENT                              Alack,
    bareheaded?                                           65
Gracious my lord, hard by here is a hovel.
Some friendship will it lend you 'gainst the tempest.
Repose you there while I to this hard house—
More harder than the stones whereof 'tis raised,
Which even but now, demanding after you,                  70
Denied me to come in—return and force
Their scanted courtesy.
LEAR                    My wits begin to turn.—
Come on, my boy. How dost, my boy? Art cold?
I am cold myself.—Where is this straw, my fellow?         75
The art of our necessities is strange
And can make vile things precious. Come, your
    hovel.—
Poor Fool and knave, I have one part in my heart
That's sorry yet for thee.                                80
FOOL ⌜*sings*⌝
    *He that has and a little tiny wit,*
        *With hey, ho, the wind and the rain,*
    *Must make content with his fortunes fit,*
        *Though the rain it raineth every day.*
LEAR
True, ⟨my good⟩ boy.—Come, bring us to this hovel.        85
                        ⌜*Lear and Kent*⌝ *exit.*

86. **brave:** fine
88–101. **When . . . used with feet:** This speech is a parody of a well-known prophecy known as "Merlin's Prophecy." The first few lines seem to present, as a vision of the future, the actual state of affairs in an imperfect world.
88. **more . . . matter:** i.e., preach virtue better than they practice it
89. **mar:** i.e., dilute
90. **nobles . . . tutors:** i.e., noblemen teach their tailors (perhaps, about what is fashionable)
91. **heretics burned:** The traditional punishment for religious **heretics** was being **burned** at the stake.
92–97. **When . . . build:** These lines represent a utopia or perfect world. **right:** just **cutpurses . . . throngs:** purse-stealers do not haunt crowds **usurers . . . field:** moneylenders count their money in public **bawds:** procurers of women as prostitutes
98. **Albion:** England
99. **confusion:** ruin
101. **going . . . feet:** i.e., walking will be done on foot

**3.3** Gloucester tells Edmund that he has decided to go to Lear's aid; he also tells him about an incriminating letter he has received about the French invasion. After Gloucester leaves to find Lear, Edmund announces his plan to betray his father to Cornwall.

2. **leave:** permission
3. **pity:** have pity on

*(continued)*

[FOOL　This is a brave night to cool a courtesan. I'll
　speak a prophecy ere I go:
　　When priests are more in word than matter,
　　When brewers mar their malt with water,
　　When nobles are their tailors' tutors,　　　　　　90
　　No heretics burned but wenches' suitors,
　　When every case in law is right,
　　No squire in debt, nor no poor knight;
　　When slanders do not live in tongues,
　　Nor cutpurses come not to throngs,　　　　　　95
　　When usurers tell their gold i' th' field,
　　And bawds and whores do churches build,
　　Then shall the realm of Albion
　　Come to great confusion;
　　Then comes the time, who lives to see 't,　　　100
　　That going shall be used with feet.
　This prophecy Merlin shall make, for I live before
　his time.
　　　　　　　　　　　　　　　　　　　*He exits.*]


### Scene 3
*Enter Gloucester and Edmund.*

GLOUCESTER　Alack, alack, Edmund, I like not this
　unnatural dealing. When I desired their leave that I
　might pity him, they took from me the use of mine
　own house, charged me on pain of perpetual
　displeasure neither to speak of him, entreat for　　5
　him, or any way sustain him.
EDMUND　Most savage and unnatural.
GLOUCESTER　Go to; say you nothing. There is division
　between the dukes, and a worse matter than that. I
　have received a letter this night; 'tis dangerous to　10
　be spoken; I have locked the letter in my closet.
　These injuries the King now bears will be revenged

8. **Go to:** an expression of impatience
11. **closet:** private chamber
13. **home:** i.e., completely; **power:** armed force; **footed:** i.e., landed
14. **incline to:** i.e., take the side of; **look:** i.e., **look** for; **privily:** secretly
16. **of:** i.e., by
19. **toward:** about to happen
21. **This . . . thee:** i.e., the forbidden kindness to the king that you are about to show
23. **This . . . deserving:** i.e., this (treachery to my father) will seem (to Cornwall) to deserve a reward

**3.4** Lear, Kent, and the Fool reach the hovel, where they find Edgar disguised as Poor Tom, a madman-beggar. When Gloucester finds them, he leads them to the shelter of a house.

----

2. **open night:** i.e., **night** in the **open** air
3. **nature:** i.e., human **nature**
10. **fixed:** lodged, rooted

home; there is part of a power already footed. We
must incline to the King. I will look him and privily
·relieve him. Go you and maintain talk with the          15
Duke, that my charity be not of him perceived. If he
ask for me, I am ill and gone to bed. If I die for it, as
no less is threatened me, the King my old master
must be relieved. There is strange things toward,
Edmund. Pray you, be careful.          *He exits.*          20

EDMUND
This courtesy forbid thee shall the Duke
Instantly know, and of that letter too.
This seems a fair deserving, and must draw me
That which my father loses—no less than all.
The younger rises when the old doth fall.          25
                         *He exits.*


### Scene 4
*Enter Lear, Kent ⌐in disguise,⌐ and Fool.*

KENT
Here is the place, my lord. Good my lord, enter.
The tyranny of the open night 's too rough
For nature to endure.          *Storm still.*
LEAR                    Let me alone.
KENT
Good my lord, enter here.          5
LEAR                    Wilt break my heart?
KENT
I had rather break mine own. Good my lord, enter.
LEAR
Thou think'st 'tis much that this contentious storm
Invades us to the skin. So 'tis to thee.
But where the greater malady is fixed,          10
The lesser is scarce felt. Thou 'dst shun a bear,
But if ⟨thy⟩ flight lay toward the roaring sea,

13. **i' th' mouth:** i.e., head-on
14. **free:** i.e., at peace
18. **as:** i.e., **as** if
19. **home:** thoroughly
23. **frank:** generous
29. **would:** i.e., that **would**
33. **bide:** suffer, endure
35. **looped and windowed:** i.e., holey (as if filled with loopholes and windows)
38. **Take physic:** i.e., cure yourself; **pomp:** i.e., you who are powerful
40. **superflux:** excess, surplus (that you have)
42. **Fathom and half:** cry of a sailor taking soundings

Thou 'dst meet the bear i' th' mouth. When the
    mind's free,
The body's delicate. ⟨This⟩ tempest in my mind          15
Doth from my senses take all feeling else
Save what beats there. Filial ingratitude!
Is it not as this mouth should tear this hand
For lifting food to 't? But I will punish home.
No, I will weep no more. [In such a night               20
To shut me out? Pour on. I will endure.]
In such a night as this? O Regan, Goneril,
Your old kind father whose frank heart gave all!
O, that way madness lies. Let me shun that;
No more of that.                                        25
KENT                   Good my lord, enter here.
LEAR
Prithee, go in thyself. Seek thine own ease.
This tempest will not give me leave to ponder
On things would hurt me more. But I'll go in.—
[In, boy; go first.—You houseless poverty—             30
Nay, get thee in. I'll pray, and then I'll sleep.]
                                   ⌐Fool⌐ *exits.*
Poor naked wretches, wheresoe'er you are,
That bide the pelting of this pitiless storm,
How shall your houseless heads and unfed sides,
Your looped and windowed raggedness defend           35
    you
From seasons such as these? O, I have ta'en
Too little care of this. Take physic, pomp.
Expose thyself to feel what wretches feel,
That thou may'st shake the superflux to them           40
And show the heavens more just.
[EDGAR ⌐*within*⌐ Fathom and half, fathom and half!
    Poor Tom!

                   *Enter Fool.*]

FOOL   Come not in here, nuncle; here's a spirit. Help
    me, help me!                                         45

48. **grumble:** i.e., mumble, mutter

50. **Away:** go away; **foul fiend:** devil (Edgar, in disguise as Poor Tom, pretends to be possessed.)

50–51. **Through . . . wind:** a line from a ballad

58. **that:** who (i.e., **the fiend** [line 56]); **his:** i.e., Poor Tom's

59. **halters:** hangman's ropes (Like **knives** and **ratsbane,** the ropes were temptations to suicide.) **porridge:** thick soup

61. **four-inched bridges:** i.e., very narrow bridges; **course:** hunt

62. **for:** as; **five wits:** five senses (According to Stephen Hawes in *The Pastime of Pleasure* [1509], the **five wits** are common wit, imagination, fantasy, estimation, and memory.)

64. **star-blasting:** i.e., the evil influence of stars; **taking:** being put under a magic spell; being attacked by disease

68. **pass:** predicament

71. **reserved:** kept, retained; **else:** otherwise

73. **pendulous:** pendent, overhanging

74. **fated:** fatefully, ominously

KENT　Give me thy hand. Who's there?

FOOL　A spirit, a spirit! He says his name's Poor Tom.

KENT　What art thou that dost grumble there i' th'
straw? Come forth.

*Enter Edgar ⌈in disguise.⌉*

EDGAR　Away. The foul fiend follows me. Through the　50
sharp hawthorn ⟨blows the cold wind.⟩ Hum! Go to
thy ⟨cold⟩ bed and warm thee.

LEAR　Didst thou give all to thy daughters? And art thou
come to this?

EDGAR　Who gives anything to Poor Tom, whom the　55
foul fiend hath led ⟨through⟩ fire and through flame,
through ⟨ford⟩ and whirlpool, o'er bog and quag-
mire; that hath laid knives under his pillow and
halters in his pew, set ratsbane by his porridge,
made him proud of heart to ride on a bay trotting　60
horse over four-inched bridges to course his own
shadow for a traitor? Bless thy five wits! Tom's
a-cold. O, do de, do de, do de. Bless thee from
whirlwinds, star-blasting, and taking! Do Poor Tom
some charity, whom the foul fiend vexes. There　65
could I have him now, and there—and there again
—and there.　　　　　　　　　*Storm still.*

LEAR

Has his daughters brought him to this pass?—
Couldst thou save nothing? Wouldst thou give 'em
all?　　　　　　　　　　　　　　　　　　70

FOOL　Nay, he reserved a blanket, else we had been all
shamed.

LEAR

Now all the plagues that in the pendulous air
Hang fated o'er men's faults light on thy daughters!

KENT　He hath no daughters, sir.　　　　　　75

LEAR

Death, traitor! Nothing could have subdued nature
To such a lowness but his unkind daughters.

79. **flesh:** i.e., bodies (See Edgar's description at 2.3.6–12 of how he will turn his body into a "horrible object.")

81. **pelican:** Young pelicans were thought to feed on their parents' blood. (See picture, page 144.)

82. **Pillicock:** a term of endearment and a name for the phallus

87. **keep . . . justice:** i.e., keep your word

87–88. **commit . . . spouse:** i.e., do **not commit** adultery

89. **array:** dress, clothing

91. **servingman:** literally, servant; figuratively, a lover (in service to his beloved)

92. **gloves:** A lover honored his mistress by wearing her glove in his hat.

98. **out-paramoured the Turk:** i.e., had sex with more women than the Turkish sultan with his harem

99. **light of ear:** i.e., ready to listen to malicious talk

101. **prey:** i.e., preying

103. **plackets:** openings in petticoats or in skirts

104. **lenders':** moneylenders'

106. **Dolphin . . . sessa:** perhaps a fragment of a song

108. **answer:** stand up to

111. **worm:** i.e., silkworm

112. **cat:** civet **cat,** from whose secretions perfume is made (See picture, page 160.) **on 's:** i.e., of us

113. **sophisticated:** not pure or genuine

113–14. **unaccommodated:** unfurnished (with items taken from other animals)

Is it the fashion that discarded fathers
Should have thus little mercy on their flesh?
Judicious punishment! 'Twas this flesh begot          80
Those pelican daughters.

EDGAR   Pillicock sat on Pillicock Hill. Alow, alow, loo,
loo.

FOOL   This cold night will turn us all to fools and
madmen.          85

EDGAR   Take heed o' th' foul fiend. Obey thy parents,
keep thy word's justice, swear not, commit not with
man's sworn spouse, set not thy sweet heart on
proud array. Tom's a-cold.

LEAR   What hast thou been?          90

EDGAR   A servingman, proud in heart and mind, that
curled my hair, wore gloves in my cap, served the
lust of my mistress' heart and did the act of
darkness with her, swore as many oaths as I spake
words and broke them in the sweet face of heaven;          95
one that slept in the contriving of lust and waked to
do it. Wine loved I ⟨deeply,⟩ dice dearly, and in
woman out-paramoured the Turk. False of heart,
light of ear, bloody of hand; hog in sloth, fox in
stealth, wolf in greediness, dog in madness, lion in          100
prey. Let not the creaking of shoes nor the rustling
of silks betray thy poor heart to woman. Keep thy
foot out of brothels, thy hand out of plackets, thy
pen from lenders' books, and defy the foul fiend.
Still through the hawthorn blows the cold wind;          105
says suum, mun, nonny. Dolphin my boy, boy, sessa!
Let him trot by.          *Storm still.*

LEAR   Thou wert better in a grave than to answer with
thy uncovered body this extremity of the skies.—Is
man no more than this? Consider him well.—Thou          110
ow'st the worm no silk, the beast no hide, the sheep
no wool, the cat no perfume. Ha, here's three on 's
are sophisticated. Thou art the thing itself; unaccommodated man is no more but such a poor, bare,

115. **lendings:** i.e., clothes
117. **naughty:** wicked
118. **wild:** uncultivated
120. **on 's:** i.e., of his
122. **Flibbertigibbet:** a name for the devil in Samuel Harsnett's *Declaration of Egregious Popish Impostures* (1603), a pamphlet Shakespeare draws on throughout for his depiction of Edgar as Poor Tom
123. **curfew:** i.e., 9 p.m., when the curfew bell was rung; **first cock:** first cock-crow of the day (i.e., dawn) See *Hamlet* 1.1.162–70.
124. **web . . . pin:** cataract of the eye; **squints:** i.e., makes squint
125. **white:** ripening
127. **Swithold:** Saint Withold, who appears in this charm against the devil in the role of an exorcist; **footed:** crossed on foot; **'old:** wold, open country
128. **nightmare:** incubus; **ninefold:** nine offspring
130. **plight:** i.e., pledge (to do no more harm)
131. **aroint:** begone, get away
137. **water:** i.e., **water newt**
139. **sallets:** tasty things
140. **ditch-dog:** dead dog thrown in a ditch; **green mantle:** scum
141–42. **tithing to tithing:** i.e., place to place (Beggars were ordered whipped from one place to the next until they returned to their own district.) **tithing:** originally the name of a community of ten families
143. **three suits:** See note to 2.2.15.
146. **deer:** animals

forked animal as thou art. Off, off, you lendings! 115
Come, unbutton here. ⌜*Tearing off his clothes.*⌝
FOOL Prithee, nuncle, be contented. 'Tis a naughty
night to swim in. Now, a little fire in a wild field
were like an old lecher's heart—a small spark, all
the rest on 's body cold. 120

*Enter Gloucester, with a torch.*

Look, here comes a walking fire.
EDGAR This is the foul ⟨fiend⟩ Flibbertigibbet. He be-
gins at curfew and walks ⟨till the⟩ first cock. He
gives the web and the pin, squints the eye, and
makes the harelip, mildews the white wheat, and 125
hurts the poor creature of earth.
　Swithold footed thrice the 'old,
　He met the nightmare and her ninefold,
　　Bid her alight,
　　And her troth plight, 130
　And aroint thee, witch, aroint thee.
KENT How fares your Grace?
LEAR What's he?
KENT Who's there? What is 't you seek?
GLOUCESTER What are you there? Your names? 135
EDGAR Poor Tom, that eats the swimming frog, the
toad, the tadpole, the wall newt, and the water;
that, in the fury of his heart, when the foul fiend
rages, eats cow dung for sallets, swallows the old
rat and the ditch-dog, drinks the green mantle of 140
the standing pool; who is whipped from tithing to
tithing, and stocked, punished, and imprisoned;
who hath ⟨had⟩ three suits to his back, six shirts to
his body,
　Horse to ride, and weapon to wear; 145
　But mice and rats and such small deer
　Have been Tom's food for seven long year.

148. **my follower:** i.e., the fiend that attends me

148, 151, 152. **Smulkin, Modo, Mahu:** names of devils in Harsnett's *Declaration*

153. **flesh and blood:** i.e., children

154. **what gets it:** i.e., parents  **gets:** i.e., begets

156–57. **suffer / T' obey:** i.e., tolerate obeying

165. **Theban:** citizen of Thebes, capital of ancient Boeotia in Greece

166. **your study:** the specialty that you study

167. **prevent:** forestall

169. **Importune:** implore, beg (accent on second syllable)

A pelican and its young. (3.4.81)
From Conrad Lycosthenes, *Prodigiorum* . . . (1557).

Beware my follower. Peace, Smulkin! Peace, thou
fiend!
GLOUCESTER, ⌜to Lear⌝
What, hath your Grace no better company?          150
EDGAR  The Prince of Darkness is a gentleman. Modo
he's called, and Mahu.
GLOUCESTER, ⌜to Lear⌝
Our flesh and blood, my lord, is grown so vile
That it doth hate what gets it.
EDGAR  Poor Tom's a-cold.          155
GLOUCESTER, ⌜to Lear⌝
Go in with me. My duty cannot suffer
T' obey in all your daughters' hard commands.
Though their injunction be to bar my doors
And let this tyrannous night take hold upon you,
Yet have I ventured to come seek you out          160
And bring you where both fire and food is ready.
LEAR
First let me talk with this philosopher.
⌜To Edgar.⌝ What is the cause of thunder?
KENT
Good my lord, take his offer; go into th' house.
LEAR
I'll talk a word with this same learnèd Theban.—          165
What is your study?
EDGAR  How to prevent the fiend and to kill vermin.
LEAR  Let me ask you one word in private.
                    ⌜They talk aside.⌝
KENT, ⌜to Gloucester⌝
Importune him once more to go, my lord.
His wits begin t' unsettle.          170
GLOUCESTER                    Canst thou blame him?
                    *Storm still.*
His daughters seek his death. Ah, that good Kent!
He said it would be thus, poor banished man.
Thou sayest the King grows mad; I'll tell thee,
    friend,          175

177. **outlawed from my blood:** i.e., (1) disinherited; (2) condemned as an outlaw
182. **cry you mercy:** i.e., excuse me
189. **keep still:** i.e., continue to stay
190. **soothe:** indulge
191. **Take . . . on:** i.e., bring him along
193. **Athenian:** i.e., philosopher
195–97. **Child . . . man:** Edgar gives to the hero of Charlemagne legends, Rowland or Roland (whose title **Child** shows that he was a candidate for knighthood), the words of the giant in "Jack and the Beanstalk." **word:** motto **still:** always

**3.5** Edmund tells Cornwall about Gloucester's decision to help Lear and about the incriminating letter from France; in return, Cornwall makes Edmund earl of Gloucester.

---

3. **censured:** judged; **that:** i.e., because; **nature:** i.e., natural affection for my father
4. **something fears:** somewhat frightens

I am almost mad myself. I had a son,
Now outlawed from my blood. He sought my life
But lately, very late. I loved him, friend,
No father his son dearer. True to tell thee,
The grief hath crazed my wits. What a night's this!          180
—I do beseech your Grace—
LEAR     O, cry you mercy, sir.
⌈*To Edgar.*⌉ Noble philosopher, your company.
EDGAR     Tom's a-cold.
GLOUCESTER, ⌈*to Edgar*⌉
In fellow, there, into th' hovel. Keep thee warm.          185
LEAR     Come, let's in all.
KENT                         This way, my lord.
LEAR, ⌈*indicating Edgar*⌉                    With him.
I will keep still with my philosopher.
KENT, ⌈*to Gloucester*⌉
Good my lord, soothe him. Let him take the fellow.          190
GLOUCESTER, ⌈*to Kent*⌉     Take him you on.
KENT, ⌈*to Edgar*⌉
Sirrah, come on: go along with us.
LEAR     Come, good Athenian.
GLOUCESTER     No words, no words. Hush.
EDGAR
Child Rowland to the dark tower came.          195
His word was still "Fie, foh, and fum,
I smell the blood of a British man."
                                        *They exit.*


## Scene 5
*Enter Cornwall, and Edmund* ⌈*with a paper.*⌉

CORNWALL     I will have my revenge ere I depart his
house.
EDMUND     How, my lord, I may be censured, that nature
thus gives way to loyalty, something fears me to
think of.          5

7. **his:** i.e., Gloucester's

8. **provoking merit:** perhaps, Edgar's virtue incited or provoked; or, perhaps, Gloucester's deserving (of death) provoked

8–9. **reprovable . . . himself:** blameworthy evil in Gloucester

12. **approves him:** i.e., proves him to be

12–13. **intelligent . . . France:** one giving information that aids the king of France

20. **apprehension:** arrest

21. **comforting:** i.e., relieving the misery of

22. **his suspicion:** i.e., Cornwall's suspicion of Gloucester

24. **my blood:** i.e., attachment to my blood relations


**3.6** Lear, in his madness, imagines that Goneril and Regan are on trial before a tribunal made up of Edgar, the Fool, Kent, and himself. Gloucester returns to announce that Lear's death is being plotted and to urge Kent to rush Lear to Cordelia at Dover.

---

2. **piece out:** i.e., increase

5. **impatience:** incapacity to endure more suffering

6. **Frateretto:** another devil found in Harsnett's *Declaration*; **Nero:** brutal and self-indulgent emperor of Rome in the first century C.E. (here doomed to fish in hell)

CORNWALL   I now perceive it was not altogether your
brother's evil disposition made him seek his death,
but a provoking merit set awork by a reprovable
badness in himself.

EDMUND   How malicious is my fortune that I must       10
repent to be just! This is the letter he spoke of,
which approves him an intelligent party to the
advantages of France. O heavens, that this treason
were not, or not I the detector.

CORNWALL   Go with me to the Duchess.                   15

EDMUND   If the matter of this paper be certain, you
have mighty business in hand.

CORNWALL   True or false, it hath made thee Earl of
Gloucester. Seek out where thy father is, that he
may be ready for our apprehension.                       20

EDMUND, ⌐*aside*¬   If I find him comforting the King, it
will stuff his suspicion more fully.—I will persevere
in my course of loyalty, though the conflict be sore
between that and my blood.

CORNWALL   I will lay trust upon thee, and thou shalt    25
find a ⟨dearer⟩ father in my love.

*They exit.*


## Scene 6
*Enter Kent ⌐in disguise,¬ and Gloucester.*

GLOUCESTER   Here is better than the open air. Take it
thankfully. I will piece out the comfort with what
addition I can. I will not be long from you.

KENT   All the power of his wits have given way to his
impatience. The gods reward your kindness!               5

⌐*Gloucester*¬ *exits.*

*Enter Lear, Edgar ⌐in disguise,¬ and Fool.*

EDGAR   Frateretto calls me and tells me Nero is an

10. **yeoman:** rank below **gentleman**

12–13. **to his son:** i.e., as a **son**

14. **before him:** i.e., **before** he has achieved the rank himself

20–59. **I will arraign . . . 'scape:** In this passage Lear stages an arraignment and trial of the absent Goneril and Regan.

20. **straight:** straightway, immediately

25. **he:** perhaps one of Poor Tom's fiends, or perhaps Lear

25–26. **Want'st . . . trial:** perhaps, "Do you lack onlookers **at** your **trial?**" or, perhaps, "Can't you see who is judging you?"

27. **Come . . . me:** the first line of a ballad first printed in 1558 (The Fool's continuation of it does not follow the original.)   **burn:** stream, brook

32. **Hoppedance:** One of Harsnett's devils is called "Hobberdidance."

33. **white:** unsmoked; **Croak not:** Edgar may be alluding to the rumbling of an empty stomach.

35. **amazed:** confused (as if lost in a maze)

37. **their evidence:** the witnesses against them

angler in the lake of darkness. Pray, innocent, and
beware the foul fiend.

FOOL  Prithee, nuncle, tell me whether a madman be a
gentleman or a yeoman.    10

LEAR  A king, a king!

[FOOL  No, he's a yeoman that has a gentleman to his
son, for he's a mad yeoman that sees his son a
gentleman before him.

LEAR]

To have a thousand with red burning spits    15
Come hissing in upon 'em!

⟨EDGAR  The foul fiend bites my back.

FOOL  He's mad that trusts in the tameness of a wolf, a
horse's health, a boy's love, or a whore's oath.

LEAR

It shall be done. I will arraign them straight.    20
⌐To Edgar.⌐ Come, sit thou here, most learnèd
justice.
⌐To Fool.⌐ Thou sapient sir, sit here. ⌐Now,⌐ you
she-foxes—

EDGAR  Look where he stands and glares!—Want'st    25
thou eyes at trial, madam?
⌐Sings.⌐ Come o'er the ⌐burn,⌐ Bessy, to me—

FOOL ⌐sings⌐

Her boat hath a leak,
And she must not speak
Why she dares not come over to thee.    30

EDGAR  The foul fiend haunts Poor Tom in the voice of
a nightingale. Hoppedance cries in Tom's belly for
two white herring.—Croak not, black angel. I have
no food for thee.

KENT, ⌐to Lear⌐

How do you, sir? Stand you not so amazed.    35
Will you lie down and rest upon the cushions?

LEAR

I'll see their trial first. Bring in their evidence.

40. **yokefellow of equity:** fellow justice in a court **of equity**
41. **Bench:** i.e., sit on the bench
41–42. **o' th' commission:** authorized to be a judge
45–48. **Sleepest . . . harm:** These lines echo songs, ballads, and catches from the period, including the nursery song "Little Boy Blue."
46. **corn:** i.e., wheat
47. **minikin:** pretty, dainty
49. **Purr the cat: Purr** is a devil named by Harsnett, although here the word may refer instead to the sound made by the cat.
51. **kicked:** i.e., she **kicked**
55. **I . . . joint stool:** a stock joke meaning "I did not notice you" (Here the fresh point may be that, while Goneril is not onstage, a stool may be.) **joint stool:** a stool made of parts joined or fitted together
56. **warped:** (1) twisted, bent; (2) perverse
57. **store:** stock, material; **on:** i.e., of
58. **Corruption in the place:** i.e., even the law court is corrupt
60. **five wits:** See note to 3.4.62.
61. **patience:** self-control
64. **counterfeiting:** i.e., disguise
67. **Avaunt:** i.e., get away
69. **or . . . or:** i.e., either . . . or

⌜*To Edgar.*⌝ Thou robèd man of justice, take thy
    place,
⌜*To Fool.*⌝ And thou, his yokefellow of equity,      40
Bench by his side. ⌜*To Kent.*⌝ You are o' th'
    commission;
Sit you, too.
EDGAR   Let us deal justly.
  ⌜*Sings.*⌝ Sleepest or wakest, thou jolly shepherd?    45
      Thy sheep be in the corn.
    And for one blast of thy minikin mouth,
      Thy sheep shall take no harm.
  Purr the cat is gray.
LEAR   Arraign her first; 'tis Goneril. I here take my oath  50
before this honorable assembly, kicked the poor
king her father.
FOOL   Come hither, mistress. Is your name Goneril?
LEAR   She cannot deny it.
FOOL   Cry you mercy, I took you for a joint stool.    55
LEAR
And here's another whose warped looks proclaim
What store her heart is made on. Stop her there!
Arms, arms, sword, fire! Corruption in the place!
False justicer, why hast thou let her 'scape?⟩
EDGAR   Bless thy five wits!    60
KENT, ⌜*to Lear*⌝
  O pity! Sir, where is the patience now
  That you so oft have boasted to retain?
EDGAR, ⌜*aside*⌝
  My tears begin to take his part so much
  They mar my counterfeiting.
LEAR   The little dogs and all,    65
  Tray, Blanch, and Sweetheart, see, they bark at me.
EDGAR   Tom will throw his head at them.—Avaunt, you
    curs!
      Be thy mouth or black or white,
      Tooth that poisons if it bite,    70

72. **brach:** bitch-hound; **lym:** bloodhound

73. **Bobtail tike:** dog with its tail cut short; **trundle-tail:** long-tailed dog

76. **hatch:** bottom half of a divided door

77. **wakes:** festivals

78. **horn:** large ox horns worn by beggars from which to drink (The phrase "my horn is dry" was a plea for more drink.) See picture, page 166.

80. **anatomize:** dissect

82. **make:** i.e., makes

83. **entertain for:** take into service as

85. **Persian:** i.e., gorgeous and exotic

88. **curtains:** i.e., imaginary bed **curtains**

90. **I'll go ... noon:** possibly an allusion to the plant called "**go to bed at noon,**" which closes itself **at noon** and remains closed until the next morning (See picture, below.)

94. **upon:** i.e., against

101. **Stand in ... loss:** i.e., will certainly be lost

Goat's beard, or "go to bed at noon." (3.6.90)
From John Gerard, *The Herball* ... (1597).

Mastiff, greyhound, mongrel grim,
Hound or spaniel, brach, or ⌜lym,⌝
Bobtail ⟨tike,⟩ or ⟨trundle-tail,⟩
Tom will make him weep and wail;
For, with throwing thus my head,                    75
Dogs leapt the hatch, and all are fled.
Do de, de, de. Sessa! Come, march to wakes
and fairs and market towns. Poor Tom, thy horn
is dry.

LEAR   Then let them anatomize Regan; see what breeds   80
about her heart. Is there any cause in nature that
make these hard hearts? ⌜*To Edgar.*⌝ You, sir, I
entertain for one of my hundred; only I do not like
the fashion of your garments. You will say they are
Persian, but let them be changed.                  85

KENT
Now, good my lord, lie here and rest awhile.

LEAR, ⌜*lying down*⌝ Make no noise, make no noise.
Draw the curtains. So, so, we'll go to supper i' th'
morning.

[FOOL   And I'll go to bed at noon.]               90

*Enter Gloucester.*

GLOUCESTER, ⌜*to Kent*⌝
Come hither, friend. Where is the King my master?

KENT
Here, sir, but trouble him not; his wits are gone.

GLOUCESTER
Good friend, I prithee, take him in thy arms.
I have o'erheard a plot of death upon him.
There is a litter ready; lay him in 't,             95
And drive toward Dover, friend, where thou shalt
   meet
Both welcome and protection. Take up thy master.
If thou shouldst dally half an hour, his life,
With thine and all that offer to defend him,        100
Stand in assurèd loss. Take up, take up,

102–3. **to some ... conduct:** i.e., quickly take you to where you can find supplies

105. **balmed:** soothed; **sinews:** nerves

107. **Stand ... cure:** i.e., are not likely to be cured

111. **bearing ... woes:** suffering **woes** like ours

112. **We ... foes:** perhaps, we almost forget our own suffering

114. **free:** carefree; **shows:** scenes

115. **sufferance:** i.e., suffering

116. **bearing:** enduring; **fellowship:** company

117. **portable:** endurable

120. **He childed ... fathered:** i.e., his children are like my father (in driving him away; or, in seeking his life)

121. **Mark ... noises:** pay attention to news of those in high places, i.e., those in power; **bewray:** reveal

124. **In thy just proof:** upon your being proved right; **repeals:** recalls; **reconciles:** i.e., **reconciles** you with your accusers

125. **What ... King:** i.e., whatever **more** happens **tonight,** may **the king** escape safely


**3.7**  Cornwall dispatches men to capture Gloucester, whom he calls a traitor. Sending Edmund and Goneril to tell Albany about the landing of the French army, Cornwall puts out Gloucester's eyes. Cornwall is himself seriously wounded by one of his own servants, who tries to stop the torture of Gloucester.

———————————

1. **Post speedily:** hasten

And follow me, that will to some provision
Give thee quick conduct.

⟨KENT                        Oppressèd nature sleeps.
This rest might yet have balmed thy broken sinews,      105
Which, if convenience will not allow,
Stand in hard cure. ⌜*To the Fool.*⌝ Come, help to
    bear thy master.
Thou must not stay behind.

GLOUCESTER⟩                    Come, come away.      110
        ⌜*All but Edgar*⌝ *exit,* ⌜*carrying Lear.*⌝

⟨EDGAR
When we our betters see bearing our woes,
We scarcely think our miseries our foes.
Who alone suffers suffers most i' th' mind,
Leaving free things and happy shows behind.
But then the mind much sufferance doth o'erskip      115
When grief hath mates and bearing fellowship.
How light and portable my pain seems now
When that which makes me bend makes the King
    bow!
He childed as I fathered. Tom, away.      120
Mark the high noises, and thyself bewray
When false opinion, whose wrong thoughts defile
    thee,
In thy just proof repeals and reconciles thee.
What will hap more tonight, safe 'scape the King!      125
Lurk, lurk.⟩
                                        ⌜*He exits.*⌝


## Scene 7
*Enter Cornwall, Regan, Goneril,* ⌜*Edmund, the*⌝ *Bastard,*
*and Servants.*

CORNWALL, ⌜*to Goneril*⌝ Post speedily to my lord your
    husband. Show him this letter. ⌜*He gives her a*
    *paper.*⌝ The army of France is landed.—Seek out
    the traitor Gloucester.        ⌜*Some Servants exit.*⌝

8. **our sister:** i.e., Goneril

8–9. **are bound:** (1) are obligated; (2) cannot fail

10–11. **Advise . . . preparation:** i.e., **advise Albany, to whom you are going,** to make speedy preparation (for war)  **festinate:** speedy, hasty

12. **to the like:** i.e., to do the same thing; **posts:** messengers

12–13. **shall be . . . intelligent:** i.e., will carry intelligence (information)

14. **lord of Gloucester:** i.e., Edmund (Oswald will immediately use the same title to refer to Edmund's father.)

18. **Hot questrists:** keen seekers

19. **the lord's:** i.e., Gloucester's

26. **Pinion:** bind

27. **pass. . . . life:** i.e., condemn him to death

29. **do a court'sy:** i.e., yield, bow down, defer

REGAN  Hang him instantly.                                            5
GONERIL  Pluck out his eyes.
CORNWALL  Leave him to my displeasure.—Edmund,
  keep you our sister company. The revenges we are
  bound to take upon your traitorous father are not
  fit for your beholding. Advise the Duke, where you    10
  are going, to a most festinate preparation; we are
  bound to the like. Our posts shall be swift and
  intelligent betwixt us.—Farewell, dear sister.—
  Farewell, my lord of Gloucester.

              *Enter* ⌜*Oswald, the*⌝ *Steward.*

  How now? Where's the King?                             15
OSWALD
  My lord of Gloucester hath conveyed him hence.
  Some five- or six-and-thirty of his knights,
  Hot questrists after him, met him at gate,
  Who, with some other of the lord's dependents,
  Are gone with him toward Dover, where they boast     20
  To have well-armèd friends.
CORNWALL  Get horses for your mistress.
                              ⌜*Oswald exits.*⌝
GONERIL  Farewell, sweet lord, and sister.
CORNWALL
  Edmund, farewell.      ⌜*Goneril and Edmund*⌝ *exit.*
          Go seek the traitor Gloucester.               25
  Pinion him like a thief; bring him before us.
                              ⌜*Some Servants exit.*⌝
  Though well we may not pass upon his life
  Without the form of justice, yet our power
  Shall do a court'sy to our wrath, which men
  May blame but not control.                            30

          *Enter Gloucester and Servants.*

                        Who's there? The
  traitor?

34. **corky:** dry and withered
40. **none:** i.e., not a traitor
46. **Naughty:** wicked
48. **quicken:** come to life
49. **my . . . favors:** perhaps, the features (face) of your host; or, perhaps, **my hospitable** kindnesses to you
50. **ruffle:** bully, treat roughly
51. **late:** recently
52. **simple-answered:** i.e., direct in answering
54. **footed:** landed
57. **guessingly set down:** i.e., written without certainty; containing only speculations

A civet cat. (3.4.112)
From Edward Topsell, *The historie of foure-footed beastes* . . . (1607).

REGAN    Ingrateful fox! 'Tis he.

CORNWALL    Bind fast his corky arms.

GLOUCESTER

   What means your Graces? Good my friends,       35
     consider
   You are my guests; do me no foul play, friends.

CORNWALL

   Bind him, I say.

REGAN               Hard, hard. O filthy traitor!

GLOUCESTER

   Unmerciful lady as you are, I'm none.         40

CORNWALL

   To this chair bind him.     ⌜*Servants bind Gloucester.*⌝
                   Villain, thou shalt find—
              ⌜*Regan plucks Gloucester's beard.*⌝

GLOUCESTER

   By the kind gods, 'tis most ignobly done
   To pluck me by the beard.

REGAN

   So white, and such a traitor?           45

GLOUCESTER            Naughty lady,
   These hairs which thou dost ravish from my chin
   Will quicken and accuse thee. I am your host;
   With robber's hands my hospitable favors
   You should not ruffle thus. What will you do?     50

CORNWALL

   Come, sir, what letters had you late from France?

REGAN

   Be simple-answered, for we know the truth.

CORNWALL

   And what confederacy have you with the traitors
   Late footed in the kingdom?

REGAN               To whose hands      55
   You have sent the lunatic king. Speak.

GLOUCESTER

   I have a letter guessingly set down

**64. Wherefore:** why

**67. I ... course:** i.e., **I am** like a bear in a bear-baiting, **tied to a stake,** facing the attack of the dogs, i.e., the **course** (See picture, below.)

**71. anointed:** i.e., with holy oil at his coronation

**73–74. buoyed up ... fires:** i.e., risen up and extinguished the stars **stellèd fires:** (1) starry fires; (2) fixed stars

**75. holp:** helped

**77–78. turn the key:** i.e., let them in

**79. All ... subscribe:** Perhaps: **All** cruel creatures, except for you, give in to feelings of compassion. **subscribe:** submit, yield

**80. wingèd vengeance:** probably, divine **vengeance**

**83. will think:** i.e., hopes, expects

A bear "tied to th' stake." (3.7.67)
From [William Lily,] *Antibossicon* (1521).

Which came from one that's of a neutral heart,
And not from one opposed.

CORNWALL   Cunning.                          60

REGAN   And false.

CORNWALL   Where hast thou sent the King?

GLOUCESTER   To Dover.

REGAN
Wherefore to Dover? Wast thou not charged at
    peril—                                   65

CORNWALL
Wherefore to Dover? Let him answer that.

GLOUCESTER
I am tied to th' stake, and I must stand the course.

REGAN   Wherefore to Dover?

GLOUCESTER
Because I would not see thy cruel nails
Pluck out his poor old eyes, nor thy fierce sister     70
In his anointed flesh stick boarish fangs.
The sea, with such a storm as his bare head
In hell-black night endured, would have buoyed up
And quenched the stellèd fires;
Yet, poor old heart, he holp the heavens to rain.     75
If wolves had at thy gate howled that stern time,
Thou shouldst have said "Good porter, turn the
    key."
All cruels else subscribe. But I shall see
The wingèd vengeance overtake such children.     80

CORNWALL
See 't shalt thou never.—Fellows, hold the chair.—
Upon these eyes of thine I'll set my foot.

GLOUCESTER
He that will think to live till he be old,
Give me some help!

    ⌐*As Servants hold the chair, Cornwall forces out*
                         *one of Gloucester's eyes.*⌐

                O cruel! O you gods!              85

88. **Hold your hand:** stop, refrain
95. **I'd . . . quarrel:** i.e., **I'd** defy you openly in this **cause; What . . . mean?:** an expression of astonishment and disbelief
96. **villain:** servant
97. **chance of anger:** i.e., risks of an angry fight
100. **mischief:** harm, injury
105. **sparks of nature:** i.e., natural feelings (as a son)
106. **quit:** requite, avenge
107. **Out:** i.e., **out** upon you (an interjection expressing abhorrence)
109. **overture:** revelation, disclosure

REGAN
  One side will mock another. Th' other too.
CORNWALL
  If you see vengeance—
⌜FIRST⌝ SERVANT                Hold your hand,
    my lord.
  I have served you ever since I was a child,        90
  But better service have I never done you
  Than now to bid you hold.
REGAN                    How now, you dog?
⌜FIRST⌝ SERVANT
  If you did wear a beard upon your chin,
  I'd shake it on this quarrel. What do you mean?        95
CORNWALL   My villain?            ⟨*Draw and fight.*⟩
⌜FIRST⌝ SERVANT
  Nay, then, come on, and take the chance of anger.
REGAN, ⌜*to an Attendant*⌝
  Give me thy sword. A peasant stand up thus?
                        ⟨*She takes a sword and runs*
                          *at him behind;*⟩ *kills him.*
⌜FIRST⌝ SERVANT
  O, I am slain! My lord, you have one eye left
  To see some mischief on him. O!        ⌜*He dies.*⌝ 100
CORNWALL
  Lest it see more, prevent it. Out, vile jelly!
              ⌜*Forcing out Gloucester's other eye.*⌝
  Where is thy luster now?
GLOUCESTER
  All dark and comfortless! Where's my son
      Edmund?—
  Edmund, enkindle all the sparks of nature        105
  To quit this horrid act.
REGAN                Out, treacherous villain!
  Thou call'st on him that hates thee. It was he
  That made the overture of thy treasons to us,
  Who is too good to pity thee.        110

111. **abused:** wronged
112. **prosper him:** cause him to flourish
115. **How look you:** i.e., **how** are **you**
117. **this slave:** i.e., the dead servant
123. **old:** usual, customary
125. **Bedlam:** i.e., Bedlam beggar, Tom o' Bedlam
126. **would:** wishes to go
126–27. **His . . . anything:** i.e., as a madman-vagabond, he can do **anything** (Anyone else would be punished for helping Gloucester.)   **roguish:** like a vagabond
128. **flax and whites of eggs:** prescribed (in the Renaissance) for wounded eyes

A Bedlam beggar. (1.2.143; 2.3.20; 3.4.43;
3.6.31, 78–79; 3.7.125; 4.1.29, 65, 90)
From *Bagford Ballads*, printed in 1878.

GLOUCESTER
O my follies! Then Edgar was abused.
Kind gods, forgive me that, and prosper him.
REGAN
Go thrust him out at gates, and let him smell
His way to Dover.
⌐*Some Servants*⌐ *exit with Gloucester.*
How is 't, my lord? How look you?    115
CORNWALL
I have received a hurt. Follow me, lady.—
Turn out that eyeless villain. Throw this slave
Upon the dunghill.—Regan, I bleed apace.
Untimely comes this hurt. Give me your arm.
⌐*Cornwall and Regan*⌐ *exit.*
⟨⌐SECOND⌐ SERVANT
I'll never care what wickedness I do    120
If this man come to good.
⌐THIRD⌐ SERVANT                    If she live long
And in the end meet the old course of death,
Women will all turn monsters.
⌐SECOND⌐ SERVANT
Let's follow the old earl and get the Bedlam    125
To lead him where he would. His roguish madness
Allows itself to anything.
⌐THIRD⌐ SERVANT
Go thou. I'll fetch some flax and whites of eggs
To apply to his bleeding face. Now heaven help him!
⌐*They*⌐ *exit.*⟩

*The Tragedy of*

# KING LEAR

ACT 4

**4.1** Edgar, still in disguise as Poor Tom, meets the blinded Gloucester and agrees to lead him to Dover.

---

1. **Yet . . . contemned:** i.e., it is **better to be** a beggar and openly despised
2. **Than . . . flattered:** i.e., **than** to be despised but **flattered**
3. **most dejected thing of:** i.e., the **thing most** cast down by (Edgar, in these lines, alludes to one's place on Fortune's wheel. When one is at the bottom of the wheel—as he thinks he is—the next turn of the wheel must bring one upward **"to laughter"** [line 6]. See pictures, pages 172 and 252.)
4. **still:** always; **esperance:** hope
6. **The . . . laughter:** i.e., any change from the worst is necessarily for the better
9. **Owes nothing to:** i.e., and therefore has **nothing to** fear from
10. **poorly led:** i.e., led by a poor peasant
11–12. **But . . . age:** i.e., **Life** yields **to** old **age** and death only because the **world,** with its strange twists and turns, **makes us hate** it.
16. **Thy comforts:** i.e., the relief that you can offer

# ACT 4

### Scene 1
*Enter Edgar ⌐in disguise.¬*

EDGAR
Yet better thus, and known to be contemned,
Than still contemned and flattered. To be worst,
The lowest and most dejected thing of Fortune,
Stands still in esperance, lives not in fear.
The lamentable change is from the best;                    5
The worst returns to laughter. [Welcome, then,
Thou unsubstantial air that I embrace.
The wretch that thou hast blown unto the worst
Owes nothing to thy blasts.] But who comes here?

*Enter Gloucester and an old man.*

My father, poorly led? World, world, O world,      10
But that thy strange mutations make us hate thee,
Life would not yield to age.

OLD MAN
O my good lord, I have been your tenant
And your father's tenant these fourscore years.

GLOUCESTER
Away, get thee away. Good friend, begone.          15
Thy comforts can do me no good at all;
Thee they may hurt.

OLD MAN                    You cannot see your way.

171

19. **want:** need
21. **Our ... us:** i.e., our resources (while in prosperity) make us careless; **mere defects:** utter deficiencies
22. **commodities:** advantages
23. **abusèd:** deceived
35. **He ... reason:** i.e., he is not completely mad
41. **wanton:** undisciplined
42. **sport:** amusement, fun
44. **trade:** i.e., occupation; **play ... sorrow:** i.e., **play** the role of a **fool** to my grieving father
45. **Ang'ring:** irritating, vexing

Fortune's wheel. (2.2.188–89; 4.1.2–6; 5.3.209)
From [John Lydgate], *The hystorye sege and dystruccyon of Troye* (1513).

GLOUCESTER
I have no way and therefore want no eyes.
I stumbled when I saw. Full oft 'tis seen          20
Our means secure us, and our mere defects
Prove our commodities. O dear son Edgar,
The food of thy abusèd father's wrath,
Might I but live to see thee in my touch,
I'd say I had eyes again.                          25

OLD MAN                    How now? Who's there?

EDGAR, ⌜aside⌝
O gods, who is 't can say "I am at the worst"?
I am worse than e'er I was.

OLD MAN                    'Tis poor mad Tom.

EDGAR, ⌜aside⌝
And worse I may be yet. The worst is not          30
So long as we can say "This is the worst."

OLD MAN
Fellow, where goest?

GLOUCESTER              Is it a beggar-man?

OLD MAN    Madman and beggar too.

GLOUCESTER
He has some reason, else he could not beg.        35
I' th' last night's storm, I such a fellow saw,
Which made me think a man a worm. My son
Came then into my mind, and yet my mind
Was then scarce friends with him. I have heard
    more since.                                    40
As flies to wanton boys are we to th' gods;
They kill us for their sport.

EDGAR, ⌜aside⌝              How should this be?
Bad is the trade that must play fool to sorrow,
Ang'ring itself and others.—Bless thee, master.   45

GLOUCESTER
Is that the naked fellow?

OLD MAN                    Ay, my lord.

GLOUCESTER
⟨Then, prithee,⟩ get thee away. If for my sake

49. **o'ertake us:** i.e., catch up to us; **twain:** two
50. **ancient:** long-established
52. **Which:** i.e., whom
54. **time's plague:** i.e., a sign of the sickness of our time
56. **Above the rest:** i.e., **above** all
57. **'parel:** apparel, clothes
58. **Come . . . will:** whatever the consequences **on 't:** of it
60. **daub it further:** i.e., act my part of Poor Tom anymore   **daub:** literally, cover over with mortar
68–70. **Obidicut, Hobbididance, Mahu, Modo, Flibbertigibbet:** all names for devils based on Harsnett's *Declaration*
70. **mopping and mowing:** grimacing and making faces; **since:** i.e., **since** then
75. **humbled . . . strokes:** i.e., reduced to a humble acceptance of **all** miseries
77. **superfluous . . . man:** he who has more than he needs and who feeds his desires
78. **slaves your ordinance:** enslaves (to his own interest) the divine decree (to share)

Thou wilt o'ertake us hence a mile or twain
I' th' way toward Dover, do it for ancient love,          50
And bring some covering for this naked soul,
Which I'll entreat to lead me.
OLD MAN   Alack, sir, he is mad.
GLOUCESTER
'Tis the time's plague when madmen lead the blind.
Do as I bid thee, or rather do thy pleasure.          55
Above the rest, begone.
OLD MAN
I'll bring him the best 'parel that I have,
Come on 't what will.                    *He exits.*
GLOUCESTER          Sirrah, naked fellow—
EDGAR
Poor Tom's a-cold. ⌈*Aside.*⌉ I cannot daub it further.   60
GLOUCESTER   Come hither, fellow.
EDGAR, ⌈*aside*⌉
And yet I must.—Bless thy sweet eyes, they bleed.
GLOUCESTER   Know'st thou the way to Dover?
EDGAR   Both stile and gate, horseway and footpath.
Poor Tom hath been ⟨scared⟩ out of his good wits.   65
Bless thee, good man's son, from the foul fiend.
⟨Five fiends have been in Poor Tom at once: of lust,
as Obidicut; Hobbididance, prince of dumbness;
Mahu, of stealing; Modo, of murder; ⌈Flibbertigib-
bet,⌉ of ⌈mopping⌉ and ⌈mowing,⌉ who since pos-   70
sesses chambermaids and waiting women. So, bless
thee, master.⟩
GLOUCESTER, ⌈*giving him money*⌉
Here, take this purse, thou whom the heavens'
    plagues
Have humbled to all strokes. That I am wretched   75
Makes thee the happier. Heavens, deal so still:
Let the superfluous and lust-dieted man,
That slaves your ordinance, that will not see
Because he does not feel, feel your power quickly.

83. **bending:** overhanging
84. **fearfully:** frighteningly; **in . . . deep:** i.e., into the waters of the English Channel, **confinèd** in the Straits of Dover between England's cliffs and France's shore
87. **rich:** i.e., valuable; **about me:** i.e., that I have with me

**4.2** Goneril and Edmund arrive at Albany and Goneril's castle. After Goneril has sent Edmund back to Cornwall, Albany enters and fiercely rebukes Goneril for her treatment of Lear. A messenger reports Gloucester's blinding and the death of the duke of Cornwall.

---

2. **Not met:** i.e., did not meet
10. **sot:** dolt, fool
12. **pleasant:** pleasing
13. **What like:** i.e., **what** he should **like**

So distribution should undo excess 80
And each man have enough. Dost thou know Dover?
EDGAR Ay, master.
GLOUCESTER
There is a cliff, whose high and bending head
Looks fearfully in the confinèd deep.
Bring me but to the very brim of it, 85
And I'll repair the misery thou dost bear
With something rich about me. From that place
I shall no leading need.
EDGAR                    Give me thy arm.
Poor Tom shall lead thee. 90
                                          *They exit.*

## Scene 2
*Enter Goneril and ⌜Edmund, the⌝ Bastard.*

GONERIL
Welcome, my lord. I marvel our mild husband
Not met us on the way.
            ⟨*Enter ⌜Oswald, the⌝ Steward.*⟩
                              Now, where's your master?
OSWALD
Madam, within, but never man so changed.
I told him of the army that was landed; 5
He smiled at it. I told him you were coming;
His answer was "The worse." Of Gloucester's
    treachery
And of the loyal service of his son
When I informed him, then he called me "sot" 10
And told me I had turned the wrong side out.
What most he should dislike seems pleasant to him;
What like, offensive.
GONERIL, ⌜*to Edmund*⌝   Then shall you go no further.

15. **cowish:** cowardly
16. **undertake:** commit himself to an enterprise; **feel wrongs:** i.e., acknowledge offenses
17. **tie ... answer:** i.e., would require him to retaliate; **wishes ... way:** hopes expressed during our journey
18. **prove effects:** i.e., be fulfilled; **brother:** i.e., brother-in-law, Cornwall
19. **musters:** gathering of soldiers; **powers:** troops
20. **change names:** i.e., exchange roles with Albany; **distaff:** spinning staff (See picture, page 184.)
22. **like:** i.e., likely
29. **Conceive:** i.e., understand (my unspoken meaning)
35. **My fool:** i.e., my husband, who is a **fool; usurps:** possesses forcibly and without right
37. **worth the whistle:** Proverbial: "It is a poor dog that is not **worth the** whistling."
40. **fear your disposition:** am fearful about your nature
41. **contemns:** despises
42. **Cannot ... itself: cannot be** securely contained within **itself;** or, can have no reliable boundaries
43–44. **herself will sliver ... sap:** i.e., tear herself away (from Lear) as if she were a branch tearing itself away from the tree that sustains it (See picture, page 192.)
45. **deadly use:** i.e., destruction (of herself and others)
46. **text:** i.e., theme of your sermon

It is the cowish terror of his spirit,                    15
That dares not undertake. He'll not feel wrongs
Which tie him to an answer. Our wishes on the way
May prove effects. Back, Edmund, to my brother.
Hasten his musters and conduct his powers.
I must change names at home and give the distaff      20
Into my husband's hands. This trusty servant
Shall pass between us. Ere long you are like to
    hear—
If you dare venture in your own behalf—
A mistress's command. Wear this; spare speech.       25
                              ⌜*She gives him a favor.*⌝
Decline your head. ⌜*She kisses him.*⌝ This kiss, if it
    durst speak,
Would stretch thy spirits up into the air.
Conceive, and fare thee well.
EDMUND
Yours in the ranks of death.          *He exits.*   30
GONERIL                          My most dear
    Gloucester!
[O, the difference of man and man!]
To thee a woman's services are due;
My fool usurps my body.                               35
OSWALD   Madam, here comes my lord.   ⟨*He exits.*⟩

                *Enter Albany.*

GONERIL
I have been worth the whistle.
ALBANY                          O Goneril,
You are not worth the dust which the rude wind
Blows in your face. ⟨I fear your disposition.          40
That nature which contemns its origin
Cannot be bordered certain in itself.
She that herself will sliver and disbranch
From her material sap perforce must wither
And come to deadly use.                               45
GONERIL   No more. The text is foolish.

51. **head-lugged:** tugged by the head (hence, bad-tempered)

53. **barbarous, degenerate:** i.e., barbarously, degenerately

54. **madded:** driven mad

55. **brother:** i.e., brother-in-law; **suffer:** allow

62. **Milk-livered:** i.e., white-livered, cowardly

63. **bear'st . . . blows:** i.e., when you are struck, you turn the other **cheek**

64–65. **discerning . . . suffering:** which can tell the difference between what must be resisted in the defense of your **honor** and what may be permitted (i.e., suffered)

66–67. **Fools . . . mischief:** i.e., only **fools** have **pity** on **villains who are punished** before **they** can do harm

69. **France:** i.e., the king of France; **noiseless:** quiet, peaceful

70. **helm:** helmet; **thy . . . threat:** i.e., begins to threaten your power

71. **moral:** i.e., moralizing

74–75. **Proper . . . woman:** i.e., the ugliness that is **proper** (appropriate) for the devil **shows** (appears) more horrible **in a woman**

76. **vain:** idle, useless

77. **changèd:** transformed; **self-covered thing:** i.e., your true nature as a fiend concealed by your womanly appearance; or, perhaps, your true nature as a woman now covered up by your fiendishness

78. **Bemonster . . . feature:** i.e., do not deform yourself into a monster  **feature:** shape; **my fitness:** appropriate for me

79. **blood:** feelings

ALBANY
Wisdom and goodness to the vile seem vile.
Filths savor but themselves. What have you done?
Tigers, not daughters, what have you performed?
A father, and a gracious agèd man,                    50
Whose reverence even the head-lugged bear would
    lick,
Most barbarous, most degenerate, have you
    madded.
Could my good brother suffer you to do it?            55
A man, a prince, by him so benefited!
If that the heavens do not their visible spirits
Send quickly down to tame ⌜these⌝ vile offenses,
It will come:
Humanity must perforce prey on itself,                60
Like monsters of the deep.⟩
GONERIL                        Milk-livered man,
That bear'st a cheek for blows, a head for wrongs;
Who hast not in thy brows an eye discerning
Thine honor from thy suffering; ⟨that not know'st    65
Fools do those villains pity who are punished
Ere they have done their mischief. Where's thy
    drum?
France spreads his banners in our noiseless land,
With plumèd helm thy state begins ⌜to threat,⌝        70
Whilst thou, a moral fool, sits still and cries
"Alack, why does he so?"⟩
ALBANY                        See thyself, devil!
Proper deformity ⟨shows⟩ not in the fiend
So horrid as in woman.                                75
GONERIL                O vain fool!
⟨ALBANY
Thou changèd and self-covered thing, for shame
Bemonster not thy feature. Were 't my fitness
To let these hands obey my blood,
They are apt enough to dislocate and tear            80

81. **Howe'er:** i.e., however much
82. **shield:** i.e., protect you (from violence at my hands)
83. **Marry:** i.e., indeed; **mew:** a sound of derision
86. **going to:** i.e., as Cornwall was **going to**
89. **he bred:** i.e., Cornwall raised; **thrilled with remorse:** pierced with compassion
90. **Opposed against:** i.e., stood in opposition to
90–91. **bending . . . To:** i.e., turning **his sword** against
92. **amongst them:** i.e., in a melee; or, between them (Cornwall and Regan)
93–94. **But . . . after:** i.e., **but not before** Cornwall suffered the wound that has since killed **him**
96. **justicers:** i.e., heavenly justices
96–97. **our . . . venge:** i.e., can so quickly avenge the **crimes** committed in our world beneath the heavens
102. **One way . . . well:** i.e., in **one way I** am glad to hear that Cornwall is dead
103. **But . . . widow:** i.e., **but** Regan now **being** a **widow**
104. **all . . . pluck:** i.e., pull down the dreams I have constructed
106. **tart:** sour

Thy flesh and bones. Howe'er thou art a fiend,
A woman's shape doth shield thee.
GONERIL    Marry, your manhood, mew—⟩

*Enter a Messenger.*

⟨ALBANY    What news?⟩
MESSENGER
O, my good lord, the Duke of Cornwall's dead,    85
Slain by his servant, going to put out
The other eye of Gloucester.
ALBANY                    Gloucester's eyes?
MESSENGER
A servant that he bred, thrilled with remorse,
Opposed against the act, bending his sword    90
To his great master, who, ⟨thereat⟩ enraged,
Flew on him and amongst them felled him dead,
But not without that harmful stroke which since
Hath plucked him after.
ALBANY                    This shows you are above,    95
You ⟨justicers,⟩ that these our nether crimes
So speedily can venge. But, O poor Gloucester,
Lost he his other eye?
MESSENGER              Both, both, my lord.—
This letter, madam, craves a speedy answer.    100
⌜*Giving her a paper.*⌝
'Tis from your sister.
GONERIL, ⌜*aside*⌝      One way I like this well.
But being widow and my Gloucester with her
May all the building in my fancy pluck
Upon my hateful life. Another way    105
The news is not so tart.—I'll read, and answer.
⟨*She exits.*⟩
ALBANY
Where was his son when they did take his eyes?
MESSENGER
Come with my lady hither.

110. **back:** i.e., going **back**

**4.3** In the French camp Kent and a Gentleman discuss Cordelia's love of Lear, which has brought her back to Britain at the head of the French army; they say that Lear is in the town of Dover, and that, though he is sometimes sane, his shame at his earlier action makes him refuse to see Cordelia.

---

5. **imports:** i.e., would cause
8. **general:** i.e., as **general**
14. **trilled:** rolled
16. **passion, who:** i.e., emotion, which

Woman with a distaff. (4.2.20)
From Johann Engel, *Astrolabium* . . . (1488).

ALBANY He is not here.
MESSENGER
No, my good lord. I met him back again. 110
ALBANY Knows he the wickedness?
MESSENGER
Ay, my good lord. 'Twas he informed against him
And quit the house on purpose, that their punishment
Might have the freer course.
ALBANY Gloucester, I live 115
To thank thee for the love thou show'd'st the King,
And to revenge thine eyes.—Come hither, friend.
Tell me what more thou know'st.
*They exit.*


⌜Scene 3⌝
⟨*Enter Kent* ⌜*in disguise*⌝ *and a Gentleman.*

KENT Why the King of France is so suddenly gone
back know you no reason?
GENTLEMAN Something he left imperfect in the state,
which since his coming forth is thought of, which
imports to the kingdom so much fear and danger 5
that his personal return was most required and
necessary.
KENT Who hath he left behind him general?
GENTLEMAN The Marshal of France, Monsieur La Far.
KENT Did your letters pierce the Queen to any demon- 10
stration of grief?
GENTLEMAN
Ay, ⌜sir,⌝ she took them, read them in my
presence,
And now and then an ample tear trilled down
Her delicate cheek. It seemed she was a queen 15
Over her passion, who, most rebel-like,
Fought to be king o'er her.
KENT O, then it moved her.

19. **Patience:** self-control
20. **Who ... goodliest:** i.e., about which would make her appear most beautiful
22. **like:** i.e., **like** sunshine and rain; **a better way:** i.e., but more lovely
24. **which:** i.e., the tears
26. **rarity most beloved:** i.e., something precious and sought after
27. **If ... it:** i.e., if sorrow could be so becoming to others
28. **Made ... question?:** i.e., did she say anything?
34. **believed:** i.e., **believed** to exist
36. **clamor moistened:** i.e., **moistened** her outburst of grief with tears
39. **conditions:** mental dispositions
40–41. **Else ... issues:** i.e., otherwise the same couple could not conceive **such different** offspring **self:** same **make:** mate, partner **issues:** offspring
44. **King:** i.e., of France; **returned:** i.e., to France
47. **better tune:** i.e., less jangled, more rational, state

GENTLEMAN
Not to a rage. Patience and sorrow ⌜strove⌝
Who should express her goodliest. You have seen          20
Sunshine and rain at once; her smiles and tears
Were like a better way. Those happy smilets
That played on her ripe lip ⌜seemed⌝ not to know
What guests were in her eyes, which parted thence
As pearls from diamonds dropped. In brief,          25
Sorrow would be a rarity most beloved
If all could so become it.
KENT     Made she no verbal question?
GENTLEMAN
Faith, once or twice she heaved the name of
"father"          30
Pantingly forth, as if it pressed her heart;
Cried "Sisters, sisters, shame of ladies, sisters!
Kent, father, sisters! What, i' th' storm, i' th' night?
Let pity not be believed!" There she shook
The holy water from her heavenly eyes,          35
And clamor moistened. Then away she started,
To deal with grief alone.
KENT                    It is the stars.
The stars above us govern our conditions,
Else one self mate and make could not beget          40
Such different issues. You spoke not with her
    since?
GENTLEMAN  No.
KENT
Was this before the King returned?
GENTLEMAN                    No, since.          45
KENT
Well, sir, the poor distressèd Lear's i' th' town,
Who sometime in his better tune remembers
What we are come about, and by no means
Will yield to see his daughter.
GENTLEMAN                    Why, good sir?          50

51. **sovereign:** overpowering; **elbows him:** i.e., jostles (his mind)

53. **from his benediction:** i.e., of his blessing

53–54. **turned ... casualties:** i.e., sent **her** away to take her chances in a **foreign** land

59. **powers:** armed forces

60. **afoot:** i.e., on the march

62. **attend:** wait upon; **dear:** important

64. **aright:** i.e., as Kent

64–65. **grieve / Lending me:** i.e., regret having extended to me

**4.4** In the French camp Cordelia orders out a search party for Lear.

---

0 SD. **Drum and Colors:** i.e., drummers and soldiers carrying banners

3–5. **fumiter, furrow-weeds, hardocks, hemlock, nettles, cuckooflowers, Darnel:** Most of these weeds and plants may be called **idle** (i.e., worthless), but some (e.g., **fumiter**) were used as medicines for diseases of the brain.

6. **our sustaining corn:** wheat, which gives us sustenance; **A century:** a troop of one hundred soldiers

9. **What ... wisdom:** i.e., **what can** human knowledge do

KENT
 A sovereign shame so elbows him—his own
  unkindness,
 That stripped her from his benediction, turned her
 To foreign casualties, gave her dear rights
 To his dog-hearted daughters—these things sting  55
 His mind so venomously that burning shame
 Detains him from Cordelia.
GENTLEMAN Alack, poor gentleman!
KENT
 Of Albany's and Cornwall's powers you heard not?
GENTLEMAN 'Tis so. They are afoot.  60
KENT
 Well, sir, I'll bring you to our master Lear
 And leave you to attend him. Some dear cause
 Will in conccalment wrap me up awhile.
 When I am known aright, you shall not grieve
 Lending me this acquaintance. I pray you, go  65
 Along with me.
          ⌜*They*⌝ *exit.*⟩


      Scene ⌜4⌝
  *Enter with Drum and Colors, Cordelia, ⟨Doctor,⟩*
    *Gentlemen, and Soldiers.*

CORDELIA
 Alack, 'tis he! Why, he was met even now
 As mad as the vexed sea, singing aloud,
 Crowned with rank fumiter and furrow-weeds,
 With hardocks, hemlock, nettles, cuckooflowers,
 Darnel, and all the idle weeds that grow  5
 In our sustaining corn. A century send forth.
 Search every acre in the high-grown field
 And bring him to our eye.   ⌜*Soldiers exit.*⌝
     What can man's wisdom

10. **his bereavèd sense:** i.e., his mind, of which he is bereaved

11. **outward worth:** i.e., wealth

14–15. **That . . . operative:** i.e., there are many medicinal plants or herbs (**simples**) that will be effective (**operative**) in inducing sleep in him

18. **unpublished:** perhaps, hidden; or, unknown; **virtues:** healing powers

19. **Spring:** grow; **Be . . . remediate:** i.e., be aids and remedies

21. **rage:** madness

22. **wants the means:** i.e., lacks the resources

29. **importuned:** importuning, pleading

30. **blown:** puffed-up, swollen; **our arms incite:** i.e., lead us to make war

**4.5** Regan questions Oswald about Goneril and Edmund, states her intention to marry Edmund, and asks Oswald to dissuade Goneril from pursuing Edmund.

---

1. **my brother's powers:** i.e., Albany's armies

In the restoring his bereavèd sense?                    10
He that helps him take all my outward worth.
⟨DOCTOR⟩    There is means, madam.
Our foster nurse of nature is repose,
The which he lacks. That to provoke in him
Are many simples operative, whose power         15
Will close the eye of anguish.
CORDELIA                                   All blest secrets,
All you unpublished virtues of the earth,
Spring with my tears. Be aidant and remediate
In the good man's ⟨distress.⟩ Seek, seek for him,     20
Lest his ungoverned rage dissolve the life
That wants the means to lead it.

*Enter Messenger.*

MESSENGER                              News, madam.
The British powers are marching hitherward.
CORDELIA
'Tis known before. Our preparation stands        25
In expectation of them.—O dear father,
It is thy business that I go about.
Therefore great France
My mourning and importuned tears hath pitied.
No blown ambition doth our arms incite,          30
But love, dear love, and our aged father's right.
Soon may I hear and see him.
                                        *They exit.*


                    Scene ⌈5⌉
        *Enter Regan and* ⌈*Oswald, the*⌉ *Steward.*

REGAN
But are my brother's powers set forth?
OSWALD                                   Ay, madam.
REGAN    Himself in person there?

4. **ado:** fuss and trouble

8. **What . . . letter:** i.e., **what** could **my sister's letter** say?

10. **is posted hence:** has hurried away

15. **nighted:** i.e., made as dark as night; **descry:** discover by observation

21. **charged my duty:** i.e., exhorted me to be dutiful

23. **Belike:** probably; or, possibly

28. **at . . . here:** when she was **here** recently

29. **eliads:** oeillades, loving glances

30. **of her bosom:** in her confidence

32. **Y' are:** i.e., you are

"She that herself will . . . disbranch. . . ." (4.2.43)
From Henry Peacham, *Minerua Britanna* . . . (1612).

OSWALD    Madam, with much ado.
Your sister is the better soldier.                                    5
REGAN
Lord Edmund spake not with your lord at home?
OSWALD    No, madam.
REGAN
What might import my sister's letter to him?
OSWALD    I know not, lady.
REGAN
Faith, he is posted hence on serious matter.          10
It was great ignorance, Gloucester's eyes being out,
To let him live. Where he arrives he moves
All hearts against us. Edmund, I think, is gone,
In pity of his misery, to dispatch
His nighted life; moreover to descry                      15
The strength o' th' enemy.
OSWALD
I must needs after him, madam, with my letter.
REGAN
Our troops set forth tomorrow. Stay with us.
The ways are dangerous.
OSWALD                          I may not, madam.            20
My lady charged my duty in this business.
REGAN
Why should she write to Edmund? Might not you
Transport her purposes by word? Belike,
Some things—I know not what. I'll love thee much—
Let me unseal the letter.                                          25
OSWALD                    Madam, I had rather—
REGAN
I know your lady does not love her husband;
I am sure of that; and at her late being here,
She gave strange eliads and most speaking looks
To noble Edmund. I know you are of her bosom.       30
OSWALD    I, madam?
REGAN
I speak in understanding. Y' are; I know 't.

33. **take this note:** i.e., **take** note of the following
35–36. **more . . . lady's:** i.e., it is **more** appropriate that **he** marry me **than** Goneril
36. **gather:** infer, guess
37. **this:** Editors and readers can only guess what Regan is sending to Edmund.
38. **thus much:** i.e., what I am telling you
39. **call . . . her:** i.e., **call** back **her** good sense

**4.6** To cure Gloucester of despair, Edgar pretends to aid him in a suicide attempt, a fall from Dover Cliff to the beach far below. When Gloucester wakes from his faint, Edgar (now in the disguise of a peasant) tells him that the gods intervened to save his life. The two meet the mad Lear, who talks with Gloucester about lechery, abuses of power, and other human follies. Lear runs off when some of Cordelia's search party come upon him. When Oswald appears and tries to kill Gloucester, Edgar kills Oswald and finds on his body a letter from Goneril to Edmund plotting Albany's death.

---

1. **that same hill:** the **hill** to which I asked to be led
8. **By:** i.e., because of

Therefore I do advise you take this note:
My lord is dead; Edmund and I have talked,
And more convenient is he for my hand          35
Than for your lady's. You may gather more.
If you do find him, pray you, give him this,
And when your mistress hears thus much from you,
I pray, desire her call her wisdom to her.
So, fare you well.          40
If you do chance to hear of that blind traitor,
Preferment falls on him that cuts him off.

OSWALD
Would I could meet ⟨him,⟩ madam. I should show
What party I do follow.

REGAN                    Fare thee well.          45

*They exit.*


Scene ⌈6⌉
*Enter Gloucester and Edgar ⌈dressed as a peasant.⌉*

GLOUCESTER
When shall I come to th' top of that same hill?

EDGAR
You do climb up it now. Look how we labor.

GLOUCESTER
Methinks the ground is even.

EDGAR                    Horrible steep.
Hark, do you hear the sea?          5

GLOUCESTER                    No, truly.

EDGAR
Why then, your other senses grow imperfect
By your eyes' anguish.

GLOUCESTER          So may it be indeed.
Methinks thy voice is altered and thou speak'st          10
In better phrase and matter than thou didst.

17. **so low:** i.e., so far down
18. **wing . . . air:** i.e., are flying halfway down
19. **gross:** large
20. **samphire:** an aromatic herb; **dreadful:** terrifying
23–24. **bark . . . buoy:** i.e., ship appears no larger than its cockboat (a small ship's boat), and her cockboat appears the size **of a buoy**
25. **for sight:** i.e., to be seen
26. **unnumbered:** innumerable; **pebble:** pebbles (of the beach)
28–29. **the . . . Topple:** i.e., the unsteadiness of my perception causes me to **topple**
33. **upright:** i.e., up into the air
35. **'s:** i.e., is
37. **Prosper . . . thee:** i.e., make it increase and make you **prosper**

EDGAR
 You're much deceived; in nothing am I changed
 But in my garments.
GLOUCESTER                   Methinks you're better spoken.
EDGAR
 Come on, sir. Here's the place. Stand still. How          15
     fearful
 And dizzy 'tis to cast one's eyes so low!
 The crows and choughs that wing the midway air
 Show scarce so gross as beetles. Halfway down
 Hangs one that gathers samphire—dreadful trade;         20
 Methinks he seems no bigger than his head.
 The fishermen that ⟨walk⟩ upon the beach
 Appear like mice, and yond tall anchoring bark
 Diminished to her cock, her cock a buoy
 Almost too small for sight. The murmuring surge          25
 That on th' unnumbered idle pebble chafes
 Cannot be heard so high. I'll look no more
 Lest my brain turn and the deficient sight
 Topple down headlong.
GLOUCESTER                   Set me where you stand.       30
EDGAR
 Give me your hand. You are now within a foot
 Of th' extreme verge. For all beneath the moon
 Would I not leap upright.
GLOUCESTER                   Let go my hand.
 Here, friend, 's another purse; in it a jewel            35
 Well worth a poor man's taking. Fairies and gods
 Prosper it with thee.       ⌜*He gives Edgar a purse.*⌝
                       Go thou further off.
 Bid me farewell, and let me hear thee going.
EDGAR, ⌜*walking away*⌝
 Now fare you well, good sir.                              40
GLOUCESTER                   With all my heart.
EDGAR, ⌜*aside*⌝
 Why I do trifle thus with his despair
 Is done to cure it.

**48. To quarrel with:** i.e., into rebellion against; **opposeless:** irresistible

**49–50. My snuff . . . out:** i.e., my useless and despised life could end itself naturally   **snuff:** partially burnt candle wick   **part:** remainder

**53. conceit:** imagination, thought

**55. Yields to:** i.e., cooperates in

**58. pass:** die

**59. What:** i.e., who

**61. aught:** anything

**63. Thou 'dst shivered:** i.e., you would have broken to pieces

**65. heavy:** i.e., solid

**67. at each:** end to end

**71. chalky bourn:** i.e., chalk cliff (of Dover)

**72. a-height:** high; **shrill-gorged:** shrill-throated, shrill-voiced

**77. beguile:** foil, cheat

GLOUCESTER          O you mighty gods!     ⟨*He kneels.*⟩
This world I do renounce, and in your sights          45
Shake patiently my great affliction off.
If I could bear it longer, and not fall
To quarrel with your great opposeless wills,
My snuff and loathèd part of nature should
Burn itself out. If Edgar live, O, bless him!—          50
Now, fellow, fare thee well.          ⟨*He falls.*⟩
EDGAR          Gone, sir. Farewell.—
And yet I know not how conceit may rob
The treasury of life, when life itself
Yields to the theft. Had he been where he thought,          55
By this had thought been past. Alive or dead?—
Ho you, sir! Friend, hear you. Sir, speak.—
Thus might he pass indeed. Yet he revives.—
What are you, sir?
GLOUCESTER          Away, and let me die.          60
EDGAR
Hadst thou been aught but gossamer, feathers, air,
So many fathom down precipitating,
Thou 'dst shivered like an egg; but thou dost
     breathe,
Hast heavy substance, bleed'st not, speak'st, art          65
     sound.
Ten masts at each make not the altitude
Which thou hast perpendicularly fell.
Thy life's a miracle. Speak yet again.
GLOUCESTER     But have I fall'n or no?          70
EDGAR
From the dread summit of this chalky bourn.
Look up a-height. The shrill-gorged lark so far
Cannot be seen or heard. Do but look up.
GLOUCESTER     Alack, I have no eyes.
Is wretchedness deprived that benefit          75
To end itself by death? 'Twas yet some comfort
When misery could beguile the tyrant's rage
And frustrate his proud will.

88. **whelked:** twisted
89. **happy father:** fortunate old man
90–92. **clearest . . . impossibilities:** i.e., most serene **gods, who** win veneration by doing what humans cannot do
94–95. **till . . . die:** i.e., until it ends; or, until I **die**
98. **free:** innocent (i.e., guilt-free); carefree
100–101. **safer sense . . . thus:** i.e., a sane mind will never allow its possessor to dress in this way
102. **touch:** censure; **coining:** making or issuing money
104. **side-piercing:** heartrending
106. **press-money:** money paid a new recruit upon enlistment (Lear speaks as if he were a recruiting officer.)
106–7. **like a crowkeeper:** i.e., inexpertly, like someone guarding a cornfield from crows
107. **Draw . . . yard:** i.e., draw your bow to a full arrow's length (the length of **a clothier's yard**)

EDGAR                    Give me your arm.
                    ⌈*He raises Gloucester.*⌉
Up. So, how is 't? Feel you your legs? You stand.          80
GLOUCESTER
Too well, too well.
EDGAR                    This is above all strangeness.
Upon the crown o' th' cliff, what thing was that
Which parted from you?
GLOUCESTER          A poor unfortunate beggar.          85
EDGAR
As I stood here below, methought his eyes
Were two full moons; he had a thousand noses,
Horns whelked and waved like the enragèd sea.
It was some fiend. Therefore, thou happy father,
Think that the clearest gods, who make them          90
    honors
Of men's impossibilities, have preserved thee.
GLOUCESTER
I do remember now. Henceforth I'll bear
Affliction till it do cry out itself
"Enough, enough!" and die. That thing you speak of,          95
I took it for a man. Often 'twould say
"The fiend, the fiend!" He led me to that place.
EDGAR
Bear free and patient thoughts.

                    *Enter Lear.*

                    But who comes here?
The safer sense will ne'er accommodate          100
His master thus.
LEAR   No, they cannot touch me for ⟨coining.⟩ I am the
    King himself.
EDGAR   O, thou side-piercing sight!
LEAR   Nature's above art in that respect. There's your          105
    press-money. That fellow handles his bow like a
    crowkeeper. Draw me a clothier's yard. Look, look,

109. **prove it:** make it good, **prove** its worth
110. **brown bills:** i.e., soldiers carrying **brown bills** (weapons painted brown to prevent rust); **O, well flown, bird:** perhaps referring to the flight of an (imaginary) arrow
111. **clout:** bull's-eye; **Hewgh:** possibly, the sound of an arrow in flight; **word:** password
116. **like a dog:** i.e., as if they were dogs fawning on me; **white hairs:** representing wisdom
119. **divinity:** theology (Compare James 5.12: "Let your yea be yea and your nay, nay.")
122. **found:** exposed; **Go to:** an expression of impatience
124. **ague-proof:** immune to chills and fevers (**Ague** is pronounced ay-gue.)
125. **trick:** peculiarity
129. **thy cause:** the accusation against you
132. **lecher:** play the lecher (i.e., copulate)
134. **got:** begotten, conceived
135. **luxury:** lechery
136–37. **whose . . . snow:** i.e., whose looks predict a cold (i.e., icily chaste) response **forks:** perhaps, instruments for propping up a woman's hair; or, perhaps, legs
137. **minces virtue:** enacts virtue mincingly (i.e., in an affected way)
138. **The fitchew:** i.e., neither the polecat
139. **soiled:** perhaps, put out to stud; or, perhaps, lively because fed with green fodder
140. **centaurs:** mythological monsters that were bestial below the waist (See picture, page 206.)
141. **girdle:** i.e., waist
142. **inherit:** possess

a mouse! Peace, peace! This piece of toasted cheese
will do 't. There's my gauntlet; I'll prove it on a
giant. Bring up the brown bills. O, well flown, bird!    110
I' th' clout, i' th' clout! Hewgh! Give the word.
EDGAR  Sweet marjoram.
LEAR  Pass.
GLOUCESTER  I know that voice.
LEAR  Ha! Goneril with a white beard? They flattered    115
me like a dog and told me I had the white hairs in
my beard ere the black ones were there. To say "ay"
and "no" to everything that I said "ay" and "no" to
was no good divinity. When the rain came to wet me
once and the wind to make me chatter, when the    120
thunder would not peace at my bidding, there I
found 'em, there I smelt 'em out. Go to. They are
not men o' their words; they told me I was everything. 'Tis a lie. I am not ague-proof.
GLOUCESTER
The trick of that voice I do well remember.    125
Is 't not the King?
LEAR                    Ay, every inch a king.
When I do stare, see how the subject quakes.
I pardon that man's life. What was thy cause?
Adultery? Thou shalt not die. Die for adultery? No.    130
The wren goes to 't, and the small gilded fly does
lecher in my sight. Let copulation thrive, for
Gloucester's bastard son was kinder to his father
than my daughters got 'tween the lawful sheets. To
't, luxury, pell-mell, for I lack soldiers. Behold yond    135
simp'ring dame, whose face between her forks
presages snow, that minces virtue and does shake
the head to hear of pleasure's name. The fitchew
nor the soiled horse goes to 't with a more riotous
appetite. Down from the waist they are centaurs,    140
though women all above. But to the girdle do the
gods inherit; beneath is all the fiend's. There's hell,

145. **civet:** musky perfume; **apothecary:** pharmacist
150. **so:** in the same way
152. **squinny:** squint; **Cupid:** the god of love, often depicted as blindfolded (See picture, page 208.)
156. **take:** believe, credit; **It is:** i.e., **it is** actually taking place
159. **case:** i.e., sockets
160. **are . . . me:** i.e., **are you with me** concerning this matter
162. **heavy case:** sad condition; **in a light:** i.e., empty
164. **feelingly:** by touch; through my feelings
167. **simple:** humble, ordinary
168. **handy-dandy:** a trick in which one asks a child to choose which of one's hands holds a treat
173. **image:** likeness, model
173–74. **a dog's . . . office:** i.e., even a dog is **obeyed** when it's in a position of power

there's darkness, there is the sulphurous pit; burn-
ing, scalding, stench, consumption! Fie, fie, fie, pah,
pah! Give me an ounce of civet, good apothecary;     145
sweeten my imagination. There's money for thee.
GLOUCESTER     O, let me kiss that hand!
LEAR     Let me wipe it first; it smells of mortality.
GLOUCESTER
O ruined piece of nature! This great world
Shall so wear out to naught. Dost thou know me?     150
LEAR     I remember thine eyes well enough. Dost thou
squinny at me? No, do thy worst, blind Cupid, I'll
not love. Read thou this challenge. Mark but the
penning of it.
GLOUCESTER
Were all thy letters suns, I could not see.     155
EDGAR, ⌜*aside*⌝
I would not take this from report. It is,
And my heart breaks at it.
LEAR     Read.
GLOUCESTER     What, with the case of eyes?
LEAR     O ho, are you there with me? No eyes in your     160
head, nor no money in your purse? Your eyes are in
a heavy case, your purse in a light, yet you see how
this world goes.
GLOUCESTER     I see it feelingly.
LEAR     What, art mad? A man may see how this world     165
goes with no eyes. Look with thine ears. See how
yond justice rails upon yond simple thief. Hark in
thine ear. Change places and, handy-dandy, which
is the justice, which is the thief? Thou hast seen a
farmer's dog bark at a beggar?     170
GLOUCESTER     Ay, sir.
LEAR     And the creature run from the cur? There thou
might'st behold the great image of authority: a
dog's obeyed in office.

175. **beadle:** inferior parish officer responsible for punishing petty offenders

177. **kind:** way

178. **usurer:** moneylender

179. **cozener:** cheat, fraud, impostor

181–82. **Plate . . . gold:** literally, cover **sin with gold** armor plate

183. **hurtless:** i.e., harmlessly

185. **able:** authorize; vouch for

192. **matter and impertinency:** sense and absurdity

198. **Mark:** pay attention

201. **This':** i.e., this is; **block:** style of hat

202. **delicate:** wonderfully ingenious

203. **put 't in proof:** i.e., **put** it to the test

A centaur. (4.6.140)
From Gabriel Rollenhagen, *Nucleus emblematum selectissimorum* . . . (1611).

Thou rascal beadle, hold thy bloody hand!      175
Why dost thou lash that whore? Strip thy own back.
Thou hotly lusts to use her in that kind
For which thou whipp'st her. The usurer hangs the
    cozener.
Through tattered clothes ⟨small⟩ vices do appear.     180
Robes and furred gowns hide all. [⌜Plate sin⌝ with
    gold,
And the strong lance of justice hurtless breaks.
Arm it in rags, a pygmy's straw does pierce it.
None does offend, none, I say, none; I'll able 'em.     185
Take that of me, my friend, who have the power
To seal th' accuser's lips.] Get thee glass eyes,
And like a scurvy politician
Seem to see the things thou dost not. Now, now,
    now, now.                                     190
Pull off my boots. Harder, harder. So.
EDGAR, ⌜*aside*⌝
O, matter and impertinency mixed,
Reason in madness!
LEAR
If thou wilt weep my fortunes, take my eyes.
I know thee well enough; thy name is Gloucester.    195
Thou must be patient. We came crying hither;
Thou know'st the first time that we smell the air
We wawl and cry. I will preach to thee. Mark.
GLOUCESTER    Alack, alack the day!
LEAR
When we are born, we cry that we are come      200
To this great stage of fools.—This' a good block.
It were a delicate stratagem to shoe
A troop of horse with felt. I'll put 't in proof,
And when I have stol'n upon these son-in-laws,
Then kill, kill, kill, kill, kill, kill!                    205

         *Enter a Gentleman* ⌜*and Attendants.*⌝

**210. natural fool of Fortune:** one born to be the plaything **of Fortune**

**214. seconds:** attendants, supporters

**215. of salt:** i.e., of tears

**218. bravely:** (1) courageously; (2) gorgeously dressed; **smug:** neat, trim in appearance

**222. an:** if

**223. Sa . . . sa:** a cry to hunting dogs to chase their prey

**224. meanest:** of lowest degree, poorest

**226. general:** universal

**227. her:** i.e., nature

**228. gentle:** noble

**229. speed:** i.e., God **speed** (May God make you prosper!)

**230. toward:** about to happen

**231. vulgar:** of common knowledge

**231–32. Everyone . . . sound:** i.e., **everyone** who can **hear hears** of the **battle** (line 230)

"Blind Cupid." (4.6.152)
Anonymous engraving inserted in Jacques Callot,
*La petite passion* . . . (n.d.).

GENTLEMAN, ⌐*noticing Lear*⌐
  O, here he is. ⌐*To an Attendant.*⌐ Lay hand upon
    him.—Sir,
  Your most dear daughter—
LEAR
  No rescue? What, a prisoner? I am even
  The natural fool of Fortune. Use me well.      210
  You shall have ransom. Let me have surgeons;
  I am cut to th' brains.
GENTLEMAN           You shall have anything.
LEAR  No seconds? All myself?
  Why, this would make a man a man of salt,    215
  To use his eyes for garden waterpots,
  ⟨Ay, and laying autumn's dust.⟩
  I will die bravely like a smug bridegroom. What?
  I will be jovial. Come, come, I am a king,
  Masters, know you that?      220
GENTLEMAN
  You are a royal one, and we obey you.
LEAR  Then there's life in 't. Come, an you get it, you
  shall get it by running. Sa, sa, sa, sa.
    ⟨*The King exits running* ⌐ *pursued by Attendants.*⌐⟩
GENTLEMAN
  A sight most pitiful in the meanest wretch,
  Past speaking of in a king. Thou hast a daughter    225
  Who redeems nature from the general curse
  Which twain have brought her to.
EDGAR  Hail, gentle sir.
GENTLEMAN    Sir, speed you. What's your will?
EDGAR
  Do you hear aught, sir, of a battle toward?    230
GENTLEMAN
  Most sure and vulgar. Everyone hears that,
  Which can distinguish sound.
EDGAR              But, by your favor,
  How near 's the other army?

**235–36. The . . . thought:** i.e., **the** sighting of the **main** part of the army is expected every hour

**238. Though that:** i.e., although; **on:** because of

**244. father:** common term of address to an old man

**245. what:** i.e., who

**246. tame:** servile, meek

**247. known:** experienced; **feeling:** deeply felt, acute

**248. pregnant:** inclined

**249. biding:** dwelling

**251–52. The bounty . . . and boot:** i.e., and, besides my thanks, I pray that you receive the gifts and blessing of heaven as your reward **To boot:** into the bargain

**253. happy:** fortunate, lucky

**256. thyself remember:** i.e., recall and repent your sins

GENTLEMAN
Near and on speedy foot. The main descry          235
Stands on the hourly thought.
EDGAR   I thank you, sir. That's all.
GENTLEMAN
Though that the Queen on special cause is here,
Her army is moved on.
EDGAR                              I thank you, sir.          240
⌜*Gentleman*⌝ *exits.*
GLOUCESTER
You ever-gentle gods, take my breath from me;
Let not my worser spirit tempt me again
To die before you please.
EDGAR   Well pray you, father.
GLOUCESTER   Now, good sir, what are you?          245
EDGAR
A most poor man, made tame to Fortune's blows,
Who, by the art of known and feeling sorrows,
Am pregnant to good pity. Give me your hand;
I'll lead you to some biding.
⌜*He takes Gloucester's hand.*⌝
GLOUCESTER                    Hearty thanks.          250
The bounty and the benison of heaven
To boot, and boot.

        *Enter* ⌜*Oswald, the*⌝ *Steward.*

OSWALD, ⌜*drawing his sword*⌝
                    A proclaimed prize! Most happy!
That eyeless head of thine was first framed flesh
To raise my fortunes. Thou old unhappy traitor,          255
Briefly thyself remember; the sword is out
That must destroy thee.
GLOUCESTER                    Now let thy friendly hand
Put strength enough to 't.
⌜*Edgar steps between Gloucester and Oswald.*⌝
OSWALD                    Wherefore, bold peasant,          260

261. **published:** proclaimed

262. **Lest:** i.e., to prevent the possibility

263. **Like:** similar

264. **Chill:** i.e., I will; **vurther 'casion:** further occasion or cause (Here Edgar assumes a dialect that signaled that the speaker was from the country.)

266. **gait:** way

267–68. **An . . . life:** if I could have been killed by mere swaggering or blustering

268–69. **'twould . . . vortnight:** it (**my life**) would **not** have been so **long as** it is **by a** fortnight

270. **che vor' ye:** I warn you; **Ise:** I will; **costard:** head (slang)

271. **ballow:** perhaps, walking stick (This word is not recorded elsewhere.)

272. **Out:** See note to 3.7.107.

273–74. **no matter . . . foins:** i.e., I do not care about your (sword) thrusts

275. **Villain:** i.e., villein, peasant

277. **about:** upon

279. **Upon:** on; **party:** side

280. **serviceable:** active and diligent in service

287. **deathsman:** executioner

288. **Leave:** i.e., give me leave; permit me; **wax:** i.e., the seal on the letter

292–93. **your will want not:** i.e., you do **not** lack the **will**

293. **fruitfully:** (1) fully, completely; (2) so as to produce good results

Dar'st thou support a published traitor? Hence,
Lest that th' infection of his fortune take
Like hold on thee. Let go his arm.
EDGAR   Chill not let go, zir, without vurther 'casion.
OSWALD   Let go, slave, or thou diest!                    265
EDGAR   Good gentleman, go your gait, and let poor
volk pass. An 'chud ha' bin zwaggered out of my
life, 'twould not ha' bin zo long as 'tis by a vort-
night. Nay, come not near th' old man. Keep out,
che vor' ye, or Ise try whether your costard or my   270
ballow be the harder. Chill be plain with you.
OSWALD   Out, dunghill.
EDGAR   Chill pick your teeth, zir. Come, no matter vor
your foins.                                 ⟨*They fight.*⟩
OSWALD, ⌜*falling*⌝
Slave, thou hast slain me. Villain, take my purse.    275
If ever thou wilt thrive, bury my body,
And give the letters which thou find'st about me
To Edmund, Earl of Gloucester. Seek him out
Upon the English party. O, untimely death! Death!
⟨*He dies.*⟩
EDGAR
I know thee well, a serviceable villain,               280
As duteous to the vices of thy mistress
As badness would desire.
GLOUCESTER   What, is he dead?
EDGAR   Sit you down, father; rest you.
Let's see these pockets. The letters that he speaks of   285
May be my friends. He's dead; I am only sorry
He had no other deathsman. Let us see.
⌜*He opens a letter.*⌝
Leave, gentle wax, and, manners, blame us not.
To know our enemies' minds, we rip their hearts.
Their papers is more lawful.     *Reads the letter.*   290
*Let our reciprocal vows be remembered. You have*
*many opportunities to cut him off. If your will want*
*not, time and place will be fruitfully offered. There is*

296–97. **supply . . . labor:** i.e., take his **place** as a reward for the **labor** (of killing him)

299. **for . . . venture:** i.e., empowered to put herself at risk for you  **venture:** an enterprise involving risk

300. **indistinguished . . . will:** boundlessness **of woman's** desire

303. **rake up:** i.e., bury in a shallow grave; **post:** messenger

304. **in the mature time:** in due **time**

305. **ungracious:** wicked

306. **death-practiced duke:** i.e., **duke** whose death has been plotted

308–10. **How stiff . . . sorrows:** i.e., **how** stubborn is **my** disgusting sanity that it keeps me standing and makes me aware **of my** great **sorrows  ingenious:** i.e., alert, fully conscious

310. **distract:** distracted, insane

312. **wrong imaginations:** false beliefs, delusions

316. **bestow:** house, lodge

**4.7**  In the French camp, Lear is waked by the doctor treating him and is reunited with Cordelia.

---

4. **o'erpaid:** i.e., to be paid too much

*nothing done if he return the conqueror. Then am I*
*the prisoner, and his bed my jail, from the loathed*          295
*warmth whereof deliver me and supply the place for*
*your labor.*
*Your (wife, so I would say) affectionate servant,*
*⟨and, for you, her own for venture,⟩          Goneril.*
O indistinguished space of woman's will!          300
A plot upon her virtuous husband's life,
And the exchange my brother.—Here, in the sands
Thee I'll rake up, the post unsanctified
Of murderous lechers; and in the mature time
With this ungracious paper strike the sight          305
Of the death-practiced duke. For him 'tis well
That of thy death and business I can tell.

GLOUCESTER
The King is mad. How stiff is my vile sense
That I stand up and have ingenious feeling
Of my huge sorrows! Better I were distract.          310
So should my thoughts be severed from my griefs,
And woes, by wrong imaginations, lose
The knowledge of themselves.          *Drum afar off.*

EDGAR          Give me your hand.
Far off methinks I hear the beaten drum.          315
Come, father, I'll bestow you with a friend.
          *They exit.*


Scene 7
*Enter Cordelia, Kent ⌜in disguise,⌝ ⟨Doctor,⟩ and*
*Gentleman.*

CORDELIA
O, thou good Kent, how shall I live and work
To match thy goodness? My life will be too short,
And every measure fail me.

KENT
To be acknowledged, madam, is o'erpaid.

5. **All . . . go:** perhaps, may **all reports** about me conform; or, perhaps, **all my reports** to you have conformed

6. **Nor . . . clipped:** i.e., neither **more nor** less

7. **suited:** dressed

8. **weeds:** clothes; **memories:** reminders

11. **to be . . . intent:** i.e., **to be** recognized would make the plan I have formed fall short

12. **My . . . not:** i.e., I ask you, as a favor, not to acknowledge me

13. **meet:** fitting

15. **sleeps:** i.e., he **sleeps**

18. **wind up:** put in tune

19. **child-changèd:** changed (driven mad) by his children

24. **I' th' sway:** i.e., according to the authority

28. **I . . . temperance:** i.e., I do not fear he will lose self-control

All my reports go with the modest truth,                    5
Nor more, nor clipped, but so.
CORDELIA                    Be better suited.
These weeds are memories of those worser hours.
I prithee put them off.
KENT                    Pardon, dear madam.                 10
Yet to be known shortens my made intent.
My boon I make it that you know me not
Till time and I think meet.
CORDELIA
Then be 't so, my good lord.—How does the King?
⟨DOCTOR⟩   Madam, sleeps still.                             15
CORDELIA   O, you kind gods,
Cure this great breach in his abusèd nature!
Th' untuned and jarring senses, O, wind up,
Of this child-changèd father!
⟨DOCTOR⟩                    So please your Majesty          20
That we may wake the King? He hath slept
    long.
CORDELIA
Be governed by your knowledge, and proceed
I' th' sway of your own will. Is he arrayed?

       *Enter Lear in a chair carried by Servants.*

GENTLEMAN
Ay, madam. In the heaviness of sleep,                      25
We put fresh garments on him.
⌜DOCTOR⌝
Be by, good madam, when we do awake him.
I doubt ⟨not⟩ of his temperance.
⟨CORDELIA                    Very well.
                              ⌜*Music.*⌝
DOCTOR
Please you, draw near.—Louder the music there.⟩           30
CORDELIA, ⌜*kissing Lear*⌝
O, my dear father, restoration hang

32. **Thy medicine:** i.e., **medicine** for you
34. **thy reverence:** i.e., you, whom they should hold in **reverence**
36. **Had you:** i.e., even if **you had; flakes:** i.e., hairs
37. **challenge:** require, demand
39. **deep:** i.e., deep-voiced; **dread-bolted thunder:** i.e., dreadful bolts of **thunder** (See note to 2.1.55.)
41. **cross-lightning:** zigzag lightning; **watch:** stay awake, stand watch; **perdu:** i.e., a *sentinel perdu,* or solitary sentinel standing watch in a very dangerous place
42. **helm:** helmet (i.e., his thin hair)
44. **Against:** i.e., by; **fain:** glad
45. **rogues forlorn:** wretched vagabonds
46. **short:** i.e., broken
48. **concluded all: all** come to an end
53. **wheel of fire:** Those condemned to death were sometimes bound to a wheel and tortured. Here, the reference to fire seems to suggest torture in hell. (See picture, page 220.)
57. **wide:** i.e., wide of the mark (in a deluded state)
60. **abused:** (1) wronged; (2) deceived; (3) worn out

Thy medicine on my lips, and let this kiss
Repair those violent harms that my two sisters
Have in thy reverence made.
KENT                              Kind and dear princess.    35
CORDELIA
Had you not been their father, these white flakes
Did challenge pity of them. Was this a face
To be opposed against the jarring winds?
⟨To stand against the deep dread-bolted thunder,
In the most terrible and nimble stroke                       40
Of quick cross-lightning? To watch, poor *perdu,*
With this thin helm?⟩ Mine enemy's dog,
Though he had bit me, should have stood that night
Against my fire. And wast thou fain, poor father,
To hovel thee with swine and rogues forlorn                 45
In short and musty straw? Alack, alack,
'Tis wonder that thy life and wits at once
Had not concluded all.—He wakes. Speak to him.
⟨DOCTOR⟩    Madam, do you; 'tis fittest.
CORDELIA
How does my royal lord? How fares your Majesty?             50
LEAR
You do me wrong to take me out o' th' grave.
Thou art a soul in bliss, but I am bound
Upon a wheel of fire, that mine own tears
Do scald like molten lead.
CORDELIA                    Sir, do you know me?             55
LEAR
You are a spirit, I know. Where did you die?
CORDELIA    Still, still, far wide.
⟨DOCTOR⟩
He's scarce awake. Let him alone awhile.
LEAR
Where have I been? Where am I? Fair daylight?
I am mightily abused; I should e'en die with pity           60

61. **thus:** i.e., in my condition
69. **fond:** silly; dazed
74. **mainly:** entirely
90. **abuse:** deceive
91. **rage:** madness, insanity
92. **danger:** i.e., dangerous
93. **even o'er:** i.e., fill in; **lost:** forgotten

"Bound upon a wheel of fire." (4.7.52–53)
From Giovanni Ferro, *Teatro d'imprese* ... (1623).

To see another thus. I know not what to say.
I will not swear these are my hands. Let's see.
I feel this pinprick. Would I were assured
Of my condition!
CORDELIA          O, look upon me, sir,          65
And hold your hand in benediction o'er me.
⟨No, sir,⟩ you must not kneel.
LEAR          Pray do not mock:
I am a very foolish fond old man,
Fourscore and upward, not an hour more nor less,          70
And to deal plainly,
I fear I am not in my perfect mind.
Methinks I should know you and know this man,
Yet I am doubtful, for I am mainly ignorant
What place this is, and all the skill I have          75
Remembers not these garments; nor I know not
Where I did lodge last night. Do not laugh at me,
For, as I am a man, I think this lady
To be my child Cordelia.
CORDELIA, ⌜*weeping*⌝ And so I am; I am.          80
LEAR
Be your tears wet? Yes, faith. I pray, weep not.
If you have poison for me, I will drink it.
I know you do not love me, for your sisters
Have, as I do remember, done me wrong.
You have some cause; they have not.          85
CORDELIA          No cause, no
cause.
LEAR  Am I in France?
KENT  In your own kingdom, sir.
LEAR  Do not abuse me.          90
⟨DOCTOR⟩
Be comforted, good madam. The great rage,
You see, is killed in him, ⟨and yet it is danger
To make him even o'er the time he has lost.⟩

95. **settling:** calming (of his mind)
100. **Holds it true:** i.e., is it a fact
103. **conductor:** leader
108. **powers ... kingdom:** i.e., armies of Britain
109. **arbitrament:** settlement of the dispute; **like:** i.e., likely
111. **My ... period:** i.e., the conclusion (of my life; or, perhaps, of my plans); **throughly wrought:** worked out completely
112. **Or ... or:** either ... or; **as ... fought:** according to the outcome of today's battle

Desire him to go in. Trouble him no more
Till further settling.                                    95
CORDELIA   Will 't please your Highness walk?
LEAR   You must bear with me.
   Pray you now, forget, and forgive. I am old and
   foolish.     ⟨*They exit. Kent and Gentleman remain.*⟩
⟨GENTLEMAN   Holds it true, sir, that the Duke of Corn-   100
   wall was so slain?
KENT   Most certain, sir.
GENTLEMAN   Who is conductor of his people?
KENT   As 'tis said, the bastard son of Gloucester.
GENTLEMAN   They say Edgar, his banished son, is with   105
   the Earl of Kent in Germany.
KENT   Report is changeable. 'Tis time to look about.
   The powers of the kingdom approach apace.
GENTLEMAN   The arbitrament is like to be bloody. Fare
   you well, sir.                          ⌜*He exits.*⌝   110
KENT
   My point and period will be throughly wrought,
   Or well, or ill, as this day's battle's fought.
                                         *He exits.*⟩

*The Tragedy of*

# KING LEAR

ACT 5

**5.1**  Albany joins his forces with Regan's (led by Edmund) to oppose the French invasion. Edgar, still in disguise, approaches Albany with the letter plotting Albany's death, and promises to produce a champion to maintain the authenticity of the letter in a trial by combat. Edmund then enters and, when alone, reflects upon his possible marriage to either Goneril or Regan and upon his intention to have Cordelia and Lear killed if the British forces are victorious.

---

1. **Know . . . hold:** i.e., learn from Albany if he is firm in his latest decision
2. **since:** i.e., **since** then
3. **alteration:** changes (of mind)
4. **constant pleasure:** settled intention
5. **man:** i.e., Oswald; **miscarried:** come to harm, perished
6. **doubted:** feared
11. **honored:** i.e., honorable
13. **forfended:** forbidden
14. **That . . . you:** i.e., you wrong yourself in having such a **thought**
15. **doubtful:** fearful
15–16. **conjunct . . . hers:** i.e., intimate with her to the fullest extent

# ACT 5

### Scene 1
*Enter, with Drum and Colors, Edmund, Regan,
Gentlemen, and Soldiers.*

EDMUND, ⌜*to a Gentleman*⌝
  Know of the Duke if his last purpose hold,
  Or whether since he is advised by aught
  To change the course. He's full of alteration
  And self-reproving. Bring his constant pleasure.
                                      ⌜*A Gentleman exits.*⌝
REGAN
  Our sister's man is certainly miscarried.                    5
EDMUND
  'Tis to be doubted, madam.
REGAN                              Now, sweet lord,
  You know the goodness I intend upon you;
  Tell me but truly, but then speak the truth,
  Do you not love my sister?                                   10
EDMUND                    In honored love.
REGAN
  But have you never found my brother's way
  To the forfended place?
⟨EDMUND    That thought abuses you.
REGAN
  I am doubtful that you have been conjunct                    15
  And bosomed with her as far as we call hers.⟩
EDMUND    No, by mine honor, madam.

**227**

20. **Fear me not:** do **not** doubt **me**
23. **bemet:** met
25. **rigor . . . state:** harshness of our government
26. **Where:** i.e., in situations **where; honest:** honorable
27. **For:** i.e., as for
28. **touches us:** concerns or moves me; **as . . . land:** i.e., in that it is a French invasion
29–30. **Not . . . oppose:** i.e., not insofar as France emboldens Lear and **others** who oppose us for **just and** serious reasons
32. **reasoned:** i.e., being discussed
34. **particular broils:** personal quarrels
36. **determine:** decide
37. **th' ancient of war:** i.e., our officers with the most military experience
38. **presently:** at once
39. **us:** i.e., me
41. **convenient:** suitable, proper

REGAN
I never shall endure her. Dear my lord,
Be not familiar with her.

EDMUND
Fear ⟨me⟩ not. She and the Duke, her husband.          20

*Enter, with Drum and Colors, Albany, Goneril, Soldiers.*

⟨GONERIL, ⌜*aside*⌝
I had rather lose the battle than that sister
Should loosen him and me.⟩

ALBANY
Our very loving sister, well bemet.—
Sir, this I heard: the King is come to his daughter,
With others whom the rigor of our state          25
Forced to cry out. ⟨Where I could not be honest,
I never yet was valiant. For this business,
It touches us as France invades our land,
Not bolds the King, with others whom, I fear,
Most just and heavy causes make oppose.          30

EDMUND
Sir, you speak nobly.⟩

REGAN          Why is this reasoned?

GONERIL
Combine together 'gainst the enemy,
For these domestic and particular broils
Are not the question here.          35

ALBANY          Let's then determine
With th' ancient of war on our proceeding.

⟨EDMUND
I shall attend you presently at your tent.⟩

REGAN    Sister, you'll go with us?

GONERIL    No.          40

REGAN
'Tis most convenient. Pray, go with us.

GONERIL, ⌜*aside*⌝
Oho, I know the riddle.—I will go.

⌜*They begin to exit.*⌝

47–48. **sound / For:** i.e., summon
49. **prove:** i.e., establish as true in a trial by combat
50. **avouchèd:** asserted; **miscarry:** lose; are killed
57. **o'erlook:** read
58. **powers:** armed forces
60. **discovery:** reconnaissance
62. **greet the time:** i.e., be ready when **the time comes**
64. **jealous:** suspicious

*Enter Edgar ⌐dressed as a peasant.⌐*

EDGAR, ⌐*to Albany*⌐
If e'er your Grace had speech with man so poor,
Hear me one word.
ALBANY, ⌐*to those exiting*⌐
              I'll overtake you.—Speak.                45
                *Both the armies exit.*
EDGAR, ⌐*giving him a paper*⌐
Before you fight the battle, ope this letter.
If you have victory, let the trumpet sound
For him that brought it. Wretched though I seem,
I can produce a champion that will prove
What is avouchèd there. If you miscarry,                50
Your business of the world hath so an end,
And machination ceases. Fortune ⟨love⟩ you.
ALBANY   Stay till I have read the letter.
EDGAR   I was forbid it.
When time shall serve, let but the herald cry                55
And I'll appear again.                *He exits.*
ALBANY
Why, fare thee well. I will o'erlook thy paper.

*Enter Edmund.*

EDMUND
The enemy's in view. Draw up your powers.
               ⌐*Giving him a paper.*⌐
Here is the guess of their true strength and forces
By diligent discovery. But your haste                60
Is now urged on you.
ALBANY                We will greet the time.
                        *He exits.*
EDMUND
To both these sisters have I sworn my love,
Each jealous of the other as the stung
Are of the adder. Which of them shall I take?                65

69. **hardly:** with difficulty
70. **Her:** i.e., Goneril's
71. **countenance:** rank and position; repute in the world
73. **taking off:** murder
76. **Shall:** i.e., they shall
76–77. **my state / Stands on me:** my position depends **on me**

**5.2**  Cordelia's French army is defeated.

---

0 SD. **Alarum:** call to arms ("All arm")
1. **father:** a polite address to an old man
5 SD. **Retreat:** trumpet call for a **retreat**
7. **ta'en:** i.e., have been taken

Both? One? Or neither? Neither can be enjoyed
If both remain alive. To take the widow
Exasperates, makes mad her sister Goneril,
And hardly shall I carry out my side,
Her husband being alive. Now, then, we'll use          70
His countenance for the battle, which, being done,
Let her who would be rid of him devise
His speedy taking off. As for the mercy
Which he intends to Lear and to Cordelia,
The battle done and they within our power,              75
Shall never see his pardon, for my state
Stands on me to defend, not to debate.
                                        *He exits.*


### Scene 2
*Alarum within. Enter, with Drum and Colors, Lear,*
*Cordelia, and Soldiers, over the stage, and exit.*
*Enter Edgar and Gloucester.*

EDGAR
Here, father, take the shadow of this tree
For your good host. Pray that the right may thrive.
If ever I return to you again,
I'll bring you comfort.
GLOUCESTER          Grace go with you, sir.          5
                                ⌜*Edgar*⌝ *exits.*
                        *Alarum and Retreat within.*

                        *Enter Edgar.*

EDGAR
Away, old man. Give me thy hand. Away.
King Lear hath lost, he and his daughter ta'en.
Give me thy hand. Come on.
GLOUCESTER
No further, sir. A man may rot even here.

**5.3**  Edmund sends Lear and Cordelia to prison and secretly commissions their assassination. Albany confronts Edmund and Goneril with their intended treachery against him and calls for the champion that Edgar said he would produce. Edgar himself, in full armor, appears to accuse Edmund of treachery. In the ensuing trial by combat, Edgar mortally wounds Edmund. Edgar reveals his identity, tells about his life as Poor Tom, and describes Gloucester's death. A messenger announces the deaths of Regan (who has been poisoned by Goneril) and Goneril (who has committed suicide). Kent, no longer in disguise, arrives in search of Lear. Edmund confesses that he has ordered the deaths of Lear and of Cordelia. While a messenger rushes to the prison to save them, Lear enters bearing the dead Cordelia. As Albany makes plans to restore Lear to the throne, Lear himself dies.

---

1. **Good guard:** i.e., guard them well
3. **censure:** pronounce judicial sentence on
5. **meaning:** purposes
7. **else:** otherwise; **false:** inconstant, fickle (**Fortune** was considered fickle because she shows favor one moment and animosity the next.)
8. **daughters ... sisters:** i.e., Goneril and Regan
18. **wear out:** outlast
20. **That ... moon:** i.e., whose fortunes change with the tides

EDGAR
　What, in ill thoughts again? Men must endure　　　10
　Their going hence even as their coming hither.
　Ripeness is all. Come on.
　[GLOUCESTER　　　　　　And that's true too.]
　　　　　　　　　　　　　　　　　*They exit.*


Scene 3
*Enter in conquest, with Drum and Colors, Edmund;*
*Lear and Cordelia as prisoners; Soldiers, Captain.*

EDMUND
　Some officers take them away. Good guard
　Until their greater pleasures first be known
　That are to censure them.
CORDELIA, ⌐*to Lear*⌐　　　　We are not the first
　Who with best meaning have incurred the worst.　　5
　For thee, oppressèd king, I am cast down.
　Myself could else outfrown false Fortune's frown.
　Shall we not see these daughters and these sisters?
LEAR
　No, no, no, no. Come, let's away to prison.
　We two alone will sing like birds i' th' cage.　　　10
　When thou dost ask me blessing, I'll kneel down
　And ask of thee forgiveness. So we'll live,
　And pray, and sing, and tell old tales, and laugh
　At gilded butterflies, and hear poor rogues
　Talk of court news, and we'll talk with them too—　15
　Who loses and who wins; who's in, who's out—
　And take upon 's the mystery of things,
　As if we were God's spies. And we'll wear out,
　In a walled prison, packs and sects of great ones
　That ebb and flow by th' moon.　　　　　　20
EDMUND　　　　　　　　　　Take them away.
LEAR
　Upon such sacrifices, my Cordelia,

23. **throw incense:** The image is of a rite of sacrifice in which those celebrating the ritual throw incense on the burnt offering. Here, it is **the gods themselves** who celebrate the sacrifice.

25. **shall:** i.e., will have to; **brand:** i.e., piece of burning wood

26. **fire us . . . foxes:** i.e., drive **us** apart with fire as **foxes** are driven out of their dens

27. **good years:** It has been suggested that this should be printed as "goodyears," and that it is a rare plural form of a term used to denote an unnamed evil power. It seems just as likely that the Folio's **good years** is the correct reading and that Lear is simply referring to the passage of time. **fell:** skin

37. **Does . . . sword:** i.e., is not fitting for a soldier

38. **bear:** allow for

41. **write "happy":** i.e., regard yourself as fortunate; **th':** thou

42. **carry it so:** i.e., **carry it** out exactly

46. **strain:** (1) disposition; (2) lineage

48. **opposites of:** opponents in

The gods themselves throw incense. Have I caught
  thee?
He that parts us shall bring a brand from heaven          25
And fire us hence like foxes. Wipe thine eyes.
The good years shall devour them, flesh and fell,
Ere they shall make us weep. We'll see 'em starved
  first.
Come.          30
          ⌜*Lear and Cordelia*⌝ *exit,* ⌜*with Soldiers.*⌝
EDMUND   Come hither, captain. Hark.
          ⌜*Handing him a paper.*⌝
Take thou this note. Go follow them to prison.
One step I have advanced thee. If thou dost
As this instructs thee, thou dost make thy way
To noble fortunes. Know thou this: that men          35
Are as the time is; to be tender-minded
Does not become a sword. Thy great employment
Will not bear question. Either say thou 'lt do 't,
Or thrive by other means.
CAPTAIN                    I'll do 't, my lord.          40
EDMUND
About it, and write "happy" when th' hast done.
Mark, I say, instantly, and carry it so
As I have set it down.
⟨CAPTAIN
I cannot draw a cart, nor eat dried oats.
If it be man's work, I'll do 't.⟩          *Captain exits.*          45

*Flourish. Enter Albany, Goneril, Regan, Soldiers* ⌜*and a
          Captain.*⌝

ALBANY, ⌜*to Edmund*⌝
Sir, you have showed today your valiant strain,
And Fortune led you well. You have the captives
Who were the opposites of this day's strife.
I do require them of you, so to use them
As we shall find their merits and our safety          50
May equally determine.

54. **retention . . . guard:** confinement under a specially **appointed guard**

55–57. **Whose . . . eyes:** i.e., Lear's old **age** and **title** will persuade the populace to take **his side,** and our own lancers (drafted from the populace) will turn against us

58. **Which:** i.e., who

61. **further space:** i.e., a later date

64–65. **And . . . sharpness:** i.e., before **the heat** of battle has cooled, **the best** of causes **are cursed by** those who have had to endure the pain of the battle

68. **by . . . patience:** a polite phrase, like "**by your leave**"

69. **hold:** regard; **but a subject of:** i.e., only as a subordinate in

71. **we list:** I choose; **grace:** confer dignity (or a title) on

72. **pleasure:** wishes; **demanded:** consulted

74. **place:** position

75. **immediacy:** i.e., direct connection to me

79. **your addition:** the title you give him

80–81. **In . . . invested:** i.e., endowed with my power and authority

81. **compeers:** is equal to

82. **That were the most:** i.e., **that** would be **the most** (that you could invest him with)

83. **Jesters . . . prophets:** Here Regan combines two proverbs: "There is many a true word spoken in jest" and "Fools [**jesters**] and children do often prophesy."

85. **That . . . asquint:** Goneril replies by alluding to another proverb: "Love, being jealous, makes a good **eye** look **asquint.**"

EDMUND  Sir, I thought it fit
　To send the old and miserable king
　To some retention ⟨and appointed guard,⟩
　Whose age had charms in it, whose title more,　　55
　To pluck the common bosom on his side
　And turn our impressed lances in our eyes,
　Which do command them. With him I sent the
　　Queen,
　My reason all the same, and they are ready　　60
　Tomorrow, or at further space, t' appear
　Where you shall hold your session. ⟨At this time
　We sweat and bleed. The friend hath lost his friend,
　And the best quarrels in the heat are cursed
　By those that feel their sharpness.　　65
　The question of Cordelia and her father
　Requires a fitter place.⟩
ALBANY　　　　　　　　Sir, by your patience,
　I hold you but a subject of this war,
　Not as a brother.　　70
REGAN　　　　　That's as we list to grace him.
　Methinks our pleasure might have been demanded
　Ere you had spoke so far. He led our powers,
　Bore the commission of my place and person,
　The which immediacy may well stand up　　75
　And call itself your brother.
GONERIL　　　　　　　　Not so hot.
　In his own grace he doth exalt himself
　More than in your addition.
REGAN　　　　　　　　In my rights,　　80
　By me invested, he compeers the best.
⟨GONERIL⟩
　That were the most if he should husband you.
REGAN
　Jesters do oft prove prophets.
GONERIL　　　　　　　Holla, holla!
　That eye that told you so looked but asquint.　　85

87. **full-flowing stomach:** i.e., with a great flow of angry words (**Stomach** often meant "anger.")

90. **the . . . thine:** Regan surrenders herself like a walled town or fortress.

91. **Witness the world:** i.e., let **the world witness**

94. **let-alone:** i.e., granting or withholding of permission

96. **Half-blooded:** illegitimate

97. **strike:** as a signal for battle

99. **On . . . treason:** for high **treason; in thine attaint:** (1) as another tainted by your crime; (2) as your accuser (as Goneril has become through Albany's possession of her letter to Edmund)

103. **subcontracted:** i.e., contracted, engaged

104. **your banns:** i.e., the proclamation of your marriage to Edmund

105. **make your loves to me:** i.e., woo me, court me

106. **bespoke:** already spoken for

107. **An interlude:** i.e., a farce (literally, a short play used to fill an interval)

112. **make it:** i.e., prove it true

113. **in nothing less:** i.e., in **no** respect **less** criminal

REGAN
Lady, I am not well, else I should answer
From a full-flowing stomach. ⌜*To Edmund.*⌝
  General,
Take thou my soldiers, prisoners, patrimony.
[Dispose of them, of me; the walls is thine.]                    90
Witness the world that I create thee here
My lord and master.
GONERIL                    Mean you to enjoy him?
ALBANY
The let-alone lies not in your goodwill.
EDMUND
Nor in thine, lord.                                               95
ALBANY                    Half-blooded fellow, yes.
REGAN, ⌜*to Edmund*⌝
Let the drum strike, and prove my title thine.
ALBANY
Stay yet, hear reason.—Edmund, I arrest thee
On capital treason; and, in ⟨thine attaint,⟩
This gilded serpent.—For your claim, fair           100
  ⟨sister,⟩
I bar it in the interest of my wife.
'Tis she is subcontracted to this lord,
And I, her husband, contradict your banns.
If you will marry, make your loves to me.           105
My lady is bespoke.
[GONERIL                    An interlude!]
ALBANY
Thou art armed, Gloucester. Let the trumpet sound.
If none appear to prove upon thy person
Thy heinous, manifest, and many treasons,           110
There is my pledge.        ⌜*He throws down a glove.*⌝
                    I'll make it on thy heart,
Ere I taste bread, thou art in nothing less
Than I have here proclaimed thee.

116. **medicine:** i.e., poison
118. **What:** i.e., whoever
121. **who not:** i.e., whoever
125. **thy single virtue:** i.e., your own strength alone
133. **quality or degree:** rank
136. **He:** i.e., Edmund
139 SD. **within:** offstage; **armed:** dressed in full armor (See picture of an armed knight, below.)

An armed knight.
From Henry Peacham, *Minerua Britanna* . . . (1612).

REGAN  Sick, O, sick!                                              115
GONERIL, ⌜*aside*⌝  If not, I'll ne'er trust medicine.
EDMUND
  There's my exchange.       ⌜*He throws down a glove.*⌝
            What in the world ⟨he is⟩
  That names me traitor, villain-like he lies.
  Call by the trumpet. He that dares approach,             120
  On him, on you, who not, I will maintain
  My truth and honor firmly.
ALBANY
  A herald, ho!
⟨EDMUND       A herald, ho, a herald!⟩
⟨ALBANY⟩
  Trust to thy single virtue, for thy soldiers,           125
  All levied in my name, have in my name
  Took their discharge.
REGAN                  My sickness grows upon me.
ALBANY
  She is not well. Convey her to my tent.
                       ⌜*Regan is helped to exit.*⌝

            *Enter a Herald.*

  Come hither, herald. Let the trumpet sound,             130
  And read out this.     ⌜*He hands the Herald a paper.*⌝
⟨CAPTAIN  Sound, trumpet!⟩
                       *A trumpet sounds.*
HERALD *reads.*
  *If any man of quality or degree, within the lists of the*
  *army, will maintain upon Edmund, supposed Earl of*
  *Gloucester, that he is a manifold traitor, let him*    135
  *appear by the third sound of the trumpet. He is bold in*
  *his defense.*          [*First trumpet* ⌜*sounds.*⌝
HERALD  Again!           *Second trumpet* ⌜*sounds.*⌝
HERALD  Again!           *Third trumpet* ⌜*sounds.*⌝
                       *Trumpet answers within.*]

            *Enter Edgar armed.*

142. **What:** who
146. **canker-bit:** destroyed like a rosebud by the cankerworm (See picture, below.)
148. **cope:** encounter
156–58. **mine    honors . . . oath . . . profession:** All these refer to Edgar's status as a knight.
159. **Maugre:** in spite of
160. **fire-new:** brand-new
163. **Conspirant:** conspiring; or, conspirator
164. **upward:** top
165. **descent:** lowest part
166. **toad-spotted:** loathsomely    tainted;    **Say thou:** i.e., if you **say**
167. **bent:** directed
170. **wisdom:** prudence

A cankerworm. (5.3.146)
From John Johnstone, *Opera aliquot* . . . (1650–62).

ALBANY, ⌐*to Herald*⌐
 Ask him his purposes, why he appears    140
 Upon this call o' th' trumpet.
HERALD        What are you?
 Your name, your quality, and why you answer
 This present summons?
EDGAR       Know my name is lost,   145
 By treason's tooth bare-gnawn and canker-bit.
 Yet am I noble as the adversary
 I come to cope.
ALBANY    Which is that adversary?
EDGAR
 What's he that speaks for Edmund, Earl of   150
  Gloucester?
EDMUND
 Himself. What sayest thou to him?
EDGAR         Draw thy sword,
 That if my speech offend a noble heart,
 Thy arm may do thee justice. Here is mine.   155
           ⌐*He draws his sword.*⌐
 Behold, it is my privilege, the privilege of mine
  honors,
 My oath, and my profession. I protest,
 Maugre thy strength, place, youth, and eminence,
 ⟨Despite⟩ thy victor-sword and fire-new fortune,  160
 Thy valor, and thy heart, thou art a traitor,
 False to thy gods, thy brother, and thy father,
 Conspirant 'gainst this high illustrious prince,
 And from th' extremest upward of thy head
 To the descent and dust below thy foot,   165
 A most toad-spotted traitor. Say thou "no,"
 This sword, this arm, and my best spirits are bent
 To prove upon thy heart, whereto I speak,
 Thou liest.
EDMUND  In wisdom I should ask thy name,  170
 But since thy outside looks so fair and warlike,

172. **that:** i.e., since; **say:** assay, sign; **breeding:** i.e., noble birth

173–74. **What . . . disdain:** i.e., **I disdain** the cautious course of claiming my right, under the rules **of knighthood**, to refuse combat with a challenger whose name and rank I do not know   **nicely:** scrupulously

175. **treasons to:** i.e., accusations of treason at

176. **the . . . lie:** i.e., **the lie** that charges me with treason, which I hate as I hate hell

177–79. **for . . . forever:** i.e., because my countercharges **glance** off your armor without even bruising you, I will now use my **sword** to open a passage to your heart, where they will **forever** lodge

180. **Save him:** i.e., let him live

181. **This is practice:** i.e., you were tricked into fighting

184. **cozened and beguiled:** duped and deceived

186. **stopple:** close with a stopple or plug; **Hold, sir:** Perhaps this repeats Albany's earlier command to Edgar to let Edmund live.

194. **Govern:** (1) restrain; (2) look after

198. **fortune on:** success over

And that thy tongue some say of breeding breathes,
[What safe and nicely I might well delay]
By rule of knighthood, I disdain and spurn.
Back do I toss these treasons to thy head,                    175
With the hell-hated lie o'erwhelm thy heart,
Which, for they yet glance by and scarcely bruise,
This sword of mine shall give them instant way,
Where they shall rest forever. Trumpets, speak!
⌜*He draws his sword.*⌝ *Alarums. Fights.*
⌜*Edmund falls, wounded.*⌝
ALBANY, ⌜*to Edgar*⌝
Save him, save him!                                           180
GONERIL                This is practice, Gloucester.
By th' law of war, thou wast not bound to answer
An unknown opposite. Thou art not vanquished,
But cozened and beguiled.
ALBANY                     Shut your mouth, dame,           185
Or with this paper shall I ⟨stopple⟩ it.—Hold, sir.—
Thou worse than any name, read thine own evil.
No tearing, lady. I perceive you know it.
GONERIL
Say if I do; the laws are mine, not thine.
Who can arraign me for 't?                                    190
ALBANY                     Most monstrous! O!
Know'st thou this paper?
⟨GONERIL⟩                   Ask me not what I know.
*She exits.*
ALBANY
Go after her, she's desperate. Govern her.
⌜*A Soldier exits.*⌝
EDMUND, ⌜*to Edgar*⌝
What you have charged me with, that have I done,              195
And more, much more. The time will bring it out.
'Tis past, and so am I. But what art thou
That hast this fortune on me? If thou 'rt noble,
I do forgive thee.

200. **charity:** i.e., forgiveness

201. **no . . . blood:** i.e., am of **no less** honorable birth or descent

202. **If more:** i.e., because I am legitimate and the firstborn; **th':** thou

204. **pleasant:** pleasure-giving

206. **thee he got:** he begot you

209. **wheel:** i.e., Fortune's **wheel,** which draws one up to a position of power and then casts one down as it continues to turn (See pictures, pages 172 and 252.) **here:** i.e., at the bottom of the wheel, where I began

217. **List:** listen to

219. **The . . . escape:** i.e., in order **to escape** from **the proclamation** condemning me to death

224. **this habit:** these garments

225. **rings:** i.e., eye sockets

229. **past:** ago

230. **success:** result

232. **flawed:** damaged

EDGAR          Let's exchange charity.        200
I am no less in blood than thou art, Edmund;
If more, the more th' hast wronged me.
My name is Edgar and thy father's son.
The gods are just, and of our pleasant vices
Make instruments to plague us.        205
The dark and vicious place where thee he got
Cost him his eyes.
EDMUND        Th' hast spoken right. 'Tis true.
The wheel is come full circle; I am here.
ALBANY, ⌜*to Edgar*⌝
Methought thy very gait did prophesy        210
A royal nobleness. I must embrace thee.
Let sorrow split my heart if ever I
Did hate thee or thy father!
EDGAR    Worthy prince, I know 't.
ALBANY    Where have you hid yourself?        215
How have you known the miseries of your father?
EDGAR
By nursing them, my lord. List a brief tale,
And when 'tis told, O, that my heart would burst!
The bloody proclamation to escape
That followed me so near—O, our lives' sweetness,    220
That we the pain of death would hourly die
Rather than die at once!—taught me to shift
Into a madman's rags, t' assume a semblance
That very dogs disdained, and in this habit
Met I my father with his bleeding rings,       225
Their precious stones new lost; became his guide,
Led him, begged for him, saved him from despair.
Never—O fault!—revealed myself unto him
Until some half hour past, when I was armed.
Not sure, though hoping of this good success,      230
I asked his blessing, and from first to last
Told him our pilgrimage. But his flawed heart
(Alack, too weak the conflict to support)

242. **period:** highest point (of woe)

243. **another:** i.e., **another** sorrowful event

244. **To amplify too much:** i.e., to increase what was already too sorrowful

245. **top extremity:** i.e., overtop the utmost point

246. **big in clamor:** i.e., loudly lamenting Gloucester's death

251. **As:** i.e., **as** if; **threw . . . father:** i.e., **threw** himself on Gloucester's body

254. **puissant:** powerful

256. **tranced:** in a trance

259. **enemy king:** Lear, who could be called Kent's **enemy** for having banished him

'Twixt two extremes of passion, joy and grief,
Burst smilingly.                                                    235
EDMUND          This speech of yours hath moved me,
And shall perchance do good. But speak you on.
You look as you had something more to say.
ALBANY
If there be more, more woeful, hold it in,
For I am almost ready to dissolve,                      240
Hearing of this.
⟨EDGAR          This would have seemed a period
To such as love not sorrow; but another,
To amplify too much, would make much more
And top extremity. Whilst I                                245
Was big in clamor, came there in a man
Who, having seen me in my worst estate,
Shunned my abhorred society; but then, finding
Who 'twas that so endured, with his strong arms
He fastened on my neck and bellowed out           250
As he'd burst heaven, threw ⌜him⌝ on my father,
Told the most piteous tale of Lear and him
That ever ear received, which, in recounting,
His grief grew puissant, and the strings of life
Began to crack. Twice then the trumpets sounded,   255
And there I left him tranced.
ALBANY                    But who was this?
EDGAR
Kent, sir, the banished Kent, who in disguise
Followed his enemy king and did him service
Improper for a slave.⟩                                       260

*Enter a Gentleman ⟨with a bloody knife.⟩*

GENTLEMAN
Help, help, O, help!
EDGAR                    What kind of help?
[ALBANY, ⌜*to Gentleman*⌝               Speak, man!]
EDGAR   What means this bloody knife?

265. **smokes:** steams
277. **compliment:** formal greeting
278. **very:** mere
280. **aye:** forever
285. **object:** spectacle

Fortune turning her wheel. (2.2.188–89; 4.1.2–6; 5.3.209)
From Gregor Reisch, *Margarita philosophica* . . . [1503].

GENTLEMAN
'Tis hot, it smokes! It came even from the heart 265
Of—O, she's dead!
ALBANY Who dead? Speak, man.
GENTLEMAN
Your lady, sir, your lady. And her sister
By her is poisoned. She confesses it.
EDMUND
I was contracted to them both. All three 270
Now marry in an instant.
[EDGAR                          Here comes Kent.

*Enter Kent.*]

ALBANY, ⌜*to the Gentleman*⌝
Produce the bodies, be they alive or dead.
                              ⌜*Gentleman exits.*⌝
This judgment of the heavens, that makes us
    tremble, 275
Touches us not with pity. O, is this he?
⌜*To Kent.*⌝ The time will not allow the compliment
Which very manners urges.
KENT                          I am come
To bid my king and master aye goodnight. 280
Is he not here?
ALBANY                  Great thing of us forgot!
Speak, Edmund, where's the King? And where's
    Cordelia?
                  *Goneril and Regan's bodies brought out.*
Seest thou this object, Kent? 285
KENT Alack, why thus?
EDMUND Yet Edmund was beloved.
The one the other poisoned for my sake,
And after slew herself.
ALBANY Even so.—Cover their faces. 290
EDMUND
I pant for life. Some good I mean to do

293–94. **my writ . . . life:** i.e., I have issued written orders commanding the death

306. **fordid:** destroyed

314. **stone:** i.e., mirror's surface

316. **promised end:** i.e., doomsday, the end of the world promised in the Bible

Despite of mine own nature. Quickly send—
Be brief in it—to th' castle, for my writ
Is on the life of Lear, and on Cordelia.
Nay, send in time.
ALBANY　　　　　　Run, run, O, run!　　　　　295

EDGAR
　To who, my lord? ⌜*To Edmund.*⌝ Who has the office?
　Send
　Thy token of reprieve.

EDMUND
　Well thought on. Take my sword. Give it the　　　300
　Captain.

EDGAR, ⌜*to a Soldier*⌝　Haste thee for thy life.
　　　　　⌜*The Soldier exits with Edmund's sword.*⌝
EDMUND, ⌜*to Albany*⌝
　He hath commission from thy wife and me
　To hang Cordelia in the prison, and
　To lay the blame upon her own despair,　　　305
　That she fordid herself.

ALBANY
　The gods defend her!—Bear him hence awhile.
　　　　　　　　　⌜*Edmund is carried off.*⌝

　　*Enter Lear with Cordelia in his arms,*
　　　⌜*followed by a Gentleman.*⌝

LEAR
　Howl, howl, howl! O, ⟨you⟩ are men of stones!
　Had I your tongues and eyes, I'd use them so
　That heaven's vault should crack. She's gone　　310
　　forever.
　I know when one is dead and when one lives.
　She's dead as earth.—Lend me a looking glass.
　If that her breath will mist or stain the stone,
　Why, then she lives.　　　　　　　　　315

KENT　　　　　　Is this the promised end?
EDGAR
　Or image of that horror?

318. **Fall and cease:** probably addressed to the heavens or the universe

333. **falchion:** sword

335. **crosses:** troubles, adversities; **spoil:** impair, weaken

337. **tell:** recognize; **straight:** straightway, in a moment

338. **loved and hated:** i.e., first **loved and** then **hated**

342. **Caius:** Kent's name when he was in disguise (This is the only time the name is used in the play.)

ALBANY　　　　　　　　　　Fall and cease.

LEAR

This feather stirs. She lives. If it be so,
It is a chance which does redeem all sorrows　　　320
That ever I have felt.

KENT　　　　　　　　　O, my good master—

LEAR

Prithee, away.

EDGAR　　　　　　'Tis noble Kent, your friend.

LEAR

A plague upon you, murderers, traitors all!　　　325
I might have saved her. Now she's gone forever.—
Cordelia, Cordelia, stay a little. Ha!
What is 't thou sayst?—Her voice was ever soft,
Gentle, and low, an excellent thing in woman.
I killed the slave that was a-hanging thee.　　　330

GENTLEMAN

'Tis true, my lords, he did.

LEAR　　　　　　　　　　Did I not, fellow?
I have seen the day, with my good biting falchion
I would have made him skip. I am old now,
And these same crosses spoil me. ⌜*To Kent.*⌝ Who　335
　are you?
Mine eyes are not o' th' best. I'll tell you straight.

KENT

If Fortune brag of two she loved and hated,
One of them we behold.

LEAR

This is a dull sight. Are you not Kent?　　　340

KENT　　　　　　　　　　　　The same,
Your servant Kent. Where is your servant Caius?

LEAR

He's a good fellow, I can tell you that.
He'll strike and quickly too. He's dead and rotten.

KENT

No, my good lord, I am the very man—　　　345

346. **see:** attend to

347. **your first ... decay:** i.e., the beginning of the change and decline of your fortunes (**Difference** may also mean "quarrel" and may refer to Lear's relations with his daughters.)

352. **fordone:** destroyed

353. **desperately:** in despair

356. **us:** i.e., ourselves

357. **bootless:** useless

361. **What ... come:** i.e., whatever opportunities that **may** become available for comforting (Lear in) **this great** decline

362. **For us, we:** i.e., as for myself, I

365. **boot:** advantage; **addition:** titles

369. **poor fool:** i.e., Cordelia (**Fool** can be a term of endearment.)

LEAR   I'll see that straight.

KENT
That from your first of difference and decay
Have followed your sad steps.

LEAR                              ⌜You⌝ are welcome
   hither.                                                        350

KENT
Nor no man else. All's cheerless, dark, and deadly.
Your eldest daughters have fordone themselves,
And desperately are dead.

LEAR                              Ay, so I think.

ALBANY
He knows not what he says, and vain is it          355
That we present us to him.

EDGAR                              Very bootless.

*Enter a Messenger.*

MESSENGER   Edmund is dead, my lord.

ALBANY   That's but a trifle here.—
You lords and noble friends, know our intent:    360
What comfort to this great decay may come
Shall be applied. For us, we will resign,
During the life of this old Majesty,
To him our absolute power; you to your rights,
With boot and such addition as your Honors        365
Have more than merited. All friends shall taste
The wages of their virtue, and all foes
The cup of their deservings. O, see, see!

LEAR
And my poor fool is hanged. No, no, no life?
Why should a dog, a horse, a rat have life,          370
And thou no breath at all? Thou'lt come no more,
Never, never, never, never, never.—
Pray you undo this button. Thank you, sir.
[Do you see this? Look on her, look, her lips,
Look there, look there!                *He dies.*⌝  375

381. **rack:** instrument of torture on which a victim's limbs were torn apart (See picture, below.)
390. **journey:** i.e., to death
394. **The oldest hath:** he who is **oldest** has

Victims tortured on a rack. (5.3.381)
From Girolamo Maggi, *De tintinnabulis liber . . .* (1689).

EDGAR He faints. ⌜*To Lear.*⌝ My lord,
 my lord!

KENT
Break, heart, I prithee, break!

EDGAR       Look up, my lord.

KENT
Vex not his ghost. O, let him pass! He hates him    380
 That would upon the rack of this tough world
 Stretch him out longer.

EDGAR      He is gone indeed.

KENT
The wonder is he hath endured so long.
He but usurped his life.            385

ALBANY
Bear them from hence. Our present business
Is general woe. ⌜*To Edgar and Kent.*⌝ Friends of my
 soul, you twain
Rule in this realm, and the gored state sustain.

KENT
I have a journey, sir, shortly to go;       390
My master calls me. I must not say no.

EDGAR
The weight of this sad time we must obey,
Speak what we feel, not what we ought to say.
The oldest hath borne most; we that are young
Shall never see so much nor live so long.     395
        *They exit with a dead march.*

# Textual Notes

The reading of the present text appears to the left of the square bracket. Unless otherwise noted, the reading to the left of the bracket is from **F,** the First Folio text (upon which this edition is based). The earliest sources of readings not in F are indicated as follows: **Q1** is the First Quarto of 1608; **Q2** is the Second Quarto of 1619; **Ed.** is an earlier editor of Shakespeare, beginning with the anonymous editor of the Second Folio of 1632. No sources are given for emendations of punctuation or for corrections of obvious typographical errors, like turned letters that produce no known word. **SD** means stage direction; **SP** means speech prefix; **uncorr.** means the first or uncorrected state of the First Folio; **corr.** means the second or corrected state of the First Folio; ~ stands in place of a word already quoted before the square bracket. ⋏ indicates the omission of a punctuation mark. There is no division into acts and scenes in Q1, only in F. Not all Q2 readings are included in these notes.

**1.1** 0. SD *Edmund*] *Bastard* Q1 *2 and often hereafter.* Cornwall] *Cornwell* Q1 4. kingdom] kingdomes Q1 5. equalities] Q1; qualities F 19. a son, sir] sir a sonne Q1 22. to] into Q1 *26 and hereafter.* SP EDMUND] *Bast.* Q1 33. SD *Sennet . . . Attendants.*] *Sound a Sennet, Enter one bearing a Coronet, then Lear, then the Dukes of Albany, and Cornwell, next Gonorill, Regan, Cordelia, with followers.* Q1 34. the] my Q1 36. lord] Leige Q1 36. SD *He exits.*] F *only* 37. shall . . . purpose] will . . . purposes Q1 38. Give me] F *only* 39. that] F *only* 40. fast] first Q1 41. from our age] of our state Q1 42. Conferring . . . strengths] Confirming . . . yeares Q1 42–48. while . . . now] F *only* 49. two great] Q1 *only* 54–55. Since . . . state] F *only* 58.

263

nature doth with merit challenge] merit doth most challenge it Q1　60. I love . . . word] I do loue . . . words Q1
62. and] or Q1　65. as . . . found] a . . . friend Q1　68.
speak] doe Q1　70. shadowy] shady Q1　70–71. and
with champains . . . rivers] F *only*　72. Albany's] *Alba-
ines* Q1　72. issue] Q1; issues F　75. of] to Q1　75.
Speak] Q1 *only*　76. I . . . that self . . . as my sister] Sir
I . . . the selfe same . . . that my sister is Q1　77. worth.
In] ~ʌ ~ Q1　79. comes too] came Q1　82. possesses]
Q1; professes F　87. ponderous] richer Q1　91. conferred . . . Goneril.—Now] confirm'd . . . *Gonorill*, but
now Q1　92. Although . . . love] Although the last, not
least in our deere loue Q1　93–94. The . . . interessed]
F (interest); F *only*　94. draw] win Q1　95. Speak] F
*only*　97–98. F *only*　99. Nothing will] How, nothing
can Q1　102. no] nor Q1　103. How . . . Cordelia] Goe
to, goe to Q1　103. speech a little] F *corr.*, Q1; speec ah
little F *uncorr.*　104. you] it Q1　110. Haply] F (Happily)　115. Q1 *only*　116. thy . . . this] this with thy
heart Q1　117. my good lord] good my Lord Q1　120.
Let] Well let Q1　122. mysteries] F2; miseries F; mis-
tresse Q1　122. night] might Q1　131. to my bosom]
F *only*　144. dowers . . . the] dower . . . this Q1　146.
with] in Q1　151. turn] turnes Q1　151. shall] still Q1
152. th' addition] the additions Q1　163. mad] Q2, F;
man Q1　163. wouldst] F (wouldest); wilt Q1　167.
falls] stoops Q1　167. Reserve thy state] Reuerse thy
doome Q1　172–73. sounds / Reverb] sound / Reuerbs
Q1　175. a] Q1 *only*　176. nor] Q1; nere F　178. being
motive] being the motiue Q1　182. SP LEAR] *Kear.* F
183. SP KENT] *Lent.* F　185. O] F *only*　185. Miscreant]
recreant Q1　186. F *only*　186. SP CORNWALL F (*Cor.*)
187. Kill . . . thy fee] Doe, kill . . . the fee Q1　188. gift]
doome Q1　191. recreant] F *only*　192. That . . . vows]
Since . . . vow Q1　193. strained] straied Q1　194.
sentence] F *uncorr.*, Q1; sentences F *corr.*　197. Five]
Foure Q1　198. disasters] diseases Q1　199. sixth] fift

Q1 204. Fare] Why fare Q1 205. Freedom] Friendship Q1 206-7. dear shelter . . . thee] protection . . . the Q1 208. justly . . . rightly] rightly . . . iustly Q1 213. SD *He exits. . . . Attendants.*] *Enter France and Burgundie with Gloster.* Q1 214. SP GLOUCESTER] Q1; *Cor.* F 215. Burgundy] *Bugundie* F 216. this] a Q1 220. Most] F *only* 221. hath] what Q1 228. more] else Q1 231. Will] Sir will Q1 233. Dowered] Couered Q1 237. in] on Q1 246. whom] that Q1 246. best] Q1 *only* 249. The . . . the] most . . . most Q1 253. your . . . affection] you . . . affections Q1 254. Fall] Falne Q1 256. Should] Could Q1 257. Majesty—] Ed.; ~. F; ~, Q1 259. well] Q1; will F 261. make known] may know Q1 263. unchaste] vncleane Q1 265. richer] rich Q1 267. That] As Q1 268. Hath . . . liking] F *corr.*, Q1; ath . . . lik ng F *uncorr.* 269. Better] Goe to, goe to, better Q1 270. t' have] t haue F 272. it but] it no more but Q1 273. Which] That Q1 276. regards] respects Q1 278. a dowry] and dowre Q1 279. king] *Leir* Q1 283. I am firm] F *only* 288. respect and fortunes] respects | Of fortune Q1 297. my] thy Q1 299. of] in Q1 301. Can] Shall Q1 309. SD *Flourish . . . exit.*] Ed.; *Flourish. Exeunt.* F; *Exit Lear and Burgundie.* Q1 310. sisters] F *corr.* (Sisters), Q1; S sters F *uncorr.* 314. Love] vse Q1 320. SP REGAN] *Gonorill* Q1 320. duty] duties Q1 321. SP GONERIL] *Regan* Q1 324. want] worth Q1 325. plighted] pleated Q1 326. with shame] shame them Q1 328. my] F *only* 329. not little] not a little Q1 335. not] Q1 *only* 338. grossly] grosse Q1 342-43. from his age to receive] to receiue from his age Q1 343. imperfections] imperfection Q1 344. the] F *only* 350. Pray you, let us sit] pray lets hit Q1 352. disposition] dispositions Q1 354. of it] on't Q1

**1.2.** 0. SD *Bastard*] *Bastard Solus.* Q1 1. SP EDMUND] Ed.; *Bast.* F (*and hereafter until line 173*), Q1 *hereafter* 4. me∧] ~? F 6. base,] ~? F 10. bastardy] Barstadie F   10–11. with "baseness," "bastardy," "base," "base"] base bastardie Q1   14. dull, stale, tired] stale dull lyed Q1   15. creating a] creating of a Q1   16. then] the Q1   18. father's] Q1; Farhers F   19. Fine . . . "legitimate"] F *only*   22. top th'] Ed.; to' th' F; tooth' Q1   25. prescribed] subscribed Q1   34. needed . . . terrible] needes . . . terrible Q1   38. SP EDMUND] Ed.; *Bast.* F; *Ba.* Q1 *corr.; omit* Q1 *uncorr.*   39. and] F *only*   41. o'erlooking] liking Q1   49. SD *reads*] *A Letter.* Q1 *after 1.48*   49. *and reverence*] F *only*   58. Sleep . . . wake] slept . . . wakt Q1   61. you to this] this to you Q1   70. his.] ~? Q1   73. before] heretofore Q1   75. heard him oft] often heard him Q1   77. declined, the] declining, his Q1   78. his] the Q1   81–82. sirrah . . . I'll] sir . . . I Q1   84. lord] Ed.; L. F; Lord Q1   86. his] this Q1   91. that] F *only*   92. writ] wrote Q1   93. other] further Q1   100–102. EDMUND . . . Earth] Q1 *only*   103. the] your Q1   106. will] shall Q1   107. find] see Q1   111. it] F *only*   114. discord] discords Q1   114. in] F *only*   114. and] F *only*   115. 'twixt] betweene Q1   115–21. This . . . graves.] F *only*   123–24. honesty! 'Tis] honest, strange Q1   124. SD *He exits.*] F *only*   126. surfeits] surfeit Q1   128–29. and stars . . . on] and the Starres . . . by Q1   130. spherical] spirituall Q1   135. on . . . a star] to . . . Starres Q1   138. Fut] Q1 *only*   139. maidenliest] F, Q1 (maidenlest)   139–40. in . . . bastardizing] of . . . bastardy Q1   140. Edgar] Q1 *only*   141. and] Q1 *only*   141. pat] out Q1   142–43. My cue . . . Tom] mine . . . them Q1   144. *Fa . . . mi*] F *only*   149. with] about Q1   150. writes] writ Q1   151–59. as . . . come] Q1 *only*   160. The] Why, the Q1   162. Ay] F *only*   164. nor] or Q1   168. until] till Q1   171. scarcely] scarce Q1   173–79. I pray . . . brother] F *only*   180. best. I] best, goe arm'd, I Q1   186. SD *Edgar exits.*] Q1 (*Fdgar*); F (*Exit.*) *1 line earlier*

**1.3.**   0. SD *Steward*] *Gentleman* Q1   3 *and hereafter in this scene.* SP OSWALD] Ed.; *Ste.* F; *Gent.* Q1   3.

Ay] Yes Q1    8. trifle.] ~ʌ Q1    14. fellows . . . to] fellow
seruants, . . . in Q1    15. distaste . . . my] dislike . . . our
Q1    17–22. Q1 *only*    23. have said] tell you Q1    24.
Well] Very well Q1    27–28. I . . . speak.] Q1 *only*    29.
very] Q1 *only*    29. course. Prepare] course, goe prepare Q1    29. SD *They exit.*] *Exit.* Q1
**1.4.**    1. well] Q1; will F    7. So . . . come] F *only*    8.
thee . . . labors] the . . . labour Q1    8. SD F; *Enter Lear.*
Q1    32. canst do] Q1; canst thou do Q2, F    38. sir] F
*only*    41–42. me—if . . . dinner. I] ~, ~ . . . ~, ~ F, Q1
44. SD *1 line later in* F *and* Q1    45. You] F *only*    46 *and
hereafter to line 357.* SP OSWALD] Ed.; *Ste.* F; *Steward*
Q1    46. *He exits*] F *only*    51. SP KNIGHT] *Kent* Q1    51.
daughter] Q1; Daughters F    54, 57, 64, 73. SP KNIGHT]
*seruant* Q1    60. of kindness] F *only*    70. purpose] pur-
port Q1    72. my] this Q1    75. well] F *only*    77. SD *1
line later in* F; F *only*    78. come . . . hither, sir] sir, come
you hither Q1    82–83. these . . . your pardon] this . . .
you pardon me Q1    90. arise. Away] F *only*    92. lubber's length again,] F, Q1 *corr.*; ~, ~ ~ʌ Q1 *uncorr.*    92.
Go to] F *only*    92–93. Have you] you haue Q1    93. So]
F *only*    94. my] F *only*    101. LEAR . . . my boy] *Kent.*
. . . Foole Q1    106. did] done Q1    111. all my] any Q1
115. dog must] dog that must Q1    116. the Lady] Ladie
oth'e Q1    118. gall] gull Q1    121. nuncle] vncle Q1
132. SP KENT] *Lear* Q1    133. 'tis] F *only*    135. nuncle]
vncle Q1    141. Dost know] Q1; Dost thou know Q2,
F    142. one] foole Q1    144–59. That . . . snatching] Q1
*only*    158. ladies] Q1 *corr.* (Ladies); lodes Q1 *uncorr.*
159–60. Nuncle, give . . . egg] giue . . . egge Nuncle
Q1    160. crowns] F, Q1 *uncorr.* (crownes); crown e s
Q1 *corr.*    164. crown] Q1; Crownes F    165. on thy]
at'h Q1    170. grace] wit Q1    172. And . . . to] They
. . . doe Q1    177. mothers] mother Q1    182. fools]
Q1; Foole F    184. learn to lie] F, Q1 *corr.* (learneto
lye); learne lye Q1 *uncorr.*    185. sirrah] F *only*    191.
thee, nuncle] F, Q1 *corr.* (thee Nuncle); theeNuncle

Q1 *uncorr.* 195. Methinks] Q1 *only* 196. thou]
F, Q1 *corr.*; tho u Q1 *uncorr.* 197. frowning] frowne
Q1 197. Now] F, Q1 *corr.* (now); thou, Q1 *uncorr.*
199. Fool. Thou] F, Q1 *corr.* (foole,thou); foole, thou
Q1 *uncorr.* 203. nor crust] neither crust Q1 203. nor
crumb] Q1; not crum F 209. riots. Sir,] Ed.; ~^ ~. F;
~,) ~^ Q1 213. it] F *only* 215. redresses] redresse Q1
218. Which] that Q1 219. Will... proceeding] must
... proceedings Q1 220. know] trow Q1 222. it's
... by it] it... beit Q1 225. I... your] Come sir, I...
that Q1 227. which... transport] that... transforme
Q1 231. This] why this Q1 234. weakens] weaknes,
or Q1 235. lethargied—Ha! Waking? 'Tis] lethergie,
sleeping, or wakeing; ha! sure tis Q1 237. SP FOOL]
F *only* 238–42. I... father.] Q1 *only* 244. This admiration, sir] Come sir, this admiration Q1 246. To] F
*only* 252. Makes it] make Q1 252. a brothel] brothell Q1 253. graced] great Q1 254. then] thou Q1
257. remainders] remainder Q1 259. Which] that Q1
266. SD *Albany*] *Duke* Q1 267. Woe] We Q1 267–68.
O... come?] Q1 *only* 269. will... horses] will that
wee prepare any horses Q1 273. F *only* 274. liest.]
list^ Q1 275. are] and Q1 280. Which] that Q1
283. Lear, Lear, Lear] *Lear, Lear* Q1 286 *and hereafter.*
SP ALBANY] *Duke* Q1 287. F *only* 289. Hear... goddess, hear] harke... Goddesse Q1 291. fruitful.] F (:);
~^ Q1 297. thwart disnatured] thourt disuetur'd Q1
299. cadent] accent Q1 301. that... feel] that shee
may feele, that she may feele Q1 303. Away, away]
goe, goe, my people Q1 303. SD F *only* 305. more
of it] the cause Q1 307. As] that Q1 307. SD F *only*
314. which] that Q1 315–17. thee worth them...
upon thee! / Th'] the worst^ ... vpon the^ Q1 317–18.
untented.../ Pierce] F, Q1 *corr.*; vntender... peruse
Q1 *uncorr.* 318. thee! Old] F (~. ~); the old Q1 320.
cast you... loose] you cast... make Q1 321. Yea, is 't

come to this?] Q1 *only* 322. Ha! Let it be so.] F *only* 322–23. I have another daughter / Who] yet haue I left a daughter, whom Q1 327. forever.] for ever, thou shalt I warrant thee Q1 327. SD Q2, F; *omit* Q1 328. that] that my Lord Q1 331. Pray . . . ho] Come sir no more Q1 332. sir] F *only* 333. tarry. Take] tary and take Q1 334–35. with thee. / A] with a Q1 339. SD F *only* 340–55. GONERIL . . . Oswald] *Gon.* What *Oswald*, ho. *Oswald.* Here Madam. | *Gon.* Q1 356. that] this Q1 357. SP OSWALD] Q1; *Stew.* F 357. Ay] Yes Q1 359. fear] feares Q1 362. And hasten] F, Q1 *corr.* (& hasten); and after Q1 *uncorr.* 362. No, no] now Q1 364. milky] F, Q1 *corr.* (milkie); mildie Q1 *uncorr.* 365. condemn] dislike Q1 366. You are] F2; Your are F; y'are Q1 366. at task for] attaskt for Q1 *corr.*; alapt Q1 *uncorr.* 367. praised] praise Q1 369. better, oft] better ought Q1

**1.5.** 0. SD F; *Enter Lear.* Q1; *Enter Lear, Kent, and Foole.* Q2 8. were] Q2, F; where Q1 11. not] nere Q1 16. can tell what] con, what Q1 17. What . . . boy] Why what canst thou tell my boy Q1 19. canst . . . stands] canst not . . . stande Q1; canst not . . . stands Q2 22. one's . . . of] his . . . on Q1 31. daughters] daughter Q1 38. indeed] F *only* 43. till] before Q1 45. not mad] F *only* 45–46. heaven! / Keep] heauen! I would not be mad, keepe Q1 47. How now] F *only* 48. SP GENTLEMAN] *Seruant* Q1 49. boy.] boy. *Exit.* Q1 50. a] F *only* 51. unless] except Q1 52. SD *They exit.*] *Exit.* Q1

**2.1.** 0. SD *severally*] *meeting* Q1 1 *and hereafter.* SP EDMUND] Ed.; *Bast.* Q1, F 2. you] Q1; your F 4. Regan] F *only* 4. this] to Q1 7. they] there Q1 8. kissing] bussing Q1 11. the dukes] the two Dukes Q1 13. do] F *only* 13. SD Q2, F; *omit* Q1 18. Which I must act . . . work] which must aske∧ . . . helpe Q1 19. SD *1 line earlier* in F; *3–4 lines earlier in* Q1 20. sir] F *only* 23. Cornwall] *Cornwall* ought Q1 27. your-

self.] your—Q1   29–30. me. / In] F (~: ~); ~ʌ ~ Q1   30.
cunning] crauing Q1   31. Draw] F *only*   33. hoa] here
Q1   34. brother] brother flie Q1   35. SD F *only*   40.
SD F; *Enter Glost.* Q1   44. Mumbling] warbling Q1
45. stand] stand's Q1   51. ho] F *only*   54. revenging]
reuengiue Q1   55. the thunder] their thunders Q1
57. in fine] in a fine Q1   59. in] with Q1   61. lanced]
Q1; latch'd F   62. And] but Q1   63. right] Q2, F; rights
Q1   72. coward] caytife Q1   78. would . . . reposal]
could . . . reposure Q1   80. I should] Q1; should I F
82. would, though] would, I, though Q1   84. practice]
pretence Q1   87. spurs] Q1; spirits F   89. O strange]
Strong Q1   90. said he] F *only*   91. Q1 *only*   91. SD
F *only, 3 lines earlier*   92. why] Q1; wher F   97. due] F
*only*   99. SD F; *Enter the Duke of Cornwall.* Q1   100.
came] F *corr.*, Q1; csme F *uncorr.*   101–2. strange
news] Q1; strangenesse F   106. O] F *only*   106. it's] is
Q1   109. O] I Q1   111. tended] tends Q1   112. bad.]
F *corr.*, Q1; ~, F *uncorr.*   113. of that consort] F *only*
116. th' expense and waste of his] these—and wast of
this his Q1 *uncorr.*; the wast and spoyle of his Q1 *corr.*
121 *and hereafter.* SP CORNWALL] *Duke* Q1   122. hear]
heard Q1   122. your] Q1; yout F   125. bewray] betray
Q1   134–35. need. Youʌ] F (~: ~ʌ); ~ʌ ~, Q1   136. sir]
F *only*   140. threading] threatning Q1   141. poise] Q1
*corr.*; prize F, Q1 *uncorr.* (prise), Q2   143. father] F, Q1
*uncorr.* (Father); Fa th er Q1 *corr.*   144. differences] F,
Q1 *corr.* (diferences); defences Q1 *uncorr.*   144. best]
F, Q1 *uncorr.*; lest Q1 *corr.*   144. thought] Q1; though
F   145. home] F, Q1 *corr.*; hand Q1 *uncorr.*   145. sev-
eral] Q1 *corr.* (seueral); F, Q1 *uncorr.* seuerall   148.
businesses] busines Q1   151. SD *Exeunt. Flourish.* F;
*Exeunt.* Q1
   **2.2.**   0. SD *and*] Q1; *aad* F   0.SD *severally*] F *only*
1 *and hereafter.* SP OSWALD] Ed.; *Stew.* F; *Steward* Q1   1.
dawning] deuen Q1 *uncorr.*; euen Q1 *corr.*   1. this] the
Q1   5. KENT I'] F *corr.* (*Kent.* I'); *Kent.* I' F *uncorr.*; *Kent.*

It' Q1   15. suited] snyted Q1 *uncorr.*; shewted Q1 *corr.*
16. worsted] Q1 *corr.*; woosted F; wosted Q1 *uncorr.*
17. action-taking, whoreson] action taking knaue, a
whorson Q1   17–18. superserviceable, finical] super-
finicall Q1   22. bitch; one whom] bitch, whom Q1   23.
clamorous] Q1 *corr.*; clamarous Q1 *uncorr.*; clamours
F   24. thy] the Q1   25. Why] F *only*   29. ago] Q1
*only* 29–30. since . . . before] since I beat thee, and
tript vp thy heeles before Q1   32. yet] F *only*   33. you,
you] you, draw you Q1   36. come with] bring Q1   43.
Strike!] Q1 *corr.* (~?); ~. F, Q1 *uncorr.*   44. Murder, mur-
der] murther, helpe Q1   44. SD *Cornwall . . . Servants.*]
*Gloster the Duke and Dutchesse* Q1   45. Part] F *only*
49–50. that | strikes] F *corr.*, Q1; that; s strikes F *uncorr.*
59. A tailor] I, a Tayler Q1   60. they] hee Q1   61. years
o'] houres at Q1   62. SP CORNWALL] *Glost.* Q1   67.
wall] walles Q1   70. sirrah] sir Q1   71. know you] you
haue Q1   75. Who] That Q1   77. the holy . . . atwain]
those . . . in twaine Q1   77. holy] F *corr.*; holly F *uncorr.*
78. too intrinse] Ed.; t'intrince F; to intrench Q1   78.
unloose] inloose Q1   81. Being . . . fire] Bring . . . stir
Q1   81. the] their Q1   82. Renege] Q1; Reuenge F   83.
gale] Q1; gall F   84. dogs] dayes Q1   86. Smile] Ed.;
Smoile F, Q1   88. drive] send Q1   93. fault] offence Q1
95. nor . . . nor] or . . . or Q1   98. Than] Q2, F; That Q1
100. some] a Q1   102. roughness] ruffines Q1   103.
nature] F *corr.* (Nature), Q1; Narure F *uncorr.*   104. An
. . . plain] he must be plaine Q1   111. faith, in] sooth,
or in Q1   112. great] graund Q1   114. On] In Q1   114.
flick'ring] Ed.; flicking F; flitkering Q1   115. mean'st
by] mean'st thou by Q1   116. dialect] dialogue Q1
121. What was] What's Q1   126. compact] coniunct Q1
128–29. man / That] man, that, / That Q1   130. self-
subdued] F *corr.*, Q1; selfe-s[inverted]ubdued F *uncorr.*
131. fleshment] flechuent Q1   131. dread] Q1; dead F
135. Fetch . . . stocks] Bring . . . stockes ho Q1   136.
ancient] ausrent Q1 *uncorr.*; miscreant Q1 *corr.*   138.

Sir] F *only*  140. employment] imployments Q1  141.
shall] should Q1  141. respect] Q1 *corr.*; respcct Q1
*uncorr.*; respects F  144. Stocking] Stobing Q1 *uncorr.*;
Stopping Q1 *corr.*  146. sit till] F *corr.*, Q1 *corr.*; set till
Q1 *uncorr.*; si ttill F *uncorr.*  149. should] could Q1
151. color] nature Q1  152. speaks] Q2, F; speake Q1
152. SD F *only, 2 lines earlier*  154–58. His . . . with] Q1
*only*  155. correctionʌ] Q1 *corr.*; ~, Q1 *uncorr.*  156.
basest] Q1 *corr.*; belest Q1 *uncorr.*  156. contemned'st]
Ed.; contaned Q1 *uncorr.*; temnest Q1 *corr.*  158. King
must] Q1; King his Master, needs must F  159. he]
hee's Q1  163. gentleman] Q2, F; Gentlemen Q1  164.
Q1 *only*  165. SP CORNWALL] Q1 *omit*  165. my good
lord] Q1; my lord Q2, F  165. SD Ed.; *Exit.* Q2, F; *omit*
Q1  166. Duke's] Q1; Duke F  170. Pray, do] Pray you
doe Q1  171. out] Q2, F; ont Q1  174. taken] tooke
Q1  174. SD Q2, F; *omit* Q1  175. saw] F, Q1 *corr.*; say
Q1 *uncorr.*  180. miracles] my rackles Q1 *uncorr.*; my
wracke Q1 *corr.*  182. most] F, Q1 *corr.*; not Q1 *uncorr.*
182. been] F, Q1 *uncorr.* (beene); bin Q1 *corr.*  183.
course,] Q1; ~. F  185. their] F, Q1 *corr.*; and Q1 *uncorr.*
185. o'erwatched] ouerwatch Q1  186. Take] F, Q1
*corr.*; Late Q1 *uncorr.*  187. shameful] Q1; shamefnll F
189. SD Q1 *only*
   **2.3.**  1. heard] heare Q1  4. unusual] Q1; vnusall
F  5. taking.] ~ʌ Q1  10. elf . . . hairs in] else . . . haire
with Q1  12. winds and persecutions] wind, and per-
secution Q1  15. and] F, Q1 *corr.; omit* Q1 *uncorr.*  15.
mortifièd arms] mortified bare armes Q1  15. armsʌ]
~, Q1; ~. F  16. Pins] F, Q1 *corr.*; Pies Q1 *uncorr.*  17.
from low farms] frame low seruice Q1 *uncorr.*; from
low seruice Q1 *corr.*  18. sheepcotes] Q1; Sheeps-
Coates F  19. Sometime] Q1; Sometimes F  20. Turly-
god] F, Q1 *corr.*; Tuelygod Q1 *uncorr.*
   **2.4.**  0. SD F; *Enter King.* Q1  0. SD *Gentleman*]
F *corr.*; *Gentlemaa* F *uncorr.*  1. home] hence Q1  2.

messenger] Q1; Messengers F   3, 68. SP GENTLEMAN]
*Knight* Q1   4. in them] F *only*   5. this] his Q1   7. Ha]
How Q1   8. thy] Q1; ahy F   9. F *only*   10. Ha, ha,
he] ha, looke he Q1   10. garters.] Q1 (~,); ~ʌ F   11.
heads] heeles Q1   12. man's] Q1; man F   22–23. yea.
/ LEAR By] yea. / *Lear.* No no, they would not. / *Kent.*
Yes they haue. / *Lear.* By Q1   24. F *only*   24. Juno]
*Iuuo* F   25. SP F *only*   26. could . . . would] would . . .
could Q1   30. might'st . . . impose] may'st . . . purpose
Q1   36. panting] Q1; painting F   39. whose] Q1; those
F   40. meiny] men Q1   46. which] that Q1   51. The]
This Q1   52–61. F *only*   63. *Hysterica*] Ed.; *Historica*
Q1, F   64. below.—] Q1 (~,); ~ʌ F   65. With] Q1; Wirh
F   65. here] F *only*   67. here] there Q1   67. SD F *only*
68. but] then Q1   69. None] No Q1   70. the] Q1; the
the F   70. number] traine Q1   77. twenty] a 100. Q1
79–80. following] following it Q1   80. upward] vp the
hill Q1   81–82. gives . . . counsel,] F *corr.* (giues . . .
counsell,), Q1; giue . . . counsellʌ F *uncorr.*   82. have]
Q1; hause F   84. which] that Q1   84. and seeks] F
*only*   86. begins] begin Q1   93. fool] F *only*   93. SD *2
lines earlier in* F   96. have] F *only*   96. all the] hard to
Q1   96. fetches,] F *corr.*; ~ʌ F *uncorr.*; Iustice, Q1   97.
The] I the Q1   103. plague, death] death, plague Q1
104. "Fiery"? What "quality"?] what fierie quality Q1
107–9. F *only*   112. fatherʌ] F, Q1 *corr.*; fate, Q1 *uncorr.*
113. his] F, Q1 *corr.*; the Q1 *uncorr.*   113. commands,
tendsʌ] Ed.; ~, ~, F; come and tendsʌ Q1 *uncorr.*; commands herʌ Q1 *corr.*   115–16. F *only*   117. "Fiery"?
The] The Q1 *uncorr.; omit* Q1 *corr.*   117. that—] that
*Lear* Q1   118. No] F, Q1 *corr.*; Mo Q1 *uncorr.*   118.
yet] F (~,); ~ʌ Q1   121. commands] Q2, F; Cõmand
Q1   129. practiceʌ *only.*] ~, ~ʌ Q1   130. Go] F *only*
130. I'd] Ile Q1   130. them.] F (~:); ~ʌ Q1   134. SD
F *only*   135. me] my heart Q1   135. my rising heart!
But down] F *only*   136. cockney] F, Q1 *corr.* (Cokney);

Coknay Q1 *uncorr.* 137. paste] F, Q1 *corr.* (pâst); past
Q1 *uncorr.* 137. knapped] rapt Q1 140. SD F; *Enter
Duke and Regan.* Q1 142. SD F *only* 144. you] Q1;
your F 146. divorce] F, Q1 *corr.* (diuorse); deuose Q1
*uncorr.* 146. mother's] Q1; Mother F 146. tomb] F,
Q1 *corr.*; fruit Q1 *uncorr.* 147. O] yea Q1 152–53.
believe∧ / With how depraved] beleeue, Of how dep-
toued Q1 *uncorr.* (depriued Q1 *corr.*) 154. you] F *only*
156. scant] slacke Q1 157–62. F *only* 165. in] on Q1
166. his] her Q1 168. pray you] pray Q1 170. her]
her Sir Q1 172. but] F *only* 178. Never] No Q1 185.
sir, fie] fie sir Q1 186. SP Q2, F; *omit* Q1 189. blis-
ter] blast her pride Q1 191. is on] F *only* 193. tender-
hefted] tender hested Q1 205. SD F *only* 208. letter]
letters Q1 209. SD *3 lines earlier in F, 2 in* Q1 212.
fickle] Q1; fickly F 212. her∧] F, Q1 *uncorr.*; ~, Q1 *corr.*
213. varlet] F, Q1 *corr.*; varlot Q1 *uncorr.* 215. SP LEAR]
*Gon.* Q1 215. stocked] struck Q1 216. SD *2 lines
earlier in* Q1, F 217. Who] *Lear.* Who Q1 218. your]
you Q1 219. Allow] F, Q1 *corr.*; alow Q1 *uncorr.* 219.
you] F *only* 223. will you] wilt thou Q1 244. hot-
blooded] F *uncorr.*; hot-bloodied F *corr.*; hot bloud in
Q1 246. beg] Q2, F; bag Q1 251. I] Now I Q1 255.
that's in] that lies within Q1 257. or] an Q1 259. call
it] F, Q1 *corr.*; callit Q1 *uncorr.* 262. when] F *corr.*, Q1;
wheu F *uncorr.* 265. so] so sir Q1 266. looked] looke
Q1 269. you old] you are old Q1 271. spoken] spoken now Q1 274. and danger] F *corr.*, Q1; anddanger
F *uncorr.* 275. Speak . . . one] Speakes . . . a Q1 293.
look] seem Q1 303. need] needes Q1 304. need]
deed Q1 306. nature] F *corr.* (Nature), Q1; Nattue F
*uncorr.* 307. is] as Q1 310–11. true need] F *corr.*, Q1;
trueneed F *uncorr.* 313. man] fellow Q1 315. daughters'] F *corr.* (Daughters), Q1; Daughte s F *uncorr.*
316. so] to Q1 317. tamely] lamely Q1 318. And] O
Q1 323. I'll∧ weep] F *corr.*, Q1; ~, ~ F *uncorr.* 325.

SD F *only* 326. into . . . flaws] in . . . flowes Q1 327.
mad] F *corr.*, Q1; mads F *uncorr.* 327. SD *Gloucester*]
Q2; *Leister* Q1 *only* 335. SP GONERIL] *Duke.* Q1 335.
purposed] puspos'd Q1 336. SP CORNWALL] *Reg.* Q1
339–40. CORNWALL . . . horse] F *only* 340. but] & Q1
341. SP CORNWALL] *Re.* Q1 341. best] good Q1 343.
high] bleak Q1 344. ruffle] russel Q1 345. scarce]
not Q1 353. Regan] *Reg.* Q1
**3.1.** 0. SD F; *Enter Kent and a Gentleman at seuerall doores.* Q1 1. Who's there] Whats here Q1 4. ele-
ments] element Q1 7–17. tears . . . all] Q1 *only* 16.
fur] Q1 *corr.* (furre); surre Q1 *uncorr.* 22. note] Arte
Q1 24. is] be Q1 26–29. Who . . . state.] F *only*
29–39. From . . . plain:] Q1 *only* 29. From] *This ed.*;
But true it is, from Q1 39–43. what . . . furnishings. F
*only* 44–46. Q1 *only* 49. am] F *only* 50. outwall] Q1
*uncorr.*; out-wall F, Q1 *corr.* 54. that] your Q1 59–61.
in . . . this] Ile this way, you that Q1
**3.2.** 0. SD *Storm still.*] F *only* 1. winds] wind
Q1 1. blow!] ~∧ F, Q1 3. our] The Q1 3. drowned]
Q1; drown F 6. of] to Q1 9. Strike] smite Q1 10.
molds] Mold Q1 11. makes] make Q1 12. holy] F,
Q1 *corr.*; holly Q1 *uncorr.* 14. in. Ask] in, and aske Q1
15. men nor fools] man nor foole Q1 18. tax] taske
Q1 20. subscription. Then] subscription, why then Q1
24. will . . . join] haue . . . ioin'd Q1 25. battles] battel
Q1 26. ho] F *only* 35. of] haue Q1 37. but] F, Q1
*corr.*; hut Q1 *uncorr.* 40. SD *2 lines earlier in F, 1 in*
Q1 44. are] sit Q1 46. wanderers] wanderer Q1 47.
make] makes Q1 51. fear] force Q1 57. simular of]
simular man of Q1 58. to] in Q1 61. concealing con-
tinents] concealed centers Q1 63. than] their Q1 69.
harder than the stones] hard then is the stone Q1 70.
you] me Q1 73. wits begin] wit begins Q1 77. And]
that Q1 77. your] you Q1 78–79. hovel.— / Poor∧]
F (~; / ~∧); ~∧ ~, Q1 79. in] of Q1 80. That's sorry]

That sorrowes Q1   81. *and*] F *only*   84. *Though*] for
Q1   85. my good] Q1 *only*   85. SD F *only*   86–103. SD
F *only*
   **3.3**  0. SD *Edmund*] and the Bastard with lights
Q1   1–2. thisʌ . . . dealing.] F (~ʌ . . . ~;); ~, . . . ~ʌ Q1
3. took from] Q2, F; tooke me from Q1   4. perpetual]
their Q1   6. or] nor Q1   8. There is division] ther's
a diuisiõ Q1   13. footed] landed Q1   14. look] seeke
Q1   17. If] though Q1   19–20. strange things toward,
Edmund] ~ ~ ~ʌ ~ F; Some strange thing toward,
*Edmund* Q1   22. Instantly] instãly Q1   25. The] then
Q1
   **3.4.**  0. SD *Fool*] F *corr.* (*Foole*), Q1; *Fo le* F *uncorr.*
2. The tyranny] F, Q1 *corr.* (the tyrranie); the the tyran-
nie Q1 *uncorr.*   3. SD F *only*   5. here] F *only*   8. con-
tentious] crulentious Q1 *uncorr.*; tempestious Q1 *corr.*
9. skin. Soʌ] F *uncorr.* (skin.so), Q1; skinso: F *corr.*   12.
thy] Q1; they F   12. roaring] F, Q1 *corr.* (roring); raging
Q1 *uncorr.*   15. This] Q1 *corr.* (this); The F, Q1 *uncorr.*,
Q2   17. beats] F, Q1 *corr.* (beates); beares Q1 *uncorr.*
17. there.] F *corr.* (~,); ~ʌ F *uncorr.*; theirʌ Q1   19.
home] sure Q1   20–21. In . . . endure] F *only*   23. gave
all] gaue you all Q1   24. lies. Let] F *corr.* (lies, let), Q1;
lie, slet F *uncorr.*   26. here] F *only*   30–31. F *only*   31.
SD F *only, 1 line earlier*   33. storm] night Q1   42–43.
SD F *only,* SD *reading "Enter Edgar, and Foole." 2 lines
earlier*   42. half, fathom and] F *corr.*; half, fathomand
F *uncorr.*   47. A spirit, a spirit] A spirit Q1   51. blows
the cold wind] Q1; blow the windes F   51. Hum!] F
*only* 52. cold] Q1 *only*   53. Didst thou give] Hast thou
giuen Q1   53. thy daughters] thy two daughters Q1
56. through] Q1; though F   56. through flame] F *only*
57. ford] Q1; Sword F   59. porridge] pottage Q1   63.
O, do de, do de, do de] F *only*   64. star-blasting] starre-
blusting Q1   66. there—and] there, and and Q1   67.
and there] F *only*   67. SD F *only*   68. Has] What Q1
69. Wouldst] didst Q1   74. light] fall Q1   82. Pillicock

Hill] pelicocks hill Q1    82. Alow, alow] a lo Q1    87.
justice] iustly Q1    97. deeply] Q1; deerely F    101.
rustling] ruslngs Q1    102. woman] women Q1    103.
brothels] brothell Q1    103. plackets] placket Q1    104.
books] booke Q1    106. says . . . nonny] hay no on ny
Q1    106. boy, sessa] my boy, caese Q1    107. SD F *only*
108. Thou] Why thou Q1    108. a] thy Q1    110. than]
but Q1    110. this?] ~∧ Q1    112. Ha] F *only*    115.
lendings] F, Q1 *corr.*; leadings Q1 *uncorr.*    116. unbutton here] on bee true Q1 *uncorr.*; on Q1 *corr.*    117. contented. 'Tis] content, this is Q1    120. on 's] in Q1    120.
SD F *4 lines earlier; Enter Gloster.* Q1 *1 line later*    122.
fiend] Q1 *only*    122. Flibbertigibbet] *Sriberdegibit* Q1
*uncorr.; fliberdegibek* Q1 *corr.*    123. till the] Q1; at F
124. gives the web and] F, Q1 *corr.* (giues the web, &);
gins the web Q1    124–25. squints . . . harelip] queues
. . . harte lip Q1 *uncorr.*; squemes . . . hare lip Q1 *corr.*
128. He met the nightmare] F, Q1 *corr.*; a nellthu night
more Q1 *uncorr.*    129. alight] O light Q1    131. witch]
F, Q1 *corr.*; with Q1 *uncorr.*    137. tadpole] F, Q1 *corr.*
(tod pole), Q1 *uncorr.* (tode pold)    137. newt] F, Q1
*corr.*; wort Q1 *uncorr.*    142. stocked, punished] stock-
punisht Q1    143. had] Q1 *only*    148. Smulkin] snul-
bug Q1    153–54. blood, my lord . . . vile / That] bloud
is growne so vild my Lord, that Q1    161. fire and food]
food and fire Q1    164. Good my] My good Q1    165.
same] most Q1    169. once more] F *only*    171. SD F
*only*    182. sir.] F *only* (~:)    185. into th'] in't Q1    195.
tower came] towne come Q1    197. SD F *only*
  **3.5.**    0. SD *Edmund*] *Bastard* Q1    1. his] the Q1
11. letter he] Q1; Letter which hee F    13. this] his Q1
14. were not] were Q1    26. dearer] Q1; deere F    26.
SD F; *Exit.* Q1
  **3.6.**    0. SD F; *Enter Gloster and Lear, Kent, Foole, and
Tom.* Q1    4. to his] to Q1    5. reward] deserue Q1    5.
SD F *only* (*Exit*), *2 lines earlier*    7. and] F *only*    12–15.
FOOL . . . LEAR] F *only*    17–59. Q *only*    23. Now] Q2; no

Q1 26. trial] Q2; tral Q1 27. *burn*] Ed.; broome Q1
38. robèd] Ed.; robbed Q1 64. They] Theile Q1 71–72.
mongrelʌ grim, / Hound] Ed.; ~, ~, ~ F; ~, ~ – ~ Q1 72.
lym] Ed.; Hym F; him Q1 73. Bobtail tike, or trundle-
tail] Q1; Or Bobtaile tight, or Troudle taile F 74. him]
them Q1 76. leapt] leape Q1 77. Do . . . Sessa] loudla
doodla Q1 82. make] makes Q1 82. these hard hearts]
this hardnes Q1 83. entertain for] entertaine you for
Q1 85. Persian] Persian attire Q1 86. and rest] F *only*
88–89. So, so . . . morning] so, so, so . . . morning, so, so,
so, Q1 90. F *only* 90. SD *placed as in* Q1; *5 lines earlier in* F 101. Take up, take up] Take vp to keepe Q1
*uncorr.*; Take vp the King Q1 *corr.* 102. me, that] F, Q1
*corr.*; ~ʌ ~ Q1 *uncorr.* 104–10. KENT . . . GLOUCESTER] Q1
*only* 110. SD F *Exeunt.*; Q1 *Exit.* 111–26. Q1 *only*
**3.7.** 0. SD *and Servants.*] F *only* 2. husband. . . .
letter.] F (~, . . . ~,); ~, . . . ~ʌ Q1 4. traitor] vilaine Q1
8. company] F, Q1 *corr.*; company company Q1 *uncorr.*
8. revenges] reuenge Q1 11. festinate] Ed.; festiuate
F; festuant Q1 11. preparation;] F (~:); ~ʌ Q1 12–13.
posts . . . intelligent] post . . . intelligence Q1 14. SD *1
line later in* Q1 18. questrists] questrits Q1 24. SD
Ed.; *Exit.* F; *Exit Gon. and Bast.* Q1 27. well] F *only*
30. SD F; *Enter Gloster brought in by two or three,* Q1,
*1 line later* 40. I'm none] I am true Q1 52. answered]
answerer Q1 66. him answer] him first answere Q1
68. Dover] Douer sir Q1 71. anointed] F, Q1 *corr.*;
aurynted Q1 *uncorr.* 71. stick] rash Q1 72. as . . .
bare] of . . . lou'd Q1 *uncorr.*; on . . . lowd Q1 *corr.* 73.
buoyed] layd Q1 *uncorr.*; bod Q1 *corr.* 74. stellèd] F,
Q1 *corr.* (stelled); steeled Q1 *uncorr.* 75. holp . . . rain]
holpt . . . rage Q1 76. howled] heard Q1 76. stern]
dearne Q1 79. subscribe] subscrib'd Q1 82. these]
those Q1 88, 94, 97, 99. SP FIRST SERVANT] Ed.; *Seru.*
F, Q1 90. you] Q2, F; *omit* Q1 97. Nay] Why Q1 99.
you have] yet haue you Q1 105. enkindle] vnbridle Q1

107. treacherous] F *only*    108. he] Q1; be F    114. SD
F *only*    119. SD *Exeunt.* F; *Exit.* Q1    120–29. Q1 *only*
120. SP SECOND SERVANT] Ed.; *Seruant* Q1    122, 128. SP
THIRD SERVANT] Ed.; *2 Seruant* Q1    125. SP SECOND SER-
VANT] Ed.; I *Ser.* Q1    126. roguish] Q1 *uncorr.*; *omit* Q1
*corr.*    129. *They exit.*] Ed.; *Exit.* Q1
**4.1.**    2. flattered.] F (~,); ~∧ Q1    4. esperance] experience Q1    6–9. Welcome . . . blasts.] F *only*    9. But
who comes] Who's Q1    9. SD F; *Enter Glost. led by an
old man* Q1, *3 lines later*    10. poorly led] Q2, F; poorlie,
leed Q1 *uncorr.*; parti, eyd Q1 *corr.*    14. these fourscore
years.] this forescore—Q1    18. You] Alack sir, you Q1
31. So] As Q1    41. flies to] flies are toth' Q1    42. kill]
bitt Q1    44. play fool] play the foole Q1    48. Then,
prithee] Q1 *only*    48. away] gon Q1    49. hence] here
Q1    52. Which] Who Q1    58. SD F *only*    60. daub]
dance Q1    62. And yet I must] F *only*    65. scared] Q1
(scard); scarr'd F    66. thee, good man's son] the good
man Q1    67–72. Five . . . master.] Q1 *only*    69–70.
Flibbertigibbet] Ed.; *Stiberdigebit* Q1    70. mopping
and mowing] Ed.; Mobing, & *Mohing* Q1    78. slaves]
stands Q1    80. undo] vnder Q1    84. fearfully] firmely
Q1    90. SD F *only*
**4.2.**    0. SD Q1; *Enter . . . Bastard, and Steward.* F    2.
SD *Enter Steward.*] Q1, *1 line later; omit* F    12. most he
should dislike] hee should most desire Q1    15. terror]
F, Q1 *corr.* (terrer); curre Q1 *uncorr.*    18. Edmund] Q2,
F; *Edgar* Q1    19. powers.] ~∧ Q1    20. names] armes
Q1    25. command] F, Q1 *corr.*; coward Q1 *uncorr.*    25.
this;] F, Q1 *corr.* (~,); ~∧ Q1 *uncorr.*    29. thee] you
Q1    30. SD F *only*    31. dear] F, Q1 *corr.* (deer), Q1
*uncorr.* (deere)    33. F *only*    34. a] F, Q1 *corr.*; *omit* Q1
*uncorr.*    35. My] F, Q1 *uncorr.*; A Q1 *corr.*    35. fool] F,
Q1 *corr.*; foote Q1 *uncorr.*    35. body] F, Q1 *uncorr.*; bed
Q1 *corr.*    36. SD *He exits.*] Q1 *only* (*Exit Stew.*); *Enter
Albany.*] F *only*    37. whistle] F, Q1 *uncorr.*; whistling

Q1 *corr.* 40–61. I . . . deep.] Q1 *only* 40. disposition.] ~ʌ Q1 41. its] Q1 *uncorr.* (it); ith Q1 *corr.* 56. benefited] Q1 *corr.*; beniflicted Q1 *uncorr.* 58. these] Ed.; this Q1 *corr.*; the Q1 *uncorr.* 60. Humanity] Q1 *corr.*; Humanly Q1 *uncorr.* 60. itself] Q1 *corr.* (it self); it selfe Q1 *uncorr.* 64. discerning] deseruing Q1 65–72. that . . . so?"] Q1 *only* 65–66. know'stʌ / Foolsʌ do] ~ʌ ~, ~ Q1 *uncorr.*; ~, ~ʌ Q1 *corr.* (know'st, foolsdo) 69. noiseless] Q1 *corr.* (noyseles); noystles Q1 *uncorr.* 70. state begins to threat] Ed.; slayer begin threats Q1 *uncorr.*; state begins thereat Q1 *corr.* 71. Whilst] Q1 *corr.* (Whil'st); Whil's Q1 *uncorr.* 74. shows] Q1 *corr.*; seemes Q2, F, Q1 *uncorr.* 75. horrid] F, Q1 *corr.*; horid Q1 *uncorr.* 77–83. Q1 *only* 83. mew] Q1 *corr.*; now Q1 *uncorr.* 83. SD F *1 line later; Enter a Gentleman* Q1 *1 line later* 84. Q1 *only* 84. SP ALBANY] Q1 *corr.* (*Alb.*), Q1 *uncorr.* (*Alb.*) 85. SP MESSENGER] F; *Gent.* Q1 89. thrilled] thrald Q1 91. thereat] Q1; threat F 96. You] F, Q1 *corr.* (you); your Q1 *uncorr.* 96. justicers] Q1 *corr.*; Iustices Q2, F, Q1 *uncorr.* 104. in] on Q1 106. tart] tooke Q1 106. SD Q1 *only* 118. SD F; *Exit.* Q1

**4.3.** 0–66. Q1 *only.* 12. sir] Ed.; say Q1 19. strove] Ed.; streme Q1 23. seemed] Ed.; seeme Q1 36. moistened] Ed.; moystened her Q1

**4.4.** 0. Scene 4] Ed.; *Scena Tertia* F 0. SD F; *Enter Cordelia, Doctor and others.* Q1 2. vexed] vent Q1 3. fumiter] Q1 (femiter); Fenitar F 6. send] is sent Q1 11. helps] can helpe Q1 12. SP DOCTOR] Q1; *Gent.* F 14. lacks.] F (~:); ~ʌ Q1 20. distress] Q1; desires F 29. importuned] important Q1 30. incite] Q2, F; in sight Q1 32. SD F; *Exit.* Q1

**4.5.** 0. Scene 5] Ed.; *Scena Quarta* F 3. there] F *only* 6. lord] Lady Q1 8. letter] Q2, F; letters Q1 13. Edmund] and now Q1 16. enemy] army Q1 17. madam] F *only* 17. letter] letters Q1 18. troops set] troope sets Q1 24. things] thing Q1 32. Y' are] for

Q1   36. more.] F (~:); ~∧ Q1   40. you] F *only*   43.
him] Q1 *only*   43. should] would Q1   44. party] Lady
Q1   45. SD F; *Exit*. Q1
**4.6.**   0. Scene 6] Ed.; *Scena Quinta* F   0. SD *Edgar*]
*Edmund* Q1   1. I] we Q1   2. up it] it vp Q1   11. In]
With Q1   17. low!] F (~,); ~∧ Q1   22. walk] Q1; walk'd
F   24. buoy] boui Q1   27. heard so] heard, its so Q1
27. high.] ~∧ Q1   44. SD Q1 *only*   49. snuff] Q2, F;
snurff Q1   50. him] F *only*   51. SD Q1 *only*   53. may]
Q2, F; my Q1   57. Friend] F *only*   57. you.] Ed.; ~∧
F, Q1   70. no] no 1 Q1   71. summit] Ed.; Somnet F;
sommons Q1   74. eyes.] F (~:); ~∧ Q1   76. death?] ~∧
Q1   77. tyrant's] Q1; Tyranrs F   80. is 't] F *only*   82.
strangeness.] F (~,); ~∧ Q1   85. beggar] Q2, F; bagger
Q1   88. enragèd] enridged Q1   90. make them] made
their Q1   95. die.] ~∧ Q1   96. 'twould] would it Q1
98. SD F; *Enter Lear mad.* Q1   3 *lines later*   100. ne'er]
Q2, F; neare Q1   102. coining] Q1; crying F   108.
piece of] F *only*   111. clout, i' th' clout! Hewgh] ayre,
hagh Q1   115. with a white beard] ha *Regan* Q1   116.
the] F *only*   118. that] F *only*   124. ague-proof] argue-
proofe Q1   127. every] Q2, F; euer Q1   127. king.] ~∧
Q1   130. die. Die] die Q1   131. does] doe Q1   137.
does] do Q1   138. to] F *only*   138. name. The] name∧
to Q1   143. sulphurous] sulphury Q1   144. consump-
tion] consumation Q1   146. sweeten] to sweeten Q1
148. Let me] Here Q1   150. Shall] should Q1   150.
Dost thou] Do you Q1   152. at] on Q1   153. this]
that Q1   153. but] F *only*   155. thy] the Q1   155. see]
see one Q1   165. this] the Q1   168. ear.] F (~:); ~∧
Q1   168. Change places and] F *only*   169. justice . . .
thief] theefe . . . Iustice Q1   174. dog's obeyed] dogge,
so bade Q1   177. Thou] thy bloud Q1   179. cozener]
Q2, F; cosioner Q1   180. clothes] raggs Q1   180.
small] Q1; great F   181. hide] hides Q1   181–87. Plate
. . . lips.] F *only*   181. Plate sin] Ed.; Place sinnes F

189–90. Now, now, now] no Q1    192. mixed,] ~∧ Q1
194. fortunes] fortune Q1    195. enough;] F (~,); ~∧ Q1
198. wawl] wayl Q1    198. Mark] marke me Q1    202.
shoe] shoot Q1    203. felt] fell Q1    203. I'll . . . proof] F
*only*    205. SD *a Gentleman*] *three Gentlemen* Q1    206.
hand] hands Q1    207. him.—Sir] Ed.; him, Sir F; him
sirs Q1    208. daughter] F *only*    211. surgeons] a chur-
gion Q1    215. a man] F *only*    217. Ay . . . dust.] Q1
*only*    218. I] *Lear.* I Q1    218. smug] F *only*    219–20.
king, / Masters] King my maisters Q1    222. Come] nay
Q1    223. by] with Q1    223. Sa . . . sa] F *only*    223. SD
Q1; *Exit.* F    225. a] one Q1    227. have] hath Q1    230.
sir] F *only*    231. vulgar.] F (~:); ~∧ Q1    232. Which]
That Q1    232. sound] sence Q1    235. speedy foot.] F
(~ ~:); speed fort∧ Q1    235. descry] descryes Q1    236.
thought] thoughts Q1    240. SD *here in* Q1; *1 line earlier in* F    246. tame to] lame by Q1    251. bounty and
the benison] F, Q1 *corr.* (benizon); bornet and beniz
Q1 *uncorr.*    252. To boot, and boot] to saue thee Q1
*uncorr.*; to boot, to boot Q1 *corr.*    254. first] F, Q1
*corr.; omit* Q1 *uncorr.*    255. old] most Q1    262. that]
F *only* 264. vurther] F *only*    266. and] F *only*    268. as
'tis] F *only*    268–69. vortnight] F, Q1 *corr.*; fortnight
Q1 *uncorr.*    269. out,] Q1 *corr.*; ~∧ F, Q1 *uncorr.*    270.
costard] F, Q1 *corr.* (Costerd); coster Q1 *uncorr.*    271.
ballow] battero Q1 *uncorr.*; bat Q1 *corr.*    274. SD Q1
*only, 2 lines earlier*    278. out∧] F, Q1 *uncorr.*; ~, Q1
*corr.*    279. English] *British* Q1 *uncorr.*; *Brittish* Q1 *corr.*
279. SD Q1 *only*    284. rest you.] ~ ~, Q1 *corr.*; ~ ~∧ Q1
*uncorr.*    285. these] his Q1    285. The] These Q1    285.
of∧] F, Q1 *uncorr.*; ~, Q1 *corr.*    286. sorry] Q2, F; sorrow Q1    288. not.] ~∧ F, Q1    289. minds, we] minds
wee'd Q1 *uncorr.*; minds wee d Q1 *corr.*    290. SD F;
*A letter.* Q1 *corr.; omit* Q1 *uncorr.*    291. our] your Q1
294. done∧] Ed.; ~. F; ~, Q1    295. jail] F (*Gaole*), Q1
*corr.* (iayle); gayle Q1 *uncorr.*    298. affectionate] your
affectionate Q1    299. *and, for you, her own for venture*]

Q1; *omit* Q2, F    300. indistinguished] Q1; indinguish'd
F    300. will] wit Q1    302. brother.—] F (~:); ~∧ Q1
302. the sands] rhe sands F    311. severed] fenced Q1
313. SD F, *2 lines earlier;* Q1 (*A drum a farre off.*)    314.
hand.] F (~:); ~∧ Q1    316. SD F; *Exit.* Q1
**4.7.**    0. SD *Doctor*] Q1 *only*    0. and] F *corr.; omit*
F *uncorr.*    0. *Gentleman*] F *only*    7. suited.] F (~,); ~∧
Q1    10. Pardon] Pardon me Q1    15 *and hereafter in
this scene.* SP DOCTOR] Q1; *Gent.* F    18. jarring] hur-
rying Q1    24. will.] F (~:); ~∧ Q1    24. SD F *only*    25.
SP GENTLEMAN] *Doct.* Q1    25. of sleep] of his sleep
Q1    27. SP DOCTOR] Ed.; *omit* F; *Gent.* Q1    27. Be by,
good madam] Good madam be by Q1    27. him.] F (~,);
~∧ Q1    28. not] Q1 *only*    29–30. Q1 *only*    35. Kind]
Klnd Q1    37. Did challenge] Had challengd Q1    38.
opposed] exposd Q1    38. jarring] warring Q1    39–42.
To . . . helm] Q1 *only*    42. helm?] ~∧ Q1    42. enemy's]
iniurious Q1    55. do you] F *only*    59. I?] ~∧ Q1    66.
your] F *corr.,* Q1; yours F *uncorr.*    66. hand] hands
Q1    67. No, sir] Q1 *only*    68. mock] Q1; mocke me
Q2, F    70. not . . . less] F *only*    80. am; I am] am Q1
92. killed] cured Q1    92–93. and . . . lost] Q1 *only*    98.
you] F *only*    99. SD Q1; *Exeunt.* F    100–112. Q1 *only*
**5.1.**    0. SD F; *Enter Edmund, Regan, and their powers.* Q1    3. He's] F, Q1 *uncorr.* (he's); hee's Q1 *corr.*    3.
alteration] F, Q1 *corr.;* abdication Q1 *uncorr.*    11. In]
I, Q1    14–16. Q1 *only*    20. me] Q1 *only*    20. SD F;
*Enter Albany and Gonorill with troupes.* Q1    21–22. Q1
*only* 22. and] Q1 *corr.;* nd Q1 *uncorr.*    23. bemet.—] F
(~:); ~∧ Q1    24. Sir . . . heard] For . . . hear Q1    26–31.
Where . . . nobly.] Q1 *only*    34. and particular broils]
and particurlar broiles F; dore particulars Q1    35. the]
to Q1    37. proceeding] proceedings Q1    38. Q1 *only*
41. Pray, go] pray you goe Q1    45. SD F *3 lines earlier;
Exeunt.* Q1 *1 line earlier*    52. And . . . ceases] F *only* 52.
love] Q1; loues F    55. the] Q1; t[inverted]he F    57.
thy] the Q1    58. view] F, Q1 *corr.;* vew Q1 *uncorr.*    59.

Here . . . guess . . . true] Hard . . . quesse . . . great Q1
63. sisters] Q2, F; sister Q1   64. stung] sting Q1   71.
countenance] countenadce Q1   72. who] that Q1   73.
the] his Q1
**5.2.** 0. SD F; *Alarum. Enter the powers of France
ouer the stage, Cordelia with her father in her hand.
Enter Edgar and Gloster.* Q1   1. tree] bush Q1   5. 1st
SD *Exit.* F; Q1 (*1 line earlier*)   5. 2nd SD *within*] F *only*
5. 3rd SD Q2, F; *omit* Q1   6. SP EDGAR] *Egdar* F; *Edg.*
Q1   10. again?] ~∧ Q1   12. all.] ~∧ F, Q1   13. F *only*
**5.3.** 0. SD F; *Enter Edmund, with Lear and Cordelia
prisoners.* Q1   2. first] F; best Q1   6. I am] am I Q1
9. No . . . no] No, no Q1   9. prison.] F (~,); ~∧ Q1   14.
hear∧ poor rogues∧] Q1; ~ (~ ~) F   27. years] F *only*
28. starved] starue Q1   30. SD Q2, F; *omit* Q1   33.
One] F, Q1 *corr.*; And Q1 *uncorr.*   44–45. Q1 *only*   45.
1st SD F *only*   45. 2nd SD F; *Enter Duke, the two Ladies,
and others.* Q1   47. well. You] F (~: ~), Q1 *corr.* (~, ~);
~∧ ~ Q1 *uncorr.*   48. Who] That Q1   49. I . . . them]
We . . . then Q1   53. send] F, Q1 *corr.*; saue Q1 *uncorr.*
54. and appointed guard] Q1 *corr.; omit* Q1 *uncorr.,*
F   55. had] F; has Q1   55. more,] F, Q1 *corr.*; ~∧ Q1
*uncorr.* 56. common] F, Q1 *corr.*; coren Q1 *uncorr.*   56.
bosom] F (bosome); bossom Q1 *uncorr.*; bossome Q1
*corr.*   56. on] of Q1   59. Queen,] ~∧ Q1   62. session.]
~∧ Q1   62–67. At . . . place.] Q1 *only*   63. We] Q1 *corr.*
(wee); mee Q1 *uncorr.*   65. sharpness] Q1 *corr.* (sharp-
nes); sharpes Q1 *uncorr.*   72. might] should Q1   75.
immediacy] imediate Q1   79. addition] aduancement
Q1   80. rights] right Q1   82. SP GONERIL] Q1; *Alb.* F
90. F *only*   93. him] him then Q1   97. SP REGAN] *Bast.*
Q1   97. thine] good Q1   99. thine attaint] Q1; thy
arrest F   101. sister] Q1; Sisters F   104. your] the Q1
105. loves] loue Q1   107. F *only*   108. SP F *only*   108.
Let . . . sound.] F *only*   108. trumpet] Trmpet F   109.
person] head Q1   112. make] proue Q1   116. medi-
cine] poyson Q1   118. he is] Q1; hes F   120. the] thy

Q1   124. Q1 *only*   125. SP Q1 *only*   128. My] This Q1
129. SD F *only, 6 lines earlier*   130. trumpet] Trumper
F   132. Q1 *only*   132. SD F *only; trumpet*] Tumpet F
133. *reads*] F *only*   133. *within*] in Q1   133. *lists*] hoast
Q1   136. *by*] at Q1   137. SD–139 SD F *only*   138. HER-
ALD Again] *Bast.* Sound? Againe? Q1   139. SD *armed*]
*at the third sound, a trumpet before him.* Q1   143.
your quality] and qualitie Q1   145. Know] O know
Q1   145–46. lost, . . . tooth∧] ∼∧ . . . ∼: F; ∼∧ . . . ∼. Q1
147. am . . . as] are I mou't / Where is Q1   148. cope]
cope with all Q1   156–57. my privilege . . . honors]
the priuiledge of my tongue Q1   159. place, youth]
youth, place Q1   160. Despite] Q1; Despise F   160.
victor-sword] victor, sword Q1   160. fortune] fortun'd
Q1   163. Conspirant] Conspicuate Q1   163. illustri-
ous] Q1; illustirous F   165. below thy foot] beneath
thy feet Q1   166. traitor. Say] ∼∧ ∼ Q1   167. are] As
Q1   170. should] sholud Q1   172. tongue] being Q1
173. F *only*   174. rule] right Q1   175. Back] Heere Q1
175. these] those Q1   176. hell-hated lie] hell hatedly
Q1   176. o'erwhelm] oreturnd Q1   177. scarcely] Q1;
scarely F   179. SD F *only, 1 line later*   181. practice]
meere practise Q1   182. war] armes Q1   182. wast]
art Q1   185. Shut] Stop Q1   186. stopple] Q1; stop
Q2, F   186. Hold, sir] F *only*   187. name] thing Q1
188. No] nay no Q1   190. can] shal Q1   191. O] F *only*
193. SP GONERIL] Q1; *Bast.* F   193. SD *3 lines earlier
in* F; *Exit. Gonorill.* Q1 *here*   198. thou 'rt] thou bee'st
Q1   204. vices∧] vertues. Q1   205. plague] scourge Q1
205–6. us. / The] F (∼: / ∼); ∼∧ ∼ Q1   208. right] truth
Q1   208. 'Tis true] F *only*   209. circle;] F (∼,); circled∧
Q1   211. nobleness.] F (∼:) ∼∧ Q1   212–13. ever I /
Did] I did euer Q1   218–19. burst! / The] F (∼. ∼); ∼∧ ∼
Q1   221. we] with Q1   226. Their] The Q1   226. lost;
became] F (∼: ∼); ∼∧ ∼ Q1   228. fault] Father Q1   232.
our] my Q1   242–60. Q1 *only*   245. extremity.] Ed.; ∼∧
Q1   251. him] Ed.; me Q1   255. crack. Twice then] ∼∧

~, ~ Q1    258. disguise] diguise Q1    260. SD F; *Enter one with a bloudie knife.* Q1    261. O, help] F *only* 262. SP EDGAR] *Alb.* Q1    263. F *only* 264.    SP EDGAR] F *only*; in Q1 *this speech is Albany's*    264. this] that Q1 266. O, she's dead] F *only*    267. F; Who man, speake? Q1    269. confesses] hath confest Q1    272–272SD F *only*    273. the] their Q1    274. judgment] Iustice Q1 275. tremble,] Q1; ~. F    276. pity. O] F; pity. *Edg.* Here comes *Kent* sir. | *Alb.* O Q1    276. is this] tis Q1    277. allow the] allow *Enter Kent* | The Q1    278. Which] that Q1    282 *and hereafter.* SP ALBANY] *Duke.* Q1    284. Cordelia?] ~^ Q1    284. SD F, *11 lines earlier; The bodies of Gonorill and Regan are brought in.* Q1, *1 line later* 300. sword. Give] sword the Captaine, | Giue Q1    302. SP EDGAR] *Duke.* Q1    308. howl! O] howle, howle, O Q1    308. you] Q1; your F    319. stirs. She] F (~, ~); ~^ ~ Q1    325. you, murderers, traitors] F (Murderors); your murderous traytors Q1    329. woman] women Q1    331. SP GENTLEMAN] *Cap.* Q1    334. him] them Q1 338. brag] bragd Q1    338. and] or Q1    340. This . . . sight] F *only*    340. you not] F; not you Q1    343. you] F *only*    347. first] life Q1    349. You are] Ed.; Your are F; You'r Q1    352. fordone] foredoome Q1    354. Ay . . . think] So thinke I to. Q1    355. says] sees Q1    355. is it] it is Q1    357. SD F, *1 line earlier; Enter Captaine.* Q1, *1 line earlier*    358. SP MESSENGER] *Capt.* Q1    361. great] F *only*    365. Honors] Q2, F; honor Q1    369. No, no, no life] no, no life Q1    370. have] Q2, F; of Q1    371. thou no] F *corr.*, Q1; thouno F *uncorr.*    371. all?] all, O Q1    372. never, never] F *only*    374–75. SD F *only*; O, o, o, o. Q1    374. this? Look] F *corr.* (Looke); this, looke F *uncorr.*    378. SP KENT] *Lear.* Q1    383. He] O he Q1    387. Is] Is to Q1    389. realm] kingdome Q1 391. me. I] and I Q1    392. SP EDGAR] *Duke.* Q1    394. hath] haue Q1    395. SD F *only*

# Appendix: 3.1.21–46

As we explain in "An Introduction to This Text," part of what distinguishes the quarto and Folio versions of *King Lear* is that occasional passages in one version do not appear in the other. Since 1725, most editors have chosen to use either the Folio or the quarto version, incorporating into their choice of version the passages found only in the other. Such a process has, in most scenes, yielded a seamless join, but it has created a significant problem in Act 3, scene 1. In that scene, in the long speech given by Kent (lines 21–46 in our edition), the traditional combination of the two versions makes less sense than one would like.

Because the traditional way of combining the Folio and quarto passages is less than successful, our edition presents this speech in the novel form proposed by Richard Knowles in his article "Revision Awry in Folio *Lear* 3.1," *Shakespeare Quarterly* 46 (1995): 32–46. Drawing on a suggestion made by Peter Blayney, Knowles proposes that the Folio and quarto passages can be combined in a way that provides a much more coherent speech.

A major difficulty in combining the quarto and Folio versions is that the speech has different purposes in the two texts. Here is the quarto version, with spelling modernized:

> Sir I do know you,
> And dare upon the warrant of my art,
> Commend a dear thing to you, there is division,
> Although as yet the face of it be covered,
> With mutual cunning, twixt *Albany* and *Cornwall*

But true it is, from *France* there comes a power
Into this scattered kingdom, who already wise in
  our negligence,
Have secret feet in some of our best ports,
And are at point to show their open banner,
Now to you, if on my credit you dare build so far,
To make your speed to Dover, you shall find
Some that will thank you, making just report
Of how unnatural and bemadding sorrow
The King hath cause to plain,
I am a gentleman of blood and breeding,
And from some knowledge and assurance,
Offer this office to you.

As Knowles points out, in this quarto version Kent conveys to the Gentleman "news of impending civil strife, informs him of French forces landed at Dover . . . , exhorts him to carry news of the king's plight to those forces, and gives assurances of his own credibility and authority in urging such a course" (p. 34).

In the 1623 Folio version, the speech begins with almost exactly the same four and a half lines with which it begins in the quarto. Then the Folio departs entirely from the quarto version. While the quarto addresses the French invasion and the need for the gentleman to go to Dover to report the king's "bemadding sorrow," the Folio speaks instead of French spies among the servants of Albany and Cornwall and of the "snuffs" (rages) and "packings" (plots) of the dukes, along with their abuse of Lear, concluding with vague reference to a mysterious "something deeper" of which the "snuffs," "packings," and abuse are perhaps only the external trappings. The speech appears in the Folio as follows (with spelling modernized):

Sir, I do know you,
And dare upon the warrant of my note

Commend a dear thing to you. There is division
(Although as yet the face of it is covered
With mutual cunning) 'twixt Albany and Cornwall:
Who have, as who have not, that their great stars
Throned and set high; servants, who seem no less,
Which are to France the spies and speculations
Intelligent of our state. What hath been seen,
Either in snuffs, and packings of the dukes,
Or the hard rein which both of them hath borne
Against the old kind king; or something deeper,
Whereof (perchance) these are but furnishings.

The Shakespeare editorial tradition since Lewis
Theobald in 1733 has generally combined these
speeches by inserting the quarto-only lines at the end of
the Folio-only lines, to produce the speech as it appears
below. (Here the quarto-only lines appear in pointed
brackets, the Folio-only lines in square brackets.)

     Sir, I do know you
And dare upon the warrant of my note
Commend a dear thing to you. There is division,
Although as yet the face of it is covered
With mutual cunning, 'twixt Albany and Cornwall,
[Who have—as who have not, that their great stars
Throned and set high?—servants, who seem no less,
Which are to France the spies and speculations
Intelligent of our state. What hath been seen,
Either in snuffs and packings of the dukes,
Or the hard rein which both of them hath borne
Against the old kind king, or something deeper,
Whereof perchance these are but furnishings—]
[But true it is, from *France* there comes a power
Into this scattered kingdom, who already,
Wise in our negligence, have secret feet
In some of our best ports and are at point
To show their open banner. Now to you:

If on my credit you dare build so far
To make your speed to Dover, you shall find
Some that will thank you, making just report
Of how unnatural and bemadding sorrow
The King hath cause to plain.
I am a gentleman of blood and breeding,
And from some knowledge and assurance offer
This office to you.]

Although the majority of editions of *King Lear* are based on the Folio, most editors, beginning with Alexander Pope in 1725, have believed that the quarto-only lines are essential to the continuity of the play's action. Knowles observes that, in particular, only in the quarto is the Gentleman whom Kent addresses directed toward Dover to find Cordelia, and it is near Dover, to which both Lear and later Gloucester will also be bound, where we find the Gentleman and Cordelia later in the play. And Knowles is not alone in contending that in an edition based, like ours, on the Folio version, editors must include the quarto lines if the scene and the play are to make sense. Knowles, however, notes the abrupt discontinuity produced in the traditional combination of the quarto and Folio versions by the quarto's words "But true it is" (which appear in the sixth line of the quarto version of the speech and the fourteenth line of Theobald's version). In the quarto text, these words constitute a confirmation of the occasion (namely, the French invasion) for which the dukes have covered their division by mutual cunning. However, when the quarto and Folio versions are combined in the way constructed by Theobald, the words "But true it is" are separated by eight lines of Folio verse from their position in the quarto text and make no sense. Depending upon Peter Blayney's unpublished analysis of what may have happened between the quarto's version of Kent's speech and the Folio's, Knowles proposes an arrangement of the versions that omits the quarto's problematic "But true it is" and adds the remaining quarto lines in two segments, the first at a point several lines earlier than in the traditional combination. (See the text, above, page 125.) The resulting speech, although still difficult, has a coherence lacking in that used by Theobald in 1733 and found in most editions of the play, including our 1993 edition.

While Knowles brings into the service of his argument a good deal of speculation about how the Folio version came to be so different from that in the quarto, it is possible to accept his solution to the problem of discontinuity presented above without embracing any of this speculation. His solution is attractive because it resolves a long-standing editorial problem, no matter how quarto and Folio came to differ.

# King Lear:
# A Modern Perspective

## Susan Snyder

Each of Shakespeare's plays creates through language its distinctive geography. In the mental map generated by *King Lear*, the action occurs largely in this or that house, as opposed to this or that town. "The kingdom" is important, but not designated places in it. Even when Lear is outlining to his daughters their shares in that kingdom, he talks of natural features rather than named sites. The striking exception to this pattern is Dover: this place is first introduced in 3.1, and named ten times thereafter, underlining its status in the action as a kind of magnet-site to which every major character except the Fool is drawn in the latter half of the play. Regan and Cornwall harp on the place-name obsessively as they interrogate the captive Gloucester:

CORNWALL  Where hast thou sent the King?
GLOUCESTER  To Dover.
REGAN
   Wherefore to Dover? Wast thou not charged at
     peril—
CORNWALL
   Wherefore to Dover? Let him answer that.
GLOUCESTER
   I am tied to th' stake, and I must stand the course.
REGAN  Wherefore to Dover?         (3.7.62–68)

The repeated questions have an immediate dramatic point, certainly: Regan and Cornwall are trying to make

293

Gloucester admit his complicity with the French force that Cordelia is leading into Britain to rescue her father. Nor is there any question why most of the characters go to Dover. That is where Cordelia will land: from her and her army, the Lear party can expect "welcome and protection" (3.6.98), and against this French expeditionary force Goneril, Regan, Edmund, and the reluctant Albany must rally on the shore to fight. But repeating and insisting on the apparently simple question "Wherefore to Dover?" generates a certain excess of meaning, and suggests that Dover has significance beyond literal location.

And indeed, when we turn our attention to Lear and Gloucester at the very center of the dramatic action, the forces that propel these characters to Dover seem more fated than comprehensible and willed. While others may wish him to seek comfort from Cordelia, the mad Lear is on his own journey of self-discovery and cannot bear the shame of such a meeting with the daughter he wronged. Gloucester, blind and despairing, seeks only death at Dover. One place is as good as another for suicide, one might think. But Gloucester takes great trouble to get to Dover cliff, as if there were some peculiar rightness about this one spot as the stage for his exhausted exit from the world. The place again assumes special meaning in his insistent "Know'st thou the way to Dover? . . . Dost thou know Dover?" (4.1.63, 81).

Paying attention to these questions—"Wherefore to Dover?" "Dost thou know Dover?"—can focus for us several kinds of dynamic that work themselves out in *King Lear*. In Gloucester's mind, the reality of Dover is a cliff, where the land ends abruptly and the sea begins: a sharp demarcation between the familiar and the unknown. After he has first caused harm by being easygoing and credulous ("I stumbled when I saw") and then suffered shocking mutilation, Gloucester's awakened self-knowledge has brought him to a physical and spiritual low point. He goes to Dover, the boundary site, to cast off the burden of his life: "From that place / I shall no leading need" (4.1.87–88). But this edge of nothingness becomes for Gloucester a place of radically new vision. Even in his own anticipating imagination, the cliff's high head "Looks fearfully in the confinèd deep" (4.1.84), as if it is gazing into the alien element. When they arrive at Dover, the words of Edgar as Poor Tom spread out the disorienting new perspective:

> How fearful
> And dizzy 'tis to cast one's eyes so low!
> The crows and choughs that wing the midway air
> Show scarce so gross as beetles. Halfway down
> Hangs one that gathers samphire—dreadful trade;
> Methinks he seems no bigger than his head.
> The fishermen that walk upon the beach
> Appear like mice. . . .
> I'll look no more
> Lest my brain turn and the deficient sight
> Topple down headlong.         (4.6.15–29)

In fact, they are nowhere near the cliff. Edgar is deceiving his father, leading him through an elaborate enactment of his despair and remorse, in order that he may put these behind him and move into a totally different posture of acceptance. This speech that so sharply images the unseen precipice brings home to us Gloucester's inner crisis and the revolution of vision he undergoes at the extremity of life.

King Lear goes through his own psychological extremities in Dover. Brought there by his adherents to be put under Cordelia's protection, he is plunged by the very prospect of that reunion into greater anguish. Lear retreats from facing the daughter he once cast off:

> A sovereign shame so elbows him—his own
>   unkindness,
> That stripped her from his benediction, turned her
> To foreign casualties, gave her dear rights
> To his dog-hearted daughters—these things sting
> His mind so venomously that burning shame
> Detains him from Cordelia.          (4.3.51–57)

At the play's opening, Lear in his rage tried to erase this unaccommodating, plain-speaking daughter, to negate both her and the filial tie between them. "Better thou / Hadst not been born"; "we / Have no such daughter, nor shall ever see / That face of hers again" (1.1.269–70, 304–6). He has struggled in the meantime to keep Cordelia and his bond to her *banished*: from his sight, from his conscious mind. Her reappearance now, asserting that bond, is like Freud's return of the repressed that stings while it clarifies. Before he can encounter her, Lear at Dover plumbs the depths of madness even more deeply (4.6). Still acting the autocratic monarch and magistrate as he reviews his archers, pardons and condemns wrongdoers, he lays hold through these fantasized scenes on truths about himself, his limitations, his participation in grimy human nature. When brought together at last with Cordelia, the shattered old man marks his own extremity by insisting he must be dead—"You do me wrong to take me out o' th' grave" (4.7.51)—but the reconciliation that follows is on very human terms: "Pray you now, forget, and forgive. I am old and foolish" (98–99).

Lear and Gloucester both go to the edge at Dover, and both come up against death (Gloucester wants to die, Lear thinks he is dead). What they achieve instead is a kind of reorientation, a transformed perspective that could not come about except by the radical revaluation that such extremities force upon them. We should recall that Dover is not just the edge of Britain but the place in that island country that is closest to foreign lands. At this farthest limit of the familiar, Lear and Gloucester confront the unknown—which is, paradoxically, their own selves. And, like the French army that pushes in at Dover, this alien force brings both great fear and deliverance.

Dover plays its part in other movements that inform *King Lear.* One of these dynamics we might call "beyond the end." It has been operating in a way since the play's opening, when Lear formally signals an end to his power through abdication but then keeps right on acting like a king, as he banishes Kent and Cordelia and travels from daughter to daughter with a royal retinue of a hundred knights. Mainly, though, it is an end to *suffering* that is repeatedly sought after, promised—and then denied. On what he believes to be Dover cliff, Gloucester thinks to shake off the world's affliction because he cannot "bear it longer" (4.6.47). But when Edgar negates this closure of self-willed death, his father is pushed to endure yet more: "Henceforth I'll bear / Affliction . . ." (93–94). Edgar himself, in his outcast state, has already experienced personally this rhythm of being pushed yet further. After the miseries of the storm, he feels himself at the lowest point of Fortune's wheel, which must therefore turn him upward again; but then his father enters with bleeding holes instead of eyes, a sight to mock any balanced prediction of Fortune's unpredictable ways. Edgar's comforting conventional image of the course of events as a wheel guided by Fortune, which dictates that "The worst returns to laughter" (4.1.6), yields at this new, overwhelming pain to something much more like the wheel that the Fool has earlier shown us, something careening downhill out of control (2.4.78–80). "Who is 't can say 'I am at the worst'?" wonders a stunned Edgar, pushed to his own new extremity; "I am worse than e'er I was" (4.1.27–28). Lear, as we have seen, avoids the closure of suffering offered by Cordelia and runs on to endure more laceration in his madness. After father and daughter are at last reconciled, the comfortable end they promise each other is foreclosed again when her forces lose the battle and they are both taken prisoner. Even in the appalling finality of Cordelia's death, Lear's own end is postponed, so that he can suffer yet further agonies over her body before exhaustion at last takes him. What the awestruck survivors record at the play's close for both Gloucester and Lear is this endurance of repeated blows, beyond the end:

> The wonder is he hath endured so long. . . .
> The oldest hath borne most. (5.3.384, 394)

The special emotional force that many feel in *King Lear* has much to do with this peculiar strategy of repeatedly suggesting a limit to pain and then frustrating the expectation; the dashed hopes of audience as well as characters intensify the suffering that follows.

Both of the dynamics so far discussed display kinds of pattern: the redemptive one of descending into the depths to be rewarded with new vision, the intensifying one of promising a stop to suffering only to bring on yet more. A third dynamic is akin to that of expectations denied, but is in its very nature more random and erratic. The Fool is its chief exponent. Through scene after scene, as the tormented king suffers one blow after another, the capering Fool by his side responds with jokes and reductive nonsense. The following short sequence may stand for many moments where heroic pathos is suddenly jarred by slapstick comedy:

LEAR
O me, my heart, my rising heart! But down!
FOOL    Cry to it, nuncle, as the cockney did to the
eels when she put 'em i' th' paste alive. She
knapped 'em o' th' coxcombs with a stick and
cried "Down, wantons, down!"    (2.4.135–39)

On Lear's towering rage and pain, the Fool superimposes a ludicrous kitchen scene with a foolish woman struggling to slap down live eels into a pastry. The degrading image complicates our sympathetic identification with Lear's royal pathos, enables simultaneously a more distanced and critical view which finds the king as foolish as that cockney and his imperious commands as ineffective as if they were addressed to a bunch of wriggling eels. With such dislocating effects, the Fool's patter again and again threatens Lear's heroic status—reduces him momentarily from his royal uniqueness to any ordinary, foolish old man, reduces his experience from world-shattering cataclysm to the commonplace, predictable fate of any father silly enough to give away his property and become dependent on his heirs. When Lear in the storm summons thunder, lightning, and torrents of rain in language of cosmic power and commands them to destroy the world that has so devastated him, the Fool thinks more prosaically that, even if it must be shared with hypocrites, "a dry house is better than this rainwater out o' door" (3.2.12–13). They are wet and unsheltered. Cosmic concerns shrink suddenly to homely needs. However titanic a figure Lear presents in the storm, we cannot shut out the other image opened by the Fool's down-to-earth practicality: that of an old man comically at odds with reality, giving orders to the universe.

The Fool disappears from the play in Act 3, but his syncopated rhythm continues, grotesque comedy repeatedly threatening tragic dignity. To some extent the Fool's role of nonsensical deflation is taken over by Lear himself. Already his early tantrums have been open to interpretation as overreactions to slights that are less than earth-shaking, bringing him close to comic self-parody. In later scenes the very language of wayward association and non sequitur that manifests his madness keeps him hovering between tragic grandeur and absurdity. The Fool is still with him when he arraigns his absent daughters in the mock trial of 3.6, but Lear is now himself a source of grotesque comedy, addressing his real grievance against Goneril to a jointstool and couching it in an absurd image: she "kicked the poor king her father" (3.6.51–52).

If Gloucester's sufferings at first seem exempt from these grace notes of absurdity, he is nevertheless exposed at "Dover cliff" to the extreme of comic degradation. After the long buildup to a dramatic suicide leap (matching his "climb" in the script), the old man simply topples over (4.6.51). That which, as an idea of an action, arouses not a smile (i.e., Edgar leading his father to a nonexistent cliff and allowing him to go through the motions of throwing himself over), when physically acted out becomes something like a clown's pratfall. At his most serious moral climax, Gloucester enacts the supreme indignity of falling on his nose. And when he intersects with Lear later in this scene, the pain of these two human ruins is punctuated by further absurdity. The mad Lear finds in his former friend only grotesque similitudes: Goneril with a white beard, a superannuated blind Cupid (4.6.115, 152).

The final absurdity, the most shattering non sequitur, is Cordelia's death. It is hard to see any dramatic logic that prepares for this death or makes it an inevitable consequence of previous action, especially when the strong redemptive movement seems to point us in just the opposite direction, i.e., to the refounded relation of an enlightened Lear to his newly valued youngest daughter. Edmund does indeed tell us that if Lear and Cordelia are captured they will be shown no mercy, and we see him sending off a captain with orders that we suspect are to be fatal for the king and his daughter, but Edmund is soon defeated by Edgar and in his dying repentance rescinds the order. He is, for no discernible reason, too late. The entrance of Lear with the dead Cordelia in his arms unites absurdity at its most cosmic with the second dynamic, expectations of better times frustrated by the blow that makes things worse than before. At the same time, this unexpected disaster violently contradicts the pronounced movement toward new wisdom through suffering.

As we live through the action of the play and experience its conclusion, how do we weight these dynamics that are similarly persistent but so radically different from each other in impact and import? Individual readers and viewers may well differ in their reactions. Does the persistent strain of reductive grotesquerie make Lear and Gloucester ironic figures rather than tragic, their actions pathetic gropings in a senseless universe? Or can they be felt as all the more heroic in triumphing over the forces of absurdity and random cruelty to arrive at an ethic of love and social obligation, an ethic no less necessary to the human community even if the larger universe is amoral? If wayward comedy attends their presentation, does the resultant laughter distance or intensify participation in their pain? Does Cordelia's death render Lear's painful progress meaningless, or does it force us to reevaluate in less sentimental terms the limits placed on any such progress by the human condition itself? At the very end, as Albany and Edgar look to a future beyond Lear, is the final stress on reordering more humanely the "gored state" (5.3.389), or rather on slogging stoically on, beyond the "promised end" which has once more been denied?

When we look away from Lear and Gloucester, the careers of other characters also defy easy moral and psychological assessment. Edgar's course is perhaps morally comprehensible in outline as he falls from high position to the condition of a destitute beggar and then wins his way back to his rightful estate, expanding his wisdom and sympathy in the process. Yet as Edgar at the play's beginning is hardly a blind, selfish Lear, we may wonder if his suffering is not more gratuitous than redemptive. Through Edgar's long engagement with the blind Gloucester, in his various disguises as beggar or countryman, the reader or viewer may well be anticipating the climactic moment when this devoted son reveals his true identity to the father who cast him off. But when it finally comes, that revelation is not shown to us but is only narrated. More unexpectedly, even shockingly, the revelation kills Gloucester. Does Gloucester's death in extremes of joy and grief fittingly conclude his long painful spiritual odyssey, or is it yet another indication that random absurdity governs events, making nonsense of Edgar's redemptive agenda? When Lear in defeat cares nothing for loss of royal power and serenely invites Cordelia to an idyllic life in prison where each will be totally absorbed in the other ("Come, let's away to prison," 5.3.9), Cordelia says nothing in response. Does Lear too unthinkingly accept the congealing of her young life with his old one, and look forward to a symbiosis that blots out her separate identity? So it could seem from the perspective of this daughter, who so firmly resisted Lear's initial wish to have all her love himself. From this point of view, in fact—the need of any child to break away from a demanding, all-engrossing parent—even the actions of Goneril and Regan escape neat categorization as unfounded pure evil. So, from another angle, does the course of Edmund, their ally in the play's oppositions of good children against bad. Even while these oppositions seem so stark as to invite a semiallegorical interpretation, Edmund can also be understood sociologically, as produced by the glaring social inequities of which this play recurrently reminds us. His malevolent ambition takes appropriate revenge on a society that has marginalized him as a bastard, automatically denying him the secure social position that otherwise his parentage and his talents would ensure.

Stark moral oppositions, then, are crossed in this complex play by trajectories of sociological and psychological questioning, just as the unexpected supplement and the random absurdity complicate Lear's and Gloucester's journeys toward insight. Like Dover, *King Lear* should act to open up vision, not close it down.

# Further Reading

In addition to the following books and articles, see www.folger.edu/shakespeare and www.folger.edu/online-resources.

## King Lear

[Abbreviations: *Ado* = *Much Ado About Nothing;* *Ant.* = *Antony and Cleopatra;* *AYLI* = *As You Like It;* *Ham.* = *Hamlet; 1H4=Henry IV, Part 1; 2H6* = *Henry VI, Part 2; Lear* = *King Lear;* *LLL* = *Love's Labor's Lost;* *MV* = *The Merchant of Venice; Oth.* = *Othello; R3* = *Richard III; Temp.* = *The Tempest; Tit.* = *Titus Andronicus; Tro.* = *Troilus and Cressida; TN* = *Twelfth Night.*]

Belsey, Catherine. "*King Lear* and the Missing Salt." In *Why Shakespeare?*, pp. 42–64. New York: Palgrave Macmillan, 2007.

Belsey examines the pervasive influence of the fireside tale genre on selected plays to argue that such stories, with their capacity to haunt the consciousness of readers and audiences, hold the key to why Shakespeare's plays have remained durable and adaptable across centuries, cultures, media, and languages. Shakespeare's retellings of riddles, tall tales, and fables of magic and witchcraft invite audiences "to feel . . . already unaccountably at home there." Belsey's focus, however, is not so much on the narrative parallels as on the differences that Shakespeare introduces in the process of reinscription. She begins the chapter on *Lear* by reading the play through the proverbial tale of a love test imposed by a rich father on his three daughters and his enraged reaction to the third daughter's response that she loves him "as fresh meat loves salt."

Incorporating elements of the Cinderella story, the tale ends happily as do all of the "intermediary versions" of the Lear narrative available to Shakespeare and his contemporaries (including chronicle accounts and the anonymous play titled *The True Chronicle History of King Leir* [published in 1605]). The play's first audience, recognizing the folktale pattern of the opening scene wherein the youngest child is conventionally the most trustworthy, "would be fully aware of the dramatic ironies involved in Lear's choice." What they could not anticipate was Shakespeare's deliberate breaking of the folktale's promise of a "happily ever after" conclusion. Noting how "the pleasure of the text does not depend on happy endings," Belsey brings Jacques Lacan's account of language as a "mismatch between words and things" to bear on the play's tragic appeal and the "logic" of its closure. Just as Lear fails in 1.1 to recognize the "inadequacy of language when it comes to defining a condition that is not purely linguistic"— i.e., Cordelia's cultural-genetic bond of kinship—so too in the final scene, when he is reduced to the howling cries of an animal (5.3.308), language proves incapable of signifying indescribable loss. The limits of language thus frame a play that dazzles with a "festival of signifiers." In reworking a simple, austere folktale, Shakespeare "evoke[s] and transform[s] a genre often dismissed as trivial and artless."

Booth, Stephen. "On the Greatness of *King Lear*." In *King Lear, Macbeth, Indefinition and Tragedy*, pp. 1–57. New Haven: Yale University Press, 1983.

For Booth, the key to *Lear*'s tragic power lies in "the fact of indefinition": "[L]iterary works we call tragedies have their value as enabling actions by which we are made capable, temporarily, of enduring manifestations of the fact that nothing in human experience is or can be definite. " His examination of the play's many "indef-initenesses" in character, plot, and language leads to the assertion that "not ending is a primary character-istic of [*Lear*]," the only Shakespeare tragedy whose exit lines indicate no immediate destination for the remaining characters to repair to: the play's survivors simply walk off the stage, not knowing who will actu-ally rule the kingdom or where exactly they are going. The final twenty lines (5.3.375–95) are emblematic of the tragedy's "manifold inconclusiveness." Booth calls *Lear* Shakespeare's "greatest achievement . . . because it is the greatest achievement of his audience." Like the titular figure, the audience endures much, being forced to confront cruelty the way the characters of the play experience it: as a constant disappointment of the persistent promise of order and resolution (see, e.g., the terrifying shock of Lear's entry at 5.3.307 SD, the dead Cordelia in his arms). *Lear* requires its characters and audience to "cope with the fact that the idea of the ultimate is only an idea" and to recognize "the infin-ity of possibility and the insufficiency of human men-tal resources to manage unstoppable improbabilities." Between the essays on *Lear* and *Macbeth*, Booth pro-vides an "interlude" (pp. 59–78) in which he compares *LLL* and *Lear* to show how inconclusiveness works in each play according to the generic requirements of comedy and tragedy.

Everett, Barbara. "The New *King Lear.*" *Critical Quar-terly* 2 (1960): 325–39.

Everett takes issue with several Christian and alle-gorical interpretations of the play, readings that owe much to A.C. Bradley's essay in *Shakespearean Tragedy* (1904)—minus his "careful reservations"—in which he suggested calling "this poem *The Redemption of King Lear.*" Among the critics she discusses are G. Wilson

Knight, R. W. Chambers, J. F. Danby, and Kenneth Muir. Claims that posit a "redeemed Lear," who loses the world in order to gain his soul, and an ending resonant with the "victory and felicity" of reconciliation and restored order cannot "be said to be 'wrong,'" but they are exclusive and they are unnecessary to explain how the play succeeds. Instead of experiencing a moral epiphany informed by Christian ethics, Lear learns that he is "'not ague-proof' [4.6.124], that he is 'a very foolish fond old man' [4.7.69]; and this in itself contains further ranges of common suffering. No moralistic outline that blurs this can be fully satisfying." Everett therefore proposes a more "metaphysical" reading that rests on the play's presentation of startling disparities— all and nothing, "extreme power and vitality embracing its antithesis"—within a single imaginative world that resists conformity with "the symbolic clarity of a Morality or the simplicity of a mystery play." In place of an "absolute dichotomy between 'the world' and 'the soul,' between 'concretes and abstracts,'" *Lear* shows "a continual relation between the two that strengthens and enriches both": see, for example, the king's final lines (5.3.370–75), which "condense the poetic experience of the play, whereby the physical and the non-physical are shown in their mysterious relationship." Ultimately, for Everett, the play exhilarates by allowing a responsive audience, within the framework of artistic design and poetic power, to endure and understand actions of great suffering and thus to master them. [The essay is reprinted in the Macmillan Shakespeare Casebook Series, *Shakespeare: King Lear* (pp. 184–202), edited by Frank Kermode (1969); and in *Major Literary Characters: King Lear* (pp. 119–31), edited by Harold Bloom (1992).]

Garber, Marjorie. "*King Lear*: The Dream of Sublimity." In *Shakespeare and Modern Culture*, pp. 231–69. New York: Pantheon Books, 2008.

Guided by the thesis that "Shakespeare makes modern culture and modern culture makes Shakespeare," Garber asks us to "reimagine . . . our own mental and emotional landscape as refracted through the prism of protean 'Shakespeare.'" Her chapter on *Lear* is indebted to R. A. Foakes's *Hamlet versus Lear* (1993), which analyzed the displacement in the 1960s of *Ham.* by *Lear* as Shakespeare's "greatest" play. For Garber, the key question is "How did [*Lear*] come to be both the icon of Shakespearean greatness for the mid-to-late twentieth century and, at the same time, the most 'modern,' modernist, and indeed postmodern of Shakespearean plays?" The answer, she suggests, lies in its combination of the "affective sublime" (Lear and Cordelia) with the "bathetic grotesque" (the Fool, the blinding of Gloucester): What previous centuries objected to as indecorous, excessive, and nihilistic "was what made the play so modern, and so devastating." Garber begins her probe of this connection with modern culture by considering the existential philosophy of Camus, who saw in Gloucester the best illustration of the absurd, and the critical views of Jan Kott, whose interpretation of the play in *Shakespeare Our Contemporary* (1964) "became vastly important for the itinerary of [*Lear*] in the theater and on film from the sixties on." She then turns to an analysis of Samuel Beckett's *Endgame* (1957) and Edward Bond's *Lear* (1971): the former exemplifies the existential *Lear* "of conscious absurdity in an already grotesque world"; the latter creates an "impassioned political social" environment governed by socioeconomic pressures. For existentialists, the Dover Cliff episode is "the emblematic 'modern' moment of Shakespeare's play"; for political, specifically Marxist, critics, the key moment comes in 3.4.32–41, when Lear senses "disparity between rich and poor, privileged and underprivileged." Garber concludes the chapter with a discussion of the mathematician and philosopher Brian Rotman's *Signifying Nothing: The Semiotics of Zero* (1987) to underscore *Lear*'s "very arithmetically minded" temper and "the relevance of zero" to the play's "thematics of 'nothing.'" As a dramatic signifier of "the emptiness, illogic, terror, and absurdity of the modern condition, [*Lear*] has been read in the twentieth and twenty-first centuries as an existential allegory [Beckett], as a social treatise [Bond], as a philosophical statement [Rotman]: an icon of modern life, not of modern man."

Hiscock, Andrew, and Lisa Hopkins, eds. *King Lear: A Critical Guide.* New York: Continuum, 2011.

The editors of this anthology state two goals in their introduction: (1) to extend reader interest in established areas of textual and critical discourse (e.g., the complex relationship between the 1608 Quarto and 1623 Folio versions of the play, performative values, and issues relating to cosmology, theology, morality, psychology, and the sociopolitical order of patriarchy); and (2) to open up "newer angles of vision on [*Lear*] by raising questions about seventeenth-century Britishness, early modern understandings of landscape . . . [and] 'self-murder,' and the implications of the insatiable appetite for Shakespearean adaptation." Following René Weis's survey of the play's reception from 1606 to the present (in editions, performances, critical debates, and adaptations) are seven new essays that aim to "bridge the gap between" past and current scholarship: Joan Fitzpatrick, "The Critical Backstory"; Ramona Wray, "*King Lear*: Performative Traditions/Interpretative Positions"; Philippa Kelly, "The Current State of Thinking on *King Lear*"; Lori Anne Ferrell, "New Directions: Promised End? *King Lear* and the Suicide-Trick"; Anthony Parr, "New Directions: 'The Wisdom of Nature': Ecological Perspectives in *King Lear*"; John J. Norton, "New Directions: *King Lear* and Protestantism"; and Willy Maley, "Critical Review: 'Great thing of us forgot'? New British Angles on *King Lear*." The final chapter by Peter Stillitoe ("*King Lear*: Resources") offers a guide to materials available for the teaching and study of the play (critical editions, online resources, films/videos/DVDs, and an annotated bibliography of the most recent publications relating to the tragedy).

Knowles, Richard. "Revision Awry in Folio *Lear* 3.1." *Shakespeare Quarterly* 46 (1995): 32–46.

Knowles examines the 1608 Quarto (Q1) and 1623 Folio (F) versions of Kent's long speech of instruction to the Gentleman in 3.1, the "centerpiece" of the scene, (1) to counter textual critics who regard F's new material as a substitute for a very different speech in Q and (2) to encourage a rethinking of the traditional conflation of the speeches (the editorial norm, since Lewis Theobald in 1733, which can be found on pages 289–90 in the Appendix to the present Folger edition). While both versions share (with slight variations) the same opening four and a half lines, F omits Q's next twelve-and-a-half, seemingly replacing them with eight new lines. Knowles finds incoherence and stylistic problems in the F speech and in the conflated arrangement noted above. Drawing on suggestions made by Peter W. M. Blayney, Knowles posits that the eight lines present only in F "are not in fact a consecutive block of text" representing "the recasting of a whole speech or substitution of one speech for another" but are two additional passages intended to "clarif[y] meaning" at "two different locations in the Q text." As such, "they are local improvements, not significant revisions." (The present edition at 3.1.21–46 follows Knowles's proposed combination of the Q and F versions of Kent's speech; see also the Appendix [pages 287–91].)

Kordecki, Lesley, and Karla Koskinen. *Re-Visioning Lear's Daughters: Testing Feminist Criticism and Theory.* New York: Palgrave Macmillan, 2010. Against the claim that *Lear*, "a monument of the patriarchal literary canon," is "irretrievably sexist," Kordecki and Koskinen seek to recover the king's three daughters from the stereotypes of good and evil that have attached to the idolized Cordelia and demonized Goneril and Regan on both the page and the stage. The authors provide line readings of every scene in which the daughters appear so as to chart their collective and individual journeys from beginning to end. Serving as a "bridge between literary criticism and theatrical possibilities," the book's feminist readings are informed by extensive critical commentary and "tested with specific renderings, placing the reader in precise theatrical moments." Kordecki and Koskinen base their readings on the 1623 Folio, which, when compared with the 1608 Quarto, yields "a more indefinite ethical atmosphere from which to view and judge Lear's daughters, thus enhancing their complexity." Central to the authors' efforts to offer a *Lear* "without innate gender bias" is the argument that all three women are products of an acutely misogynistic environment created by their father, a world established before the start of the play and one in which each daughter must navigate her own course as she seeks "an active, meaningful role within a patriarchal society." Following an introductory essay that addresses the limitations of established readings and traditional performance decisions ("The Problem with *Lear*") are ten chapters: (1) The Trial: Goneril, Politician and Appeaser, 1.1; (2) The Trial: Regan, Soldier and Enabler, 1.1; (3) The Trial: Cordelia, Heir Apparent and Zealot, 1.1; (4) Goneril Makes Her Stand: Queen and Mother, 1.3 and 4; (5) The Sisters Unite: Kingship and Kinship, 2.1 and 2; (6) Regan and Torture: Abuser and Abused, 3.7; (7) The Sisters and Edmund: Agency and Sexuality, 4.2 and 4 [Q4.5]); (8) Cordelia Returns: Sinner and Saint, 4.3 [Q4.4] and 7; (9) Homeland Security: Defeat and Denial, 5.1, 2, 3 (Cordelia); and (10) Patriarchy Restored: Duplicity and Death, 5.3 (Goneril and Regan).] A bibliography concludes the volume.

Mack, Maynard. *King Lear: In Our Time*. Berkeley: University of California Press, 1965.

In the three chapters that make up this highly influential study ("Actors and Redactors," "Archetype, Parable, and Vision," and "Action and World"), Mack considers aspects of *Lear*'s stage history, explores its literary and imaginative sources, and reflects on what in the play "speaks most immediately to us" in our own time. The chapter on the play's theatrical afterlife includes discussion of Nahum Tate's 1681 adaptation (which dominated the English stage for 157 years), a brief overview of many notable Lears (among them David Garrick, Edmund Kean, William Charles Macready, John Gielgud, Laurence Olivier, Michael Redgrave, Charles Laughton, and Paul Scofield), and a critique of the "rationalizing" efforts of directors such as Herbert Blau and Peter Brook who, eager to "motivate the [play's] bizarre actions . . . in some 'reasonable' way," favor subtext over text. Mack contends that after the horrors of two world wars and Auschwitz, our modern temper shares a particular affinity "with the play's jagged violence, its sadism, madness, and processional of deaths, its wild blends of levity and horror, selfishness and selflessness, and the anguish of its closing scene." Turning from stage history to "the genetic pole," Mack focuses not on specific sources (e.g., Holinshed's *Chronicles*, *A Mirror for Magistrates*, Edmund Spenser's *The Faerie Queene*, and Sir Philip Sidney's *Arcadia*) but on "the traditions of thought and feeling in terms of which [Shakespeare] shaped his materials"; these "cogent influences" include folktales, medieval morality drama (with its homiletic structure and emblematic characters), and pastoral romance (the conventional pattern of which Shakespeare turns into the "greatest anti-pastoral ever penned").

The final chapter outlines reasons for *Lear*'s appeal to the modern age, describes the dominant mood of the drama as "imperative," and refutes both Christian readings that sentimentalize the ending and nihilist readings that find only absurdity in the play's world: "Existence is tragic in *Lear* because existence is inseparable from relation; we are born from and to it. . . . Man's tragic fate, as *Lear* presents it, comes into being with his entry into relatedness, which is his entry into humanity." Mack concludes with the claim that tragedy never "tells us what to think" but "shows us what we are and may be."

Maus, Katherine Eisaman. "Vagabond Kings: Entitlement and Distribution in *2 Henry VI* and *King Lear.*" In *Being and Having in Shakespeare*, pp. 99–132, esp. pp. 112–31. Oxford: Oxford University Press, 2013.

Maus uses the history plays, *MV*, and *Lear* to explore the problem of property and identity, i.e., the relation between who a person is and what he or she has. Countering some materialist critics who view "being" (subject) and "having" (object) as one and the same—who believe that objects, in other words, "constitute subjects"—she advocates a more "dialectical and mutually constitutive" interrelationship in which persons relate to each other by way of things in an ever-changing context of social situations, economic transactions, and legal arrangements. Maus focuses her discussion of *Lear*'s "poetics of property" on the figure of the "'vagabond king,' theoretically entitled but actually dispossessed," to argue that the play "coordinate[s] problems of entitlement with conundrums about distributive justice, raising fundamental questions about property relations and social organization." The opening scene, wherein Lear's plan to divide the kingdom "construes sovereignty as a form of property right," quickly establishes the relationship between person and property as "double": Lear's love test presumes that the two are inextricable—that a "bequest of wealth is the same as . . . 'love' "; Cordelia, Kent, and France, however, argue for their distinction, that love is "something other" (see 1.1.275–77). In the "wild spaces" of *Lear's* middle acts, "where property rights are uncertain or are not worth asserting," the struggle to distinguish between what is superfluous to the human condition and what is necessary operates at its most extreme (see 3.4.32–41 and 4.1.77–81). When Lear tears off his clothes at 3.4.116, he "leans simultaneously on both contradictory wings of the paradoxical relation between being and having": "If . . . property, 'the superflux' . . . makes us human [see 2.4.304–7], it is apparently by" divesting oneself of "add-ons" and empathizing with others "that we become humane." Prompted by the ambiguity surrounding the inheritance of the kingdom at the end of Act 5, Maus asks, "Who would want to rule Britain, and why?" The "apocalyptic language [of 5.3.316–17] suggests the extent to which the traumas of the play have made inheritance impossible. And it is impossible . . . primarily . . . because the . . . very desirability of property, and the importance of asserting title to it, itself is at last emptied out."

McEachern, Claire. "Fathering Himself: A Source Study of Shakespeare's Feminism." *Shakespeare Quarterly* 39 (1988): 269–90.

McEachern combines source study and feminism to investigate Renaissance patriarchy through a study of fathers and daughters as presented in Shakespeare's plays, with special emphasis on *Ado* and *Lear*. Viewing sources as "cultural context" rather than as "sites of mere borrowing," she considers the playwright's transformation of the Lear story, as found in Holinshed's *Chronicles* and the anonymous play *King Leir*, in terms of his reaction to ideologies of dominant male authority. A key difference between the source material and Shakespeare's tragedy lies in the motivation of the old king regarding his youngest daughter's imminent marriage. The question of political succession motivates the earlier Leirs, the protagonist of the anonymous text actually desiring his favorite daughter's public profession of love so that he might manipulate her into marrying the most politically appropriate husband. The motivation of Shakespeare's Lear, in contrast, is complicated by a second set of pressures, this one more personal than political: namely, the preservation of his authority over the family unit. Driven more by emotional desire and the pain of losing his cherished daughter to another family, this Lear tries to force Cordelia "to buy her dowry with the very capital she herself must use to marry: her love." His demand for absolute love, which renders marriage impossible, reveals his wish to keep her as a possession rather than relinquish her according to the "social demands of exogamy." The dowry negotiation is not, then, the usual one between two men but between a father and his daughter, and "it is the father who subverts the conventions of patriarchy in defying its demand for male alliance through marriage": "[R]ather than simply presenting a patriarch's control over a woman, Shakespeare investigates the incestuous possessiveness that exogamy counteracts." By letting us see Lear abuse his authority over Cordelia, Shakespeare undermines our confidence "in the power that we invest in kings and fathers . . . [and] exposes . . . the coercive pressures of patriarchy."

Novy, Marianne. *"King Lear:* Outsiders in the Family *and* in the Kingdom." In *Shakespeare and Outsiders*, pp. 121–46. Oxford Shakespeare Topics. Oxford: Oxford University Press, 2013.

In contrast to the mythic/psychoanalytic approach of Leslie Fiedler in *The Stranger in Shakespeare* (1972), Novy draws on social, economic, and political history to examine representations of difference and exclusion in *MV, TN, Oth., Lear,* and (briefly) *Temp.* In *Lear,* Shakespeare deals with two aspects of exclusion: outsiders in the family (the bastard and the difficult elder parent) and in the kingdom itself (the homeless poor and the mad). Images of being either a literal or figurative outsider are iterative in both the Lear and Gloucester plots. At a time "when poverty was marked by the increased visibility of bastards, elderly poor, and beggars," Edmund, Lear, and Edgar (as Poor Tom) give dramatic voice to "outsider" issues specific to each of those conditions; Kent, Gloucester, and the Fool serve as further reflections of the outsider's homeless status. While Goneril and Regan reveal themselves "as moral outsiders," Cordelia, whose initial asides and subsequent disinheritance and banishment make her "look . . . like an outsider onstage," is "an insider to the play's value system," one that prioritizes sympathy as "a human quality, not simply a feminine one." Nowhere else in his treatment of other kinds of outsiders (whether ethnic or religious) does Shakespeare make "the theme of sympathy so explicit," as most of the play's "social outsiders come together in a community to help [the old king]." Novy concludes that *Lear* "is not just a play about homelessness, but also one about the pain and yet the importance of home and families." Revealing serious flaws in both fathers and children, *Lear* nevertheless "draws readers and audiences into identifying with characters on both sides of the generational divide as it proceeds to its poignant reunions and its painful final bereavement."

Ryle, Simon. "*King Lear* and Film Space: Something from Nothing." In *Shakespeare, Cinema and Desire: Adaptation and Other Futures of Shakespeare's Language*, pp. 36–84. New York: Palgrave Macmillan, 2014. Rather than focusing on the "political [and] . . . institutional desires" that occupy cultural materialists, Ryle emphasizes the "desire inbuilt in Shakespeare's language," which "impel[s] ever new Shakespeares" and needs to be read "through its heterogeneous intersections with modernity." To this end, the book examines issues that are central to both Shakespeare and film: "media technologies, narrative territories and flows, mourning and loss, the voice, the body, sexuality and gender." The chapter on *Lear* explores how the play's "somethings from nothings" are translated into the cinematic space of five films: namely, Akira Kurosawa's *Ran* (*Chaos*, 1985), Peter Brook's *King Lear* and Grigori Kozintsev's *Korol Lir* (both made in 1971), Jean Luc Godard's *King Lear* (1987), and Kristian Levring's *The King Is Alive* (2000). Central to Ryle's analysis are the poststructuralist views of Jacques Lacan and Jacques Derrida. Among Ryle's observations is his discussion of a scene in Kurosawa that depicts the Lear-figure Hidetora sinking to the ground as burning arrows whistle past him in a moment of symbolic death; emerging from this chaos, his blank eyes drained of life, he appears as "something *undead*," a figure of "fearful and uncanny dimensions." Commenting on how Edgar's invocation of Dover Cliff (4.6.15–29) creates a "self-conscious non-space" that only the eyeless Gloucester can fully inhabit, Ryle notes Brook's image of father and son appearing as fragmented bodies framed against the whiteness of the sky as they approach this "nothing cliff." Kozintsev, who wrote that his film's centralized concept of empty space and individual shapes was inspired by a Japanese Zen garden, links the blinding of Gloucester to a sexual act between Edmund and Goneril by means of a cut in the image track matching Gloucester's scream to a bedroom where we see Goneril lacing up a boot and Edmund putting on his belt: the effect "literalizes, in film space, the connections between Dover [the play's most vivid image of nothing], Gloucester's emptied eye sockets, and Goneril's genitalia that are foregrounded in Regan's questions [at 3.7.64, 68; and 5.1.12–13]." The "audiovisual disjunction" of Godard's avant-garde cinematography rethinks Cordelia's initial "Nothing" as an embodied failure of language, with the word projected on the voicetrack over images of her mute body. Levring's adaptation, which depicts stranded tourists rehearsing *Lear* in the desert, "approaches Shakespeare's nothing through questions of performativity," the vision of the naked Poor Tom being the image that most intrigues the director. Ryle concludes that in *Lear* Shakespeare "locates a series of *somethings from nothings*: the fecundity of the 'round-wombed' prostitute [Edmund's mother, 1.1.14]; Lear as residue living beyond symbolic death; the emotional proximity of [Dover] Cliff. These 'substitutive significations' (to borrow Derrida's phrase) insinuate themselves at the place of loss. As modern reduplications of the ongoing process of substitutive signification, cinematic adaptations and critical theory each constitute a compelling approach to Shakespeare's nothing."

Snyder, Susan. "*King Lear* and the Psychology of Dying." *Shakespeare Quarterly* 33 (1982): 449–60.
Recognizing that all tragedy "addresses the necessity of dying" (even when the tragic protagonist does not actually die), Snyder proposes that because of its "peculiar blend of dignity and defeat," tragedy embodies two reactions to death. The first is that death is right and natural, since humans are governed by nature's laws of growth and decay. Against this reaction, however, is set our implicit protest that death is wrong, unfairly imposed upon us by some external enemy. In *Lear*, wherein dying is "a kind of subtext," Snyder finds an "undeniable special potency [that] may derive from this direct appeal" to our ambivalent responses toward death. Structuring her analysis of the play around the tenets of Elisabeth Kübler-Ross's influential *Death and Dying* (1969), which outlined five stages in the dying process—denial, anger, bargaining, depression, and acceptance—Snyder locates naturalistic and symbolic correspondences to these stages in Lear's and Gloucester's loss of power ("which is . . . what dying is about"), in their intense physical and mental suffering ("the dying experience of dislocation and disintegration has seldom found fuller dramatic expression than in Lear's madness"), and in the double deaths of Lear and Cordelia, which "act out the paradox of mortality as both unnatural [Cordelia's (5.3.308–11, 370–71)] and inevitable (the old and exhausted king's [5.3.384])." Snyder concludes that "our pleasure in tragedy [may be] owing in part to its power of bringing together what in our psyches simply coexist unrelated, these two reactions of recognition and resistance—bringing them together, not in resolution . . . but in energizing interaction."

Stewart, Alan. "The Matter of Messengers in *King Lear*." In *Shakespeare's Letters*, pp. 193–230. Oxford: Oxford University Press, 2008.

Within the context of the materiality and proto-
cols of letter writing in early modern England, Stewart offers new readings of *Ham.*, *Lear*, *Ant.*, *MV*, and
*1H4*. If we can recapture "what it meant to write,
send, receive, read, and archive a letter," we will better understand "how and why Shakespeare put letters on stage in virtually all of his plays"—nowhere,
however, more frequently and intricately plotted than
in *Lear*. Stewart focuses on "the personally conveyed
letter, with its particular dynamics of delivery, reception, report and response," to argue that messengers
not only matter but are, in the case of *Lear*, "the matter" (see 2.2.45–52): the playwright's decision to imply
(see 2.1.117–20) rather than stage the reception of
two letters to Regan—Goneril's by way of her steward
Oswald and Lear's by way of an apparent stranger, the
disguised Kent—"throws our attention onto the messengers rather than the letters they carry, thus identifying the play as "a matter of messengers." Building on
Richard Halpern's argument that the central conflict in
*Lear* is not between Edmund and Kent, as respective
representatives of the new and old orders, but between
Oswald (the play's real "new man") and Kent, Stewart
explores "this opposition [as it] play[s] out through
their differing versions of what constitutes a proper
messenger." The balance of the chapter considers how
various types of letters are used to dramatic effect in
the play: (1) closet letters, i.e., letters without messengers; (2) undirected letters that create geographical/
spatial confusion for readers and audiences because
they "circulate at high speed, miraculously reaching
characters on the run, in disguise, and moving swiftly
between multiple locales"; (3) "preposterous letters"
that confuse because the timing of their reception
seems off; and (4) letters whose messengers are interrupted. "With its letters forged, intercepted, delivered
by men in disguise, delivered by no apparent means,

thrown in at casements, and undelivered, [*Lear*] can be seen as [Shakespeare's] most advanced exploration of the myriad problems and challenges facing communication via letters in the early modern world."

Taylor, Gary, and Michael Warren, eds. *The Division of the Kingdoms: Shakespeare's Two Texts of "King Lear."* Oxford: Clarendon Press, 1983.

Two versions of Shakespeare's *Lear* were published in the first quarter of the seventeenth century: the 1608 Quarto (Q1; reprinted in 1619 [Q2]) and the 1623 First Folio edition (F). The wide discrepancies between these versions (F, for instance, is missing about 300 lines present in Q1) are the subject of this collection of twelve new essays. Among the differences (and their implications for interpretation) noted by the volume's contributors are F's omission of much of the mock trial (Roger Warren); the treatments of Goneril (Randall McLeod), Kent (Michael Warren), and the Fool (John Kerrigan); the handling of the role of the king and the ending (Thomas Clayton); and speech prefixes (Beth Goldring). Other essays deal with the editorial practice of conflation (Steven Urkowitz), censorship (Taylor), Folio editors and compositors (Paul Werstine), and the fluctuating variation associated with "author, annotator, or actor?" (MacD. P. Jackson). The volume argues that the tradition of conflated texts has now died and that the play(s) must be thought of as distinct—each representing authoritative stages of composition; consequently, they must be issued today in separate editions. Although there is no consensus among the volume's contributors concerning this theory of the *Lear* texts, Gary Taylor's essay ("The Date and Authorship of the Folio Version," pp. 351–451) attempts to prove that the Folio text is a Shakespearean revision of Q1, and that this revision dates from 1609–10. An introduction by Stanley Wells ("The Once and Future *King Lear*," pp. 1–22) briefly examines the origins of both texts and their relationship to each other. Wells posits that "split[ting] asunder the two texts of [*Lear*] is a work of restoration, not of destruction"; in the process, "we shall gain a pair of legitimate—though not identical—twins." A select bibliography follows three appendices: "Emendations Affecting Rare Vocabulary in the Two Texts of '[*Lear*],'" "Rare Vocabulary in the Two Texts of '[*Lear*],'" and "Internal Links in '[*Lear*],' '*Tro.*,' '*R3*,' and '*Titus.*'" [For more on the differences between the Quarto and Folio versions, see "An Introduction to This Text" in the present edition (pages lii–lxii).]

Young, David. "The Natural Fool of Fortune: *King Lear.*" In *The Heart's Forest: A Study of Shakespeare's Pastoral Plays*, pp. 73–103. New Haven: Yale University Press, 1972.

In the chapter on *Lear*, Young outlines the play's relation to the pastoral tradition, finding that the tragedy follows the tripartite pattern of pastoral romance as developed in Spain and Italy, and then elaborated in England: the pattern involves banishment from society (whether established as the court or the city), a period of sojourn in a natural setting (that "acts as a mirror to the mind"), and eventual return. Young contends that *Lear* employs this pattern in order ultimately to negate it, a claim he illustrates in part by examining the "curious kinship" between *Lear* and the pastoral romantic comedy *AYLI*, two plays that share plot devices of the typical pastoral narrative and a fundamental concern with the "nature of Nature." Each, however, reveals a radically different natural setting: the pleasant and artificial forest of Arden offers "a protective fantasy that keeps the bitter weather and the suffering of unaccommodated man at bay"; the "harsh and fearsome" wilderness—"intensely realized" with the terrors of a wild storm and such "unpleasant realities" as Bedlam beggars and Poor Tom's diet (3.4.136–47)—removes all such assurances. The natural world of *Lear*, in fact, is so "far from the norm of Renaissance pastoral romance" (see 4.6.119–24) that it may be classified as pastoral "turned inside out," its characters denied the healing consolations that traditionally accompany the sojourn in the world of nature. Even the king's willing renunciation of political power and courtly life (5.3.10–20), a staple of pastoral, does not insure him against further suffering, the play's most devastating blow to follow before the end of the scene. Viewed in light of Cordelia's death, *Lear* "appears as a play in which man and nature keep coming together, only to be inexorably separated." Having redefined pastoral conventions, *Lear* "drives on to challenge basic assumptions about the essential harmony of man and nature," the very core of the pastoral genre. In an appendix on the staging of pastorals (pp. 196–204), Young advocates "experimentation with more stylized treatments" of setting, characterization, acting, costume, makeup, structure, and atmosphere. Such "careful rethinking" may yield productions of *Lear* "that explore the symbolic and 'metatheatrical' elements of the play to greater effect."

## Shakespeare's Language

Abbott, E. A. *A Shakespearian Grammar.* New York: Haskell House, 1972.

This compact reference book, first published in 1870, helps with many difficulties in Shakespeare's language. It systematically accounts for a host of differences between Shakespeare's usage and sentence structure and our own.

Blake, Norman. *Shakespeare's Language: An Introduction.* New York: St. Martin's Press, 1983.

This general introduction to Elizabethan English discusses various aspects of the language of Shakespeare and his contemporaries, offering possible meanings for hundreds of ambiguous constructions.

Dobson, E. J. *English Pronunciation, 1500–1700.* 2 vols. Oxford: Clarendon Press, 1968.

This long and technical work includes chapters on spelling (and its reformation), phonetics, stressed vowels, and consonants in early modern English.

Hope, Jonathan. *Shakespeare's Grammar.* London: Arden Shakespeare, 2003.

Commissioned as a replacement for Abbott's *Shakespearian Grammar,* Hope's book is organized in terms of the two basic parts of speech, the noun and the verb. After extensive analysis of the noun phrase and the verb phrase come briefer discussions of subjects and agents, objects, complements, and adverbials.

Houston, John. *Shakespearean Sentences: A Study in Style and Syntax.* Baton Rouge: Louisiana State University Press, 1988.

Houston studies Shakespeare's stylistic choices, considering matters such as sentence length and the relative positions of subject, verb, and direct object. Examining plays throughout the canon in a roughly chronological, developmental order, he analyzes how sentence structure is used in setting tone, in characterization, and for other dramatic purposes.

Onions, C. T. *A Shakespeare Glossary.* Oxford: Clarendon Press, 1986.
This revised edition updates Onions's standard, selective glossary of words and phrases in Shakespeare's plays that are now obsolete, archaic, or obscure.

Robinson, Randal. *Unlocking Shakespeare's Language: Help for the Teacher and Student.* Urbana, Ill.: National Council of Teachers of English and the ERIC Clearinghouse on Reading and Communication Skills, 1989.
Specifically designed for the high-school and undergraduate college teacher and student, Robinson's book addresses the problems that most often hinder present-day readers of Shakespeare. Through work with his own students, Robinson found that many readers today are particularly puzzled by such stylistic characteristics as subject-verb inversion, interrupted structures, and compression. He shows how our own colloquial language contains comparable structures, and thus helps students recognize such structures when they find them in Shakespeare's plays. This book supplies worksheets—with examples from major plays—to illuminate and remedy such problems as unusual sequences of words and the separation of related parts of sentences.

Williams, Gordon. *A Dictionary of Sexual Language and Imagery in Shakespearean and Stuart Literature.* 3 vols. London: Athlone Press, 1994.
Williams provides a comprehensive list of words to which Shakespeare, his contemporaries, and later Stuart writers gave sexual meanings. He supports his identification of these meanings by extensive quotations.

## Shakespeare's Life

Baldwin, T. W. *William Shakspere's Petty School.* Urbana: University of Illinois Press, 1943.

Baldwin here investigates the theory and practice of the petty school, the first level of education in Elizabethan England. He focuses on that educational system primarily as it is reflected in Shakespeare's art.

Baldwin, T. W. *William Shakspere's Small Latine and Lesse Greeke.* 2 vols. Urbana: University of Illinois Press, 1944.

Baldwin attacks the view that Shakespeare was an uneducated genius—a view that had been dominant among Shakespeareans since the eighteenth century. Instead, Baldwin shows, the educational system of Shakespeare's time would have given the playwright a strong background in the classics, and there is much in the plays that shows how Shakespeare benefited from such an education.

Beier, A. L., and Roger Finlay, eds. *London 1500–1700: The Making of the Metropolis.* New York: Longman, 1986.

Focusing on the economic and social history of early modern London, these collected essays probe aspects of metropolitan life, including "Population and Disease," "Commerce and Manufacture," and "Society and Change."

Chambers, E. K. *William Shakespeare: A Study of Facts and Problems.* 2 vols. Oxford: Clarendon Press, 1930.

Analyzing in great detail the scant historical data, Chambers's complex, scholarly study considers the nature of the texts in which Shakespeare's work is preserved.

Cressy, David. *Education in Tudor and Stuart England.* London: Edward Arnold, 1975.
This volume collects sixteenth-, seventeenth-, and early eighteenth-century documents detailing aspects of formal education in England, such as the curriculum, the control and organization of education, and the education of women.

Duncan-Jones, Katherine. *Shakespeare: An Ungentle Life.* London: Arden Shakespeare, 2010.
This biography, first published in 2001 under the title *Ungentle Shakespeare: Scenes from His Life,* sets out to look into the documents from Shakespeare's personal life—especially legal and financial records—and it finds there a man very different from the one portrayed in more traditional biographies. He is "ungentle" in being born to a lower social class and in being a bit ruthless and more than a bit stingy. As the author notes, "three topics were formerly taboo both in polite society and in Shakespearean biography: social class, sex and money. I have been indelicate enough to give a good deal of attention to all three." She examines "Shakespeare's uphill struggle to achieve, or purchase, 'gentle' status." She finds that "Shakespeare was strongly interested in intense relationships with well-born young men." And she shows that he was "reluctant to divert much, if any, of his considerable wealth towards charitable, neighbourly, or altruistic ends." She insists that his plays and poems are "great, and enduring," and that it is in them "that the best of him is to be found."

Dutton, Richard. *William Shakespeare: A Literary Life.* New York: St. Martin's Press, 1989.

Not a biography in the traditional sense, Dutton's very readable work nevertheless "follows the contours of Shakespeare's life" as it examines Shakespeare's career as playwright and poet, with consideration of his patrons, theatrical associations, and audience.

Honan, Park. *Shakespeare: A Life*. New York: Oxford University Press, 1998.

Honan's accessible biography focuses on the various contexts of Shakespeare's life—physical, social, political, and cultural—to place the dramatist within a lucidly described world. The biography includes detailed examinations of, for example, Stratford schooling, theatrical politics of 1590s London, and the careers of Shakespeare's associates. The author draws on a wealth of established knowledge and on interesting new research into local records and documents; he also engages in speculation about, for example, the possibilities that Shakespeare was a tutor in a Catholic household in the north of England in the 1580s and that he acted particular roles in his own plays, areas that reflect new, but unproven and debatable, data—though Honan is usually careful to note where a particular narrative "has not been capable of proof or disproof."

Potter, Lois. *The Life of William Shakespeare: A Critical Biography*. Malden, Mass.: Wiley-Blackwell, 2012.

This critical biography of Shakespeare takes the playwright from cradle to grave, paying primary attention to his literary and theatrical milieu. The chapters "follow a chronological sequence," each focusing on a handful of years in the playwright's life. In the chapters that cover his playwriting years (5–17), each chapter focuses on events in Stratford-upon-Avon and in London (especially in the commercial theaters) while giving equal space to discussions of the plays and/or poems Shakespeare wrote during those years. Filled with information from Shakespeare's literary and theatrical worlds, the biography also shares frequent insights into how modern productions of a given play can shed light on the play, especially in scenes that Shakespeare's text presents ambiguously.

Schoenbaum, S. *William Shakespeare: A Compact Documentary Life.* New York: Oxford University Press, 1977.

Schoenbaum's evidence-based biography of Shakespeare is a compact version of his magisterial folio-size *Shakespeare: A Documentary Life* (New York: Oxford University Press, 1975). Schoenbaum structures his readable "compact" narrative around the documents that still exist which chronicle Shakespeare's familial, theatrical, legal, and financial existence. These documents, along with those discovered since the 1970s, form the basis of almost all Shakespeare biographies written since Schoenbaum's books appeared.

## Shakespeare's Theater

Bentley, G. E. *The Profession of Player in Shakespeare's Time, 1590–1642.* Princeton: Princeton University Press, 1984.

Bentley readably sets forth a wealth of evidence about performance in Shakespeare's time, with special attention to the relations between player and company, and the business of casting, managing, and touring.

Berry, Herbert. *Shakespeare's Playhouses.* New York: AMS Press, 1987.

Berry's six essays collected here discuss (with illustrations) varying aspects of the four playhouses in which Shakespeare had a financial stake: the Theatre in Shoreditch, the Blackfriars, and the first and second Globe.

Berry, Herbert, William Ingram, and Glynne Wickham, eds. *English Professional Theatre, 1530–1660.* Cambridge: Cambridge University Press, 2000.
Wickham presents the government documents designed to control professional players, their plays, and playing places. Ingram handles the professional actors, giving as representative a life of the actor Augustine Phillips, and discussing, among other topics, patrons, acting companies, costumes, props, playbooks, provincial playing, and child actors. Berry treats the twenty-three different London playhouses from 1560 to 1660 for which there are records, including four inns.

Cook, Ann Jennalie. *The Privileged Playgoers of Shakespeare's London.* Princeton: Princeton University Press, 1981.
Cook's work argues, on the basis of sociological, economic, and documentary evidence, that Shakespeare's audience—and the audience for English Renaissance drama generally—consisted mainly of the "privileged."

Dutton, Richard, ed. *The Oxford Handbook of Early Modern Theatre.* Oxford: Oxford University Press, 2011.
Dutton divides his study of the theatrical industry of Shakespeare's time into the following sections: "Theatre Companies," "London Playhouses," "Other Playing Spaces," "Social Practices," and "Evidence of Theatrical Practices." Each of these sections is further subdivided, with subdivisions assigned to individual experts. W. R. Streitberger treats the "Adult Playing Companies to 1583"; Sally-Beth MacLean those from

1583 to 1593; Roslyn L. Knutson, 1593–1603; Tom Rutter, 1603–1613; James J. Marino, 1613–1625; and Martin Butler, the "Adult and Boy Playing Companies 1625–1642." Michael Shapiro is responsible for the "Early (Pre-1590) Boy Companies and Their Acting Venues," while Mary Bly writes of "The Boy Companies 1599–1613." David Kathman handles "Inn-Yard Playhouses"; Gabriel Egan, "The Theatre in Shoreditch 1576–1599"; Andrew Gurr, "Why the Globe Is Famous"; Ralph Alan Cohen, "The Most Convenient Place: The Second Blackfriars Theater and Its Appeal"; Mark Bayer, "The Red Bull Playhouse"; and Frances Teague, "The Phoenix and the Cockpit-in-Court Playhouses." Turning to "Other Playing Spaces," Suzanne Westfall describes how "'He who pays the piper calls the tune': Household Entertainments"; Alan H. Nelson, "The Universities and the Inns of Court"; Peter Greenfield, "Touring"; John H. Astington, "Court Theatre"; and Anne Lancashire, "London Street Theater." For "Social Practices," Alan Somerset writes of "Not Just Sir Oliver Owlet: From Patrons to 'Patronage' of Early Modern Theatre," Dutton himself of "The Court, the Master of the Revels, and the Players," S. P. Cerasano of "Theater Entrepreneurs and Theatrical Economics," Ian W. Archer of "The City of London and the Theatre," David Kathman of "Players, Livery Companies, and Apprentices," Kathleen E. McLuskie of "Materiality and the Market: The Lady Elizabeth's Men and the Challenge of Theatre History," Heather Hirschfield of "'For the author's credit': Issues of Authorship in English Renaissance Drama," and Natasha Korda of "Women in the Theater." On "Theatrical Practices," Jacalyn Royce discusses "Early Modern Naturalistic Acting: The Role of the Globe in the Development of Personation"; Tiffany Stern, "Actors' Parts"; Alan Dessen, "Stage Directions and the Theater Historian"; R. B. Graves, "Lighting";

Lucy Munro, "Music and Sound"; Dutton himself, "Properties"; Thomas Postlcwait, "Eyewitnesses to History: Visual Evidence for Theater in Early Modern England"; and Eva Griffith, "Christopher Beeston: His Property and Properties."

Greg, W. W. *Dramatic Documents from the Elizabethan Playhouses.* 2 vols. Oxford: Clarendon Press, 1931.
Greg itemizes and briefly describes almost all the play manuscripts that survive from the period 1590 to around 1660, including, among other things, players' parts. His second volume offers facsimiles of selected manuscripts.

Harbage, Alfred. *Shakespeare's Audience.* New York: Columbia University Press, 1941.
Harbage investigates the fragmentary surviving evidence to interpret the size, composition, and behavior of Shakespeare's audience.

Keenan, Siobhan. *Acting Companies and Their Plays in Shakespeare's London.* London: Bloomsbury Arden Shakespeare, 2014.
Keenan "explores how the needs, practices, resources and pressures on acting companies and playwrights informed not only the performance and publication of contemporary dramas but playwrights' writing practices." Each chapter focuses on one important factor that influenced Renaissance playwrights and players. The initial focus is on how "the nature and composition of the acting companies" influenced the playwrights who wrote for them. Then, using "the Diary of theatre manager Philip Henslowe and manuscript playbooks showing signs of theatrical use," Keenan examines the relations between acting companies and playwrights. Other influences include "the

physical design and facilities of London's outdoor and indoor theatrical spaces" and the diverse audiences for plays, including royal and noble patrons.

Shapiro, Michael. *Children of the Revels: The Boy Companies of Shakespeare's Time and Their Plays.* New York: Columbia University Press, 1977.
Shapiro chronicles the history of the amateur and quasi-professional child companies that flourished in London at the end of Elizabeth's reign and the beginning of James's.

## The Publication of Shakespeare's Plays

Blayney, Peter W. M. *The First Folio of Shakespeare.* Hanover, Md.: Folger, 1991.
Blayney's accessible account of the printing and later life of the First Folio—an amply illustrated catalogue to a 1991 Folger Shakespeare Library exhibition—analyzes the mechanical production of the First Folio, describing how the Folio was made, by whom and for whom, how much it cost, and its ups and downs (or, rather, downs and ups) since its printing in 1623.

Hinman, Charlton. *The Norton Facsimile: The First Folio of Shakespeare.* 2nd ed. New York: W. W. Norton, 1996.
This facsimile presents a photographic reproduction of an "ideal" copy of the First Folio of Shakespeare; Hinman attempts to represent each page in its most fully corrected state. This second edition includes an important new introduction by Peter W. M. Blayney.

Hinman, Charlton. *The Printing and Proof-Reading of the First Folio of Shakespeare.* 2 vols. Oxford: Clarendon Press, 1963.

In the most arduous study of a single book ever undertaken, Hinman attempts to reconstruct how the Shakespeare First Folio of 1623 was set into type and run off the press, sheet by sheet. He also provides almost all the known variations in readings from copy to copy.

Werstine, Paul. *Early Modern Playhouse Manuscripts and the Editing of Shakespeare.* Cambridge: Cambridge University Press, 2012.

Werstine examines in detail nearly two dozen texts associated with the playhouses in and around Shakespeare's time, conducting the examination against the background of the two idealized forms of manuscript that have governed the editing of Shakespeare from the twentieth into the twenty-first century—Shakespeare's so-called foul papers and the so-called promptbooks of his plays. By comparing the two extant texts of John Fletcher's *Bonduca*, one in manuscript and the other printed in 1647, Werstine shows that the term "foul papers" that is found in a note in the *Bonduca* manuscript does not refer, as editors have believed, to a species of messy authorial manuscript but is instead simply a designation for a manuscript, whatever its features, that has served as the copy from which another manuscript has been made. By surveying twenty-one texts with theatrical markup, he demonstrates that the playhouses used a wide variety of different kinds of manuscripts and printed texts but did not use the highly regularized promptbooks of the eighteenth-century theaters and later. His presentation of the peculiarities of playhouse texts provides an empirical basis for inferring the nature of the manuscripts that lie behind printed Shakespeare plays.

# Key to Famous Lines and Phrases

Ingratitude, thou marble-hearted fiend . . .
[*Lear*—1.4.270]

How sharper than a serpent's tooth it is
To have a thankless child.       [*Lear*—1.4.302–3]

Blow winds, and crack your cheeks! Rage, blow!
[*Lear*—3.2.1]

I am a man
More sinned against than sinning.
[*Lear*—3.2.62–63]

The worst is not
So long as we can say "This is the worst."
[*Edgar*—4.1.30–31]

As flies to wanton boys are we to th' gods;
They kill us for their sport.
[*Gloucester*—4.1.41–42]

'Tis the time's plague when madmen lead the blind.
[*Gloucester*—4.1.54]

Ay, every inch a king.
[*Lear*—4.6.127]

Through tattered clothes small vices do appear.
Robes and furred gowns hide all. Plate sin with gold,
And the strong lance of justice hurtless breaks.
[*Lear*—4.6.180–83]

337

...I am bound
Upon a wheel of fire, that mine own tears
Do scald like molten lead.        [*Lear*—4.7.52–54]


Men must endure
Their going hence even as their coming hither.
Ripeness is all.                  [*Edgar*—5.2.10–12]


Her voice was ever soft,
Gentle, and low, an excellent thing in woman.
                                  [*Lear*—5.3.328–29]